Prehistoric Pottery Across the Baltic

Regions, Influences and Methods

Edited by

Paul Eklöv Pettersson

BAR International Series 2785

2016

First Published in 2016 by
British Archaeological Reports Ltd
United Kingdom

BAR International Series 2785

Prehistoric Pottery Across the Baltic

ISBN: 978 1 4073 1463 1

Printed in England

All BAR titles are available from:

British Archaeological Reports Ltd
Oxford
United Kingdom
Phone +44 (0)1865 310431
Fax +44 (0)1865 316916
Email: info@barpublishing.com
www.barpublishing.com

Contents

Preface

Pottery Across the Baltic, the name of this publication as well as the name of the conference held at Lund University; refers to the study of ceramic materials within the modern countries bordering the Baltic Sea. During three days in March 2013 archaeologists from ten different countries gathered in Lund, to discuss current results, methods and interpretations with their colleagues. The presentations held focused on a variety of topics including regionalities, continental influences, borders, decorations, morphology, temper, clay choice, dating methods, technical ceramics, household pottery, asbestos ware, firing techniques, manufacturing methods etcetera. This publication compiles the contributions of thirteen authors in nine articles. Although the large part of the conference took place at the Laboratory of Ceramic Research, Lund University we also like to thank the open-air museum *Vikingatider* and the ceramic workshop *Wallåkra* for guiding and hosting a nice excursion in Skåne. We also like to take the opportunity to thank all those who have helped in the work with this publication.

Paul Eklöv Pettersson (M.A.), Thomas Eriksson (Ph.D.) & Anders Lindahl (Prof.)
Lund, November 2015

List of Participants

Many thanks to the participants and session holders:

Agnieszka, Czekaj-Zastawny. Institute of Archaeology and Ethnology, Polish Academy of Science, Krakow, Poland (presented)

Asplund, Henrik. University of Turku

Bacunic F. Imelda. University of Gothenburg

Björkli, Birgitte. Museum of Cultural History, Norway

Blank, Malou. University of Gothenburg

Botwid, Katarina. Lund University (presented)

Dumpe, Baliba. National History Museum of Latvia (presented)

Eklöv Pettersson Paul. Lund University (presented)

Eriksson, Thomas. Lund University & County administrative board Gävleborg (presented & session holder)

Fredriksen Ditlef. Per. University of Oslo (presented)

Hagberg, Christoffer. Lund University

Hartz, Sönke. Archäologisches Landesmuseum Schloss Gottorf, Schleswig (presented)

Hop Henriette University of Bergen (presented)

Hulthén, Birgitta. Lund University

Jacek, Kabaciński. Institute of Archaeology and Ethnology, Polish Academy of Science, Poznań, Poland. (presented)

Jörgensen L. Anne. Lund University

Kniesel, Jutta. Christian-Albrechts University, Kiel

Kotula, Andreas. University of Greifswald (presented)

Kristoffersen E. Siv. University of Stavanger (presented)

Larsson, Åsa. Societas Archaeologica Upsaliensis (SAU), Sweden (presented)

Lindahl, Anders. Lund University (presented & session holder)

Macheridis, Stella. Lund University

Nielsen O Poul. The National Museum of Denmark

Philippsen, Bente. Aarhus University (presented)

Pikirayi, Innocent. University of Pretoria

Piliciauskas, Gytis. Lithuanian Institute of History (presented)

Pääkönen, Mirva. University of Turku

Ragnesten, Ulf. Göteborg City Museum

Rosberg, Simon. Lund University

Rödsrud Løchsen. Christian. Museum of Cultural History, Norway (presented)

Sahlen, Daniel. Stockholm University (presented)

Skriver Søren, Tillisch. Saxo institute, University of Copenhagen (presented)

Stilborg, Ole. Stilborgs Keramiska Analys & Stockholm University (presented & session holder)

Sulte, Alise. Latvia University (presented)

Terberger, Thomas. Department of Prehistory, University of Greifswald, Germany (presented)

Thielen, Laura. Hamburg University (presented)

Wennberg, Tom. Göteborg City Museum

The conference committee: Thomas Eriksson, Paul Eklöv Pettersson and Anders Lindahl

Asbestos Ceramics along the West Norwegian Coast – Influences, Age and Morphology in the Bronze Age–Early Pre-Roman Iron Age (ca. 1700–400 BC)

Henriette Maria Børslid Hop

Department of Archaeology, History, Cultural Studies and Religion
University of Bergen

Henriette.Hop@uib.no

Abstract: This paper is largely based on my master thesis (Hop 2011) that focused on the little known asbestos ceramics from the regions of Hordaland, Rogaland and Vest-Agder (hereby referred to collectively as southwestern Norwegian asbestos ceramics), dated to the Bronze Age and the pre-Roman Iron Age. The point of departure for the discussions in this article is a comparison of the morphology and age of the southwestern Norwegian asbestos ceramics to the typological-chronological framework suggested by studies of the north-western Norwegian asbestos ceramics after Anne Ågotnes (1986) and the Late Bronze Age Risvik ceramics following Dag Andreassen (2002). The data strongly suggests that the fairly common practice of using the Risvik ceramics as a reference point or archetype for all west Norwegian asbestos ceramics is misleading. Previous research has pointed to the fact that although the practice of asbestos tempering is originally Arctic, asbestos ceramics were adapted into the local material repertoire in regions that were culturally connected to South Scandinavia (e.g. Prescott 1991; Ågotnes 1986). Furthermore, it is questioned whether perhaps Nordic Bronze Age pottery styles influenced the asbestos ceramics along the west Norwegian coast.

Key words: Asbestos pottery; Bronze Age; Early Iron Age; West Norway; Morphology and shape

Asbestos ceramics in Norway – a brief outline

The practice of asbestos tempering in ceramics originated in eastern Finland around 5500–5000 BP and expanded to northern Fennoscandia and northwest Russia in the Late Neolithic/Early Metal Age (Pesonen 1996, p. 28). In Norway, asbestos tempered ceramics can be divided into *Arctic* and *Nordic* groups (Table. 1). Although this division is obviously a simplification of the pre-historic reality, I consider it to be necessary for analytical purposes. The Arctic group includes five of the six asbestos tempered types described by Roger Jørgensen and Bjørnar Olsen in their publication on asbestos-ceramic groups in northern Norway from 1988: the Late Neolithic Lovozero and Pasvik ceramic, Textile and Imitated Textile in the Metal Age, and Kjelmøy ceramic in the Late Metal Age/Iron Age, the latter is a style considered more or less equivalent to the Finnish Särasniemi II and the Swedish Norrländsk asbestos ceramics (Carpelan 1979, p. 17).

The Nordic group consists of the geographically defined north-western Norwegian asbestos ceramic and southwestern Norwegian asbestos ceramic found along the Norwegian west coast and fjord areas from the Early Bronze Age to the pre-Roman Iron Age, as well as the Risvik ceramic from the Late Bronze Age/pre-Roman Iron Age (Fig. 1). The Nordic asbestos ceramics existed in environments affiliated with the Nordic Bronze Age complex (Carpelan 1979, p. 17). Although asbestos ceramics were an inherently northern innovation, they were developed and transformed in local contexts through large parts of Scandinavia after the expansion in the Early Metal Age. As they were adapted into the local technical and symbolic ceramic repertoire in western Norway, asbestos ceramics existed as part of local ceramic traditions where Nordic Bronze Age pottery styles were the primary influence.

In all probability, the asbestos ceramics were locally made as the clay qualities differ within each region and the raw asbestos and/or clay are found in relation to asbestos ceramics in several contexts (Ågotnes 1986, p. 94-95; Kutshcera 1995, p. 14; Engedal et al. 2006, p. 22; Hop 2011, p. 50). Furthermore, x-ray diffraction analysis of local clay and asbestos ceramics was carried out on a sherd from the site Voll in Rennesøy, and confirmed that the ceramics were made from local clay (Høgestøl 1995, p. 124). The Nordic Bronze Age pottery was developed from continental traditions (essentially the ceramics of the Lausitzian and Tumulus cultures) and has a more selective range of forms and preferences than the continental traditions. According to Henrik Thrane, this is what defines the Nordic Bronze Age pottery as 'an entity of its own' (2008, p. 247). Apparently, the only clear link between the

Table 1: Timeline of the ceramic groups mentioned in the text

BC	Arch. period	Arctic asbestos ceramics		BC	Arch. period	Nordic asbestos ceramics	South-Scandinavian Bronze Age-ceramics
2000	Late Stone Age	*Pasvik* (inland)	*Lovozero* (coastal)	2000	LN		
1900				1900			Late Neolithic/Early Bronze Age types, "Kümmerkeramik"
1800				1800			
1700	Early metal age		*Textile/imitated textile ceramics*	1700	EBA I	Regional asbestos ceramic groups:	
1600				1600			"M.Rasmussen phase 3"
1500				1500	EBA II	*southwestern norwegian/*	
1400				1400		*northwestern norwegian*	
1300				1300	EBA III		
1200				1200			
1100				1100	LBA IV		Late Bronze Age types *"A-group"*
1000				1000			
900		*Kjelmøy*		900	LBA V		
800				800		*Risvik*	"B-group"
700				700	LBA VI		
600				600			
500				500	PR.IA		
400				400			
300- AD				300-AD			

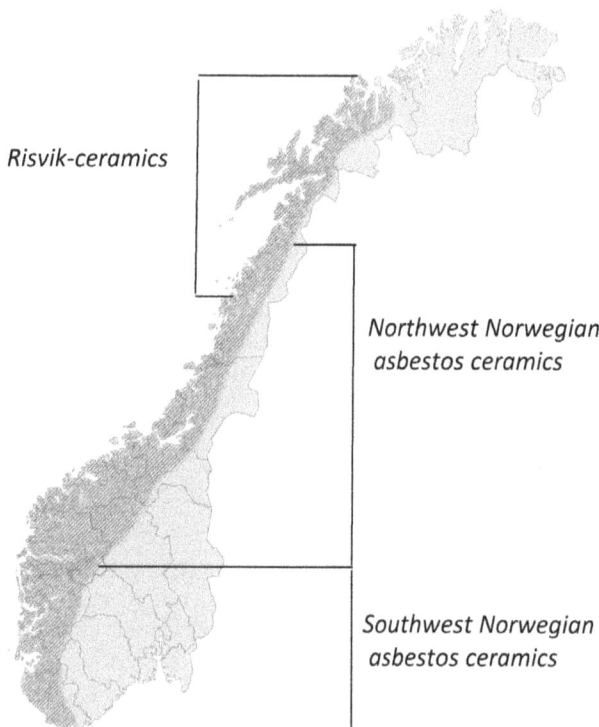

Risvik-ceramics

Northwest Norwegian asbestos ceramics

Southwest Norwegian asbestos ceramics

Fig. 1: Map showing the geographical regions of the three Nordic asbestos ceramic groups (mapdata from norgeskart. no).

Nordic asbestos pottery and the Fennoscandian (Arctic) asbestos ceramic tradition is the actual technology of asbestos tempering (Munch 1962, p. 22; Carpelan 1979,

p. 17; Ågotnes 1986, p. 116). Although there are local variations within the craft to consider, the west Norwegian Bronze Age pottery existed and was developed under the general influence of a common Nordic repertoire of pottery styles.

Studies on Bronze Age ceramics in western Norway

Research and publications dealing with pottery of 'South Scandinavian types' has been practically non-existent in Norwegian Bronze Age research since Håkon Shetelig (1911) and Eyvind De Lange (1913) touched upon the subject more than a century ago. Although several researchers have pointed out the potential of and need for a typological/ chronological treatment of the undecorated, coarse pottery from the Bronze Age and the Early Iron Age (as pointed out by, for example, Wangen 2009, p. 75), the general attitude towards this category of finds is that the pottery is too dull, too limited in number and too fragmented to make sense of. One exception is the Late Bronze Age *face urns* (funerary urns with stylized faces) from Rogaland and Aust-Agder that have been the subject of some research (Haavaldsen 1985; Johansen 1986; Aasbøe 2006, 2008; Kneisel 2012) and which have provided valuable insights into a local variant of the European face-urn tradition. Parallels to the Norwegian urns are found in Denmark, Poland and even, in one case, Italy (Løken 2006). My ongoing PhD project will in due course contribute to the established knowledge on Bronze Age pottery in Norway, as it focuses on pottery from Norwegian Bronze Age graves. The main focuses of the study are upon the chronology and regional traditions of the pottery from Norwegian Bronze Age graves, comprising of the asbestos ceramics and the 'other' variants (South Scandinavian style ceramics/non-asbestos tempered) as regional groups that display differing degrees of mutual influences.

Studies on Nordic Asbestos ceramics

As opposed to the South Scandinavian pottery types, asbestos ceramics have recurrently been addressed in discussions about identity and cultural relations along the west Norwegian coast (e.g. Bakka 1976; Prescott 1991; Engedal 2010; Hop 2011). In 1986 Ågotnes published an article on asbestos ceramics from northwest Norway that focused on the geographical distribution of finds and a typological-chronological framework for the asbestos ceramics spanning from the Early Bronze Age to the early pre-Roman Iron Age. There are many new finds to consider since the publication of that article, a great many from what was then the southernmost 'border' of asbestos ceramics—the Sognefjord. However, the main conclusions of her study remain relevant. She also points to the fact that although the aspect of asbestos tempering relates the ceramic in some respects to the northern and eastern parts of Scandinavia, the north-western Norwegian asbestos pottery is culturally associated with the Nordic Bronze Age complex (Ågotnes 1986, p. 114–116).

The southwestern Norwegian asbestos ceramics

As noted, localities with asbestos ceramics south of the Sognefjord are a fairly recent discovery. In Rogaland, several ceramic finds were re-classified as asbestos tempered during the recent revision of the museum collections. To my knowledge there are at least 22 archaeological sites containing asbestos ceramics in southwest Norway. The sites can be classified as 'settlement/activity sites', with the exception of one votive context (Østre Hauge, Lista in Vest-Agder) and one dubious grave-find (Holmen, Bjerkreim in Rogaland). Asbestos ceramics from 19 of the 22 sites were available for visual examination. The geographical distribution of the 19 sites included in this analysis is seen in Fig. 2. The studied assemblage consists of 721 sherds/1.94 kg. Some of the results were compared with reference to Ågotnes' (1986) study of asbestos ceramics from the regions of Sogn and Fjordane, Møre og Romsdal and Nordland (northwestern Norwegian asbestos ceramics) and Andreassen's (2002) study of the Risvik ceramics from Nordland and Troms (Hop 2011, p. 69 ff.). This comparison is relevant in order to detect regional patterns and to evaluate the material against the chronological frame that is currently available.

Contexts

Sherds from settlements/activity sites have been recovered from cultural layers or agricultural/settlement layers, in mound fillings, and as single finds. The site Tjelmeland, Etne was test-excavated twice (Kutschera 1995; Madsen

1995), but never fully excavated. The amount of asbestos ceramics found at Tjelmeland consisted of 246 sherds—a substantial amount when compared to most Early Bronze Age sites with pottery in southwest Norway. The quantity and nature of the artifacts, as well as the thickness and intensity of the cultural layer in which the ceramics were found (C14 dated to Early Bronze Age II/III), suggests that this is a result of an occupation of a certain length and intensity. There were no postholes, hearths or other settlement structures at this site, possibly due to the fact that only a small part of the area was excavated (Madsen 1995, p. 14–15). A similar situation was seen at the site of Hollve in Granvin where 33 sherds of asbestos ceramics were found in a black, fatty layer packed with coal and fire-cracked stones and interpreted as a refuse area / midden. The layer was C14 dated in a sequence of six samples, with the focal point in the Early Bronze Age II/III—a result that corresponded well with the typological implications of asbestos ceramics and the lithic techniques/materials. The excavated area constitutes only a small part of the plain, and no structures were discovered. However, traces of domesticated barley in the botanical samples suggest cereal cultivation at the site, or in close proximity to the site (Halvorsen 2012; Hop and Lødøen 2013). It has been noted that in the South Scandinavian Early Bronze Age, the waste areas were normally organized away from the building/living area (Sofaer et al. 2010, p. 186). It is plausible to link this observation with sites such as Hollve and Tjelmeland where the cultural layers are indicative of settlement activity although no such structures were actually discovered.

A common archaeological situation in Rogaland, is the discovery of ceramic sherds from activity layers under grave mounds, namely old settlement remains with no persuasive contextual relation to the grave monuments. Such contexts are mainly connected to the extensive grave-mound excavations that went on in the early 1900s, conducted by the museum curator Tor Helliesen. In several of Helliesens' accounts, pottery from layers underneath the mounds was described (or at least registered in the museum protocol) as grave-urns, although descriptions from excavation reports indicate that these finds were probably settlement debris from layers stratigraphically below the burial mound. The finds from Røyneberg, Søre Sunde, Håvik, and Byberg are all examples of this. There is, however, one dubious grave context in southwest Norway where asbestos ceramics were present: Holmen in Bjerkreim, Rogaland. This site—a mound—was excavated by Einar Østmo in 1973. According to him, the sherds (originally not observed as being asbestos tempered) were found in a vertical position among stones in a coal-scattered layer at the bottom level of the mound. There were no evidences of skeletal remains, a pit or a chamber construction to effectively verify this as a grave context. The interpretation of the sherds as a grave-find is questionable, an opinion expressed also by the excavator (Østmo 1973).

The single votive deposit in this study comes from the southernmost locality of Østre Hauge in Farsund, Vest-

Fig. 2: Distribution map of sites with southwest Norwegian asbestos ceramics included in this study: ●= Settlement/activity sites; ▲= Votive context (map-data from open access resources at www.norgeskart.no).

Agder. The find was discovered on a platform in a bog amongst a layer of ash, and consisted of a flint dagger of the VI type (Lomborg 1973, p. 75), a spoon-shaped flint scraper and five sherds of asbestos pottery (allegedly, several sherds were observed but not collected) (Johansen 1986, p.89). The artefacts were located alongside one large and several smaller stones. Ceramics are rarely found in Bronze Age votive contexts (Jensen 1997, p. 174; Melheim 2006, p. 52) and the fact that the sherds are asbestos tempered makes this find even more unusual.

Morphological features of the southwestern Norwegian asbestos ceramics

The analysed material is highly fragmented, and there are no complete vessels /assemblages of sherds that can be informatively reconstructed. Despite the obvious difficulties of attempting to analyse a highly fragmented material, the visual examination and documentation has nonetheless revealed some features (as well as confirming absence

of other features) that are chronologically informative in a regional and comparative perspective. Firstly, I will present a brief account on the age span of the southwestern Norwegian asbestos ceramics. Furthermore, I attempt to describe some of the *general* morphological features of this group (for a more detailed description, see Hop 2011) and I will bring attention to some of the traits of the Risvik and northwestern Norwegian asbestos ceramics that illustrate the chronological and morphological differences to the southwestern Norwegian asbestos ceramics.

Age

Five of the sites from southwest Norway are C14 dated, and an equal number of sites are dated on the premise of contextual relation to typologically datable finds (Table 2). The remaining sites cannot be given a more precise date than Early Bronze Age or Bronze Age in general. The finds cover the entire chronological span of the Bronze Age as well as one sample from the pre-Roman Iron Age. However,

6

Table 2: Datings of sites with southwestern Norwegian asbestos ceramics (All C14 dates calibrated by the oxcal program)

Site	Dated on the basis of:	Archaeological Period
Kråkås, Askøy	Typology. Contextual relation to pressure flaked flint debris	BA
Bjorvollen, Stend	Stratigraphic relation with BA-layer	BA
Samnøy, Fusa	Stratigraphic relation with BA-layer	BA
Kvitevoll, Halsnøy (felt A)	Typology. Contextual relation to pressure flaked tools (from layer older than 1350 BC)	EBA
Kvitevoll, Halsnøy, (felt B)	C14. From fencing with pottery and burnt clay. 2360+-40 BP/Cal. 520-380 BC	PR.IA
Tjelmeland, Etne	C14. From cultural layer 3060+-35 BP/Cal.1415-1165 BC, 2995+-35 BP/Cal.1256-1135 BC	EBA II/III
Hollve, Granvin	C14. Dating sequence from cultural layer: 2840+-30 BP/Cal.1050-910 BC, 2470+-30 BP/760-680 BC, 3060+-30 BP/Cal.1390-1210 BC, 3240+-30 BP/1610-1450 BC, 3390+-30 BP/Cal.1740-1560, 3500+-30 BP/Cal.1890-1740	EBA II/III (Mainly)
Vestbø, Vindafjord	Typology. Contextual relation to soapstone vessel sherds	LBA/PR.IA
Håvik, Karmøy		BA
Galta, Rennesøy	Dating from nearby hearth suggest LBA V, relation between the ceramic and the hearth is uncertain	BA
Voll, Rennesøy	C14. charred remains on asbestos ceramic sherd. 3050+-65 BP/Cal. 1301 ± 86 BC.	EBA II/III
Søre Sunde, Stavanger	Ceramic attributes indicative of EBA	BA (EBA)
Røyneberg, Sola	Ceramic attributes indicative of EBA	BA (EBA)
Byberg, Sola		BA
Jåsund, Sola	C14Typology. From dated layer. 2670+-40 BP/Cal 910-790 BC - *mininum age of the pottery.*	LBA V *or EBA*
Hana, Sandnes	Ceramic attributes	EBA
Varhaug, Hå		BA
Holmen, Bjerkreim		BA
Østre Hauge, Lista	Typology. Contextual relation to flint dagger and spoon-shaped scraper	EBA I/II

the main dating frame of the southwestern Norwegian asbestos ceramic is in the Montelius period II and III, as exemplified by C14 dated samples from Tjelmeland, Hollve, Voll, Kvitevoll site A and Håvik, as well as typological datings to the Early Bronze Age at Røyneberg, Hana and possibly also Jåsund. The ceramics from Jåsund were found in a layer C14 dated to the Late Bronze Age IV—a result that should be regarded as a minimum date for the ceramics since it is most likely contextually related to older layers (Fyllingen 2011, p. 8–9). In addition, the type VI flint dagger and the spoon shaped scraper in the votive deposit from Østre Hauge can be dated typologically to the Early Bronze Age I/II.

Sherd thickness and temper

As mentioned, the numbers of finds analysed from southwest Norway total approximately 721 sherds/1.94 kg—a small amount considering that the assemblage comes from a total of 22 sites. The majority of sherds are thin-walled and light-weight, ranging from 3–7 mm for rim-sherds 3–15 mm for base-sherds, and 3–14 mm for the body sherds (Hop 2011, p. 75). The asbestos fibres are cut or shredded; a method whose result produces a distinctively different product to the finely crushed or pulverized asbestos tempering that is distinctive of the bucket shaped pots of the Late Roman/Migration period, as is commonly found

in these geographical areas. The length and width of the asbestos fibres varies greatly, even within the same sherd/ vessel. The bottom half of the vessels are typically densely tempered, in contrast to the more sparingly tempered rim and neck sherds.

Shapes

The material finds point toward simple shapes, usually small vessels with barrel- or situla-shaped profiles. There are hardly any features that are indicative of articulated profile shapes and only one sherd with a possible 'bulb' (Norwegian: *vulst*)—features that are chronologically attributed to the ceramic traditions of the Late Bronze Age and are thus absent in this Early Bronze Age assemblage. The steepness of the angle from the foot to the belly varies, as well as the curvature of the belly sherds. The base is flat; there are no sherds in the assemblage that indicate a rounded base or an overall spherical/rounded vessel shape (as is commonly proposed for the Risvik pottery). Bases both with and without marked feet are present. Overall there are great variations in the shapes of rim sherds, even within the same site (Hop 2011, Fig. 5, p. 68).

There are two reconstruction-drawings from the sites at Rennesøy, Rogaland (Fig. 3) that, in my opinion, illustrate the general character of the southwestern Norwegian

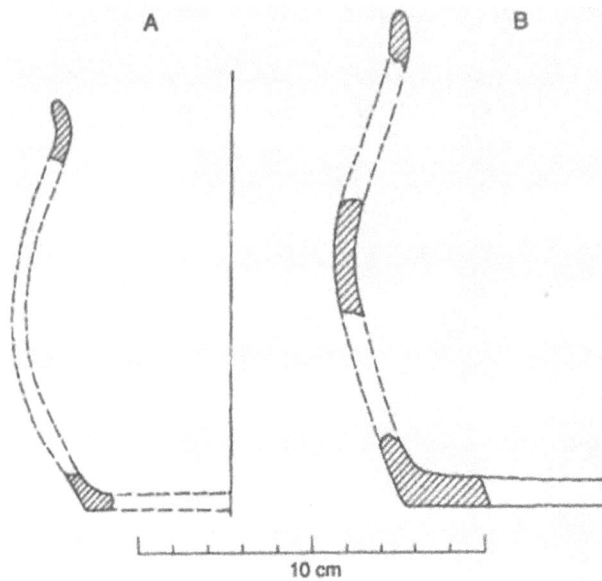

Fig. 3: Vessel profiles of asbestos ceramics found at Rennesøy, Rogaland (Høgestøl 1995, fig.20, p. 134. Drawing by Mydland, L./Hølland Berg, A.)

asbestos ceramics, although there are, of course, variations within this theme (Hop 2011, p. 68). It was remarked that the asbestos ceramics from Rennesøy had no morphological link with the Risvik ceramics (Høgestøl 1995, p. 135). It is perhaps no wonder that these Early Bronze Age asbestos ceramic finds are not comparative to the Late Bronze Age Risvik ceramics.

South Scandinavian pottery in the Early Bronze Age

In general, Early Bronze Age pottery is notoriously difficult to classify due to its plain and somewhat inconsistent shapes, undecorated surfaces and coarseness. Also, the material is usually highly fragmented, implying that the overall ceramic quality was poor (Sofaer et al. 2010 p. 188; Rasmussen 1993b, p. 87). As mentioned, ceramics are typically under- researched with regards to the Norwegian Bronze Age and it is thus necessary to consult South Scandinavian chronologies. Henrik Thrane has proposed a threefold division of the Bronze Age ceramics in Denmark building on Marianne Rasmussen's studies of Early Bronze Age settlement ceramics (1993a, 1993b) and Jørgen Jensen's chronological study of Late Bronze Age settlement ceramics (1977). In order to describe the pottery tradition in the Late Neolithic/Early Bronze Age, Thrane has adapted the term 'Kümmerkeramik', originally used on the pottery of the Early Bronze Age 'Elp culture' in the Netherlands (Fokkens and Fontinjn 2013, p.553). The second stage is 'Rasmussen phase III' which can be regarded as the predecessor of the many changes that come about in the ceramic repertoire of the Late Bronze Age (Thrane 2008, p. 249).

Northwestern Norwegian asbestos ceramics – context, age and morphology

In 1986, Ågotnes published an article on asbestos ceramics from northwestern Norway. The focus was placed on

mapping the geographical distribution of finds and suggesting a typological-chronological framework for the asbestos ceramics spanning from the Early Bronze Age to the pre-Roman Iron Age. Her research emphasizes that although the asbestos tempering relates the ceramic in some respects to the northern and eastern parts of Scandinavia, the asbestos pottery found in northwest Norway is culturally associated with the Nordic Bronze Age complex (Ågotnes 1986, p. 114–116).

Ågotnes' analysis included asbestos tempered ceramics from Nordland to Sogn og Fjordane, with emphasis on Sunnmøre (Fig. 1). Sunnmøre is considered to be the core area of asbestos ceramics, with numerous sites from the Early Bronze Age to the pre-Roman Iron Age. The contexts include settlements and rock-shelters, as well as graves. The asbestos ceramics found in north-western Norway are not a distinctive 'type' like that of Risvik because the pottery found in the northwest encompasses asbestos ceramics from the Early Bronze Age to the pre-Roman Iron Age in an analytically defined region. Some of the vessels clearly resemble the Risvik pottery (Ågotnes 1986, p. 86), for instance the Late Bronze Age Flatebakken assemblage (Ågotnes 1976), while other finds display features that are seemingly closer to the Early Bronze Age ceramics found in South Scandinavia. Despite some overlapping tendencies, the chronological ordering of the sherds revealed that there was a development from thin-walled vessels in the Early Bronze Age to thicker walls (frequently with bulbs) in the Late Bronze Age (Fig. 4). The Late Bronze Age vessel-profile is most commonly concave–convex with a straight or flattened rim edge. The base is either rounded or flat, and the vessel-shape is commonly spherical/rounded. A common feature of the north-western Norwegian asbestos ceramics (as well as the Risvik ceramics) dating from the Late Bronze Age is the bulb. In some instances the bulb separates surface textures as a smoothed neck from a coarse-surfaced belly (Ågotnes 1986, p. 92)

The Risvik ceramics – context, age and morphology

The Risvik type was first described and named by Guttorm Gjessing (1942, p. 278) and was further studied by Jens Storm Munch (1962), Roger Jørgensen and Bjørnar Olsen (1988), and Andreassen (2002). Socio-culturally, the Risvik ceramics are linked to groups of late hunter/ gatherers with an evolving agricultural economy—a result of the intensified contacts with South Scandinavia that are evident in the archaeological record from this period (Jørgensen and Olsen 1988; Bakka 1976; Andreassen 2002; Arntzen 2012). Perhaps in lack of an alternative term, Risvik has frequently been used by archaeologists to describe asbestos ceramics 'outside' of the Arctic sphere, covering what is here referred to as 'Nordic Asbestos ceramics'. The morphological characteristics of the Risvik ceramics according to Gjessing (1942), Munch (1962), Jørgensen and Olsen (1988), and Andreassen (2002), can be summarized as follows: Risvik vessels are generally small with an almost spherical shape and rounded base. The rim/neck area is smoothed or polished in contrast to the

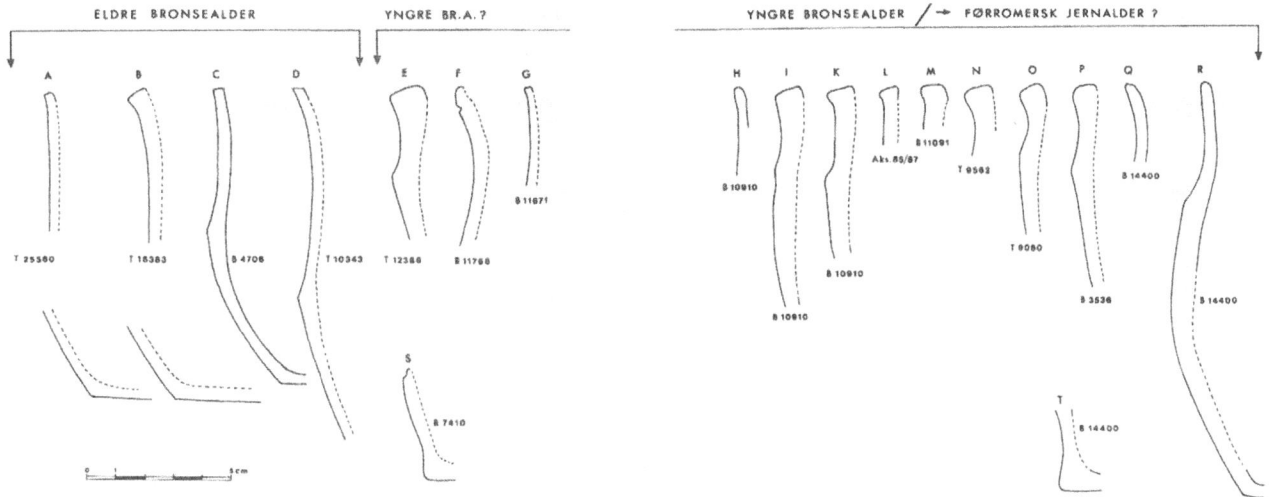

Fig. 4: The chronological development of northwestern Norwegian asbestos ceramic (Ågotnes 1986, fig.12, p. 112-113. Drawing by Tangedal, L.)

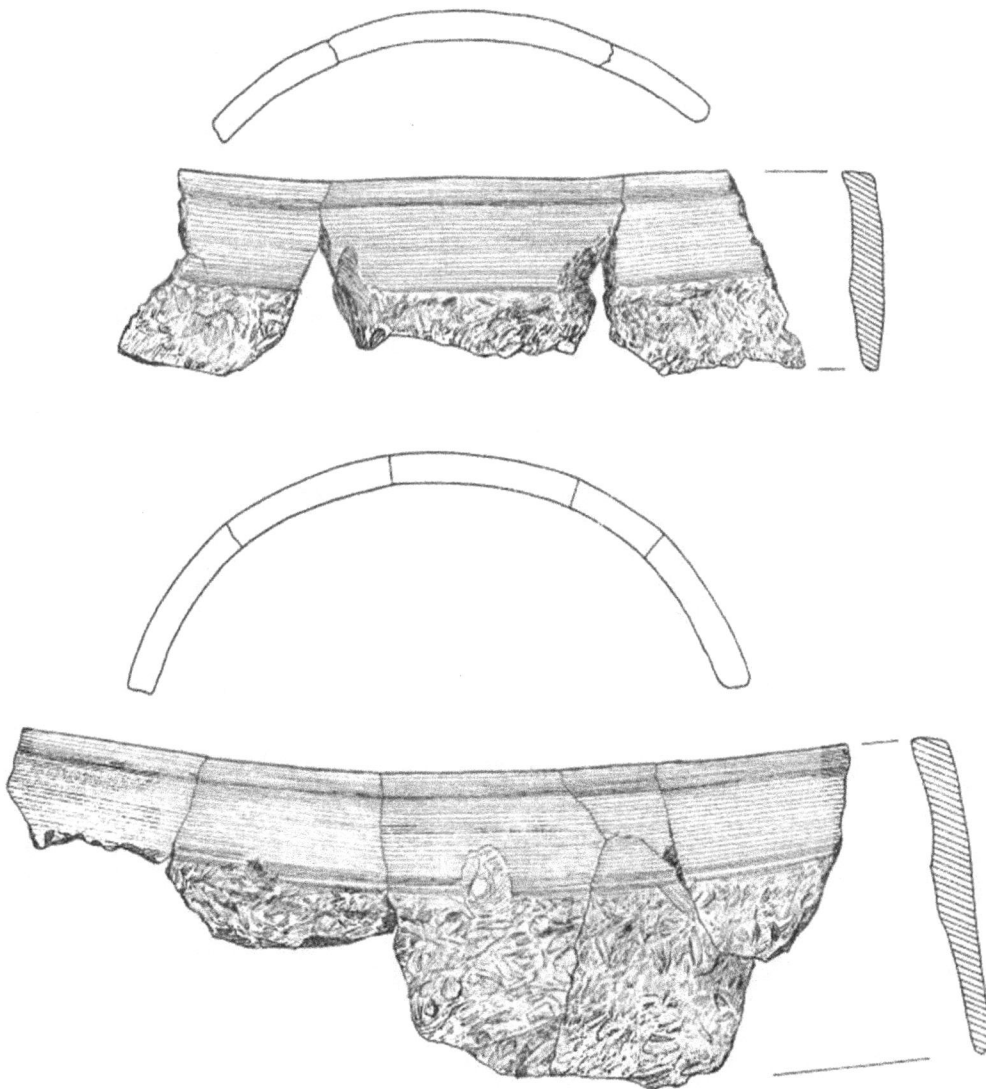

Fig. 5: Risvik ceramics from Skjevika, Meløy in Nordland. The coarse area under the bulb is produced by dense asbestos tempering and gives the impression of a "rusticated" surface (From Munch 1962, fig. 3 p. 9. Drawing by Aune, O.)

coarse surface of the belly which is commonly separated by a bulb. The vessel walls are around 1 cm thick and the rim is usually thickened (Fig. 5). The asbestos fibres are generally short and thick as opposed to the long, thin fibres that are more typical of the Arctic styles. Radiological datings from a number of Risvik-ceramic sites, as well as

AMS datings on charred remains on vessels (Andreassen 2002, p. 64; Jørgensen and Olsen 1988, p. 62), propose that the main time-span for Risvik ceramics was 800–400 BC (Andreassen 2002, p. 71).

South Scandinavian influences on Risvik ceramics

Andreassen points to the fact that several of the Risvik-ceramic sites have stratigraphically older layers with finds of Textile ceramics and hence proposes Textile ceramics as the *precursor* to the Risvik type (2002, p. 115). As mentioned, Risvik ceramics are connected to the agricultural expansion in the North in the Late Bronze Age/ pre-Roman Iron Age, and Andreassen argues further that the development from Textile ceramics signals a shift in orientation of socio-economic contacts from east to south (Andreassen 2002, p. 114–118). However, the question of possible influences for the development of Risvik ceramics is left unaddressed. Considering that there is a stylistic leap from Textile to Risvik and that South Scandinavian impacts are otherwise evident (for example in the increase of Nordic bronze artefacts and with the agricultural/economic development in the region), it is not inconceivable that a South Scandinavian influence in the Late Bronze Age affected the ceramic craft and consequently the development of the Risvik ceramics.

The term *Risvik ceramics* describes a distinct ceramic type within a limited time-frame and is perhaps to be considered a distinct local Late-Bronze-Age-style of the northern and north-western Norwegian regions. As the forerunner, it seems that Textile ceramics were bound to the east, but as the orientation toward South Scandinavia was intensified in the Late Bronze Age, the ceramic technology developed accordingly. Considering that the Risvik ceramics are synchronous with the agricultural expansion to the North, it is proposed that the style developed under influence of the B-group ceramics—a ceramic type that is common in settlement contexts in South Scandinavia around 825–500 BC (Stilborg 2002a, p. 86). In my opinion there are noticeable stylistic similarities between Risvik and the South Scandinavian 'B-group' pottery (Fig. 6).

The 'B-group' ceramics are common on Late Bronze Age settlements in Denmark and southern Sweden (Björhem and Säfvestad 1993; Stilborg 2002a, p. 86-87). In south and east Norway there are some, although few, known finds of this type from settlements, a votive find (Meling 2010) as well as grave contexts (Haavaldsen 1986; Johansen 1986). The B-group covers the Montelius Bronze Age periods V/VI, making it chronologically synchronous with Risvik. Characteristic for the B-type is the smoothed/ polished rim area and the rough surface of the belly, produced by rustication. The rusticated belly is frequently separated from the smoothed rim by, for example, incised decoration and/or different moulded features such as a bulb (Stilborg 2002a, p. 86–87). Furthermore, the coarse belly of the B-group was produced by rustication while the rough surface of the Risvik vessels was created by heavy inclusions of short and thick asbestos fibres.

Fig. 6: Sherds of the B-group type, from Tornesvatnet, Haugesund in Rogaland. Note the smoothed belt under the rim and the bulb that marks the transition to the rusticated belly (Photo: Hop, H.)

The concurrence in datings and particular morphological features makes it plausible that the Risvik ceramics were developed under influence of the South Scandinavian B-type pottery. It is tempting to see the rough surface of the Risvik ceramics, created by heavy tempering of short and wide asbestos fibres, as a local variation of the rusticating technique that was adjusted to fit the local asbestos tempering tradition.

It seems like a bit of a paradox that the concentration of early finds of asbestos tempered ceramics along the coast comes from regions furthest away from the focal points of the asbestos tradition. However, it seems far-fetched to consider the asbestos tempering trait as a local southwest Norwegian innovation, considering the extensive Fennoscandian asbestos ceramic tradition and the fact that northern influences, such as slate arrowheads, are evident in the southwestern Norwegian archaeological assemblage at least from the Middle Neolithic period (Prescott 1991, p. 94). If we accept the premise that the technology of asbestos tempering was adapted from Fennoscandia, and that it was further developed and transformed within the context of local ceramic production, we can follow Christopher Prescott's understanding of the asbestos ceramics as being a distinctly local material expression in a periphery of the South Scandinavian Bronze Age complex: western Norway (1991, p. 95).

Summing up

As previously mentioned, there are no grave contexts containing asbestos ceramics in southwest Norway. All of the finds (with the exception of the votive find from Østre Hauge, Lista) are likely to be interpreted as remains from settlement activities. Asbestos tempered pottery is, in most instances, found together with 'regular' pottery at the settlement sites, indicating that asbestos ceramics were perhaps reserved for specific purposes in the domestic sphere. A consideration of the special properties of asbestos and why it was preferred as clay temper is an issue that cannot be discussed further here (however, for some insights on this topic, see Hulthén 1991; Espelund 1992; Lavento 1995; Sundquist 2000).

North-western Norway is recognized as a core area of Nordic asbestos ceramics, and there are finds covering the entire chronological scope from the Early Bronze Age to the pre-Roman Iron Age—finds that model the typological-chronological framework suggested by Ågotnes (1986). In comparison with southern and northern contexts, it is evident that some of the general traits in the chronology are relevant to the Nordic asbestos tradition as a whole. Even though local variations complicate this picture, the general development can be summed up as follows: in the Early Bronze Age the vessel walls are thin, the base is flat and the shapes are simple, and often unrestricted. In the Late Bronze Age the vessel walls are thicker and the base is either rounded or flat. A common variation is the smoothed belt under the rim with a bulb separating the belly that is commonly rough, like the Risvik style. On the whole, this description of the chronological change is generally consistent with the one proposed by Ågotnes (1986).

The southwest Norwegian asbestos ceramics are found in settlements throughout the Bronze Age, with a marked concentration in the Early Bronze Age. The absence of asbestos ceramics in south Norwegian Bronze Age graves are consistent with the general absence of the ceramics in Early Bronze Age graves in northern Europe, but is in contrast to the trend in north-western Norway, where the focal point for asbestos ceramics in graves is actually in the Early Bronze Age. This observation indicates that regional variation, influences and questions of identity can be fruitful topics for future studies of the uncharted subject of Norwegian Bronze Age ceramics. Asbestos ceramics seems like a good place to start.

Acknowledgement

I would like to thank Ole Stilborg for an especially important and thought-provoking comment after my talk at the Prehistoric Pottery across the Baltic Basin conference in Lund 2013.

Bibliography

Aasbøe, M. (2006) *Sørnorske ansiktsurner – en studie av lokal kontekst og interregionale kontakter.* Upublisert hovedfagsavhandling. Bergen: Universitetet i Bergen.

Aasbøe, M. (2008) *Norwegian face-urns: local context and interregional contacts.* In Fahlander, F., Østigaard, T. (eds.), The Materiality of Death: Bodies, Burials, Beliefs, 105–113. Oxford: Bar International Series.

Andreassen, D. M. (2002) *Risvikkeramikk – en analyse av teknologisk stil på Nordkalotten i sein steinbrukende tid.* Upublisert hovedfagsavhandling. Tromsø: Universitetet i Tromsø.

Arntzen, J. (2012) *Jordbruksboplasser fra bronsealder og førromersk jernalder i Nord-Norge: Veien videre.* In F. Kaul, Sørensen, L. (eds.), Agrarsamfundenes ekspansion i nord: symposium på Tanums Hällristningsmuseum, Underslös, Bohuslan, 25-29. maj 2011, 183–194. København:Nationalmuseet.

Bakka, E. (1976) *Arktisk og Nordisk i bronsealderen i Nordskandinavia.* Miscellanea 25, 4-58. Trondheim: Det kongelige norske videnskabers selskab.

Björhem, N. and Säfvestad, U. (1993) *Fosie IV. Bebyggelse under brons och järnålder.* Malmöfynd 6. Malmö: Malmö Museer.

Carpelan, C. (1979) *Om asbestkeramikens historia i Fennoskandien.* Finskt museum, 85, 5–25.

De Lange, E. (1913) *Et par vestlandske urnegraver fra yngre bronsealder.* Oldtiden – tidsskrift for norsk forhistorie, Bind III, 41–57.

Espelund, A. (1992) *Tidlig jernframstilling i asbestkeramikk? Kommentar til B.Hulthen.* Fornvännen 87, 259–260.

Engedal, Ø, Handeland, H and Kristoffersen, K. (2006) *Arkeologiske granskninger på Kvitevoll gnr.198 bnr.1-2 Halsnøy, Kvinnherad kommune.* Upublisert rapport. Bergen: Bergen Museum.

Engedal, Ø. (2010) *The Bronze Age of Northwestern Scandinavia.* Dissertation for the degree doctor philosophiae. Bergen: University of Bergen.

Fokkens, H. and Fontijn. H (2013) The Bronze Age in the low countries. In Harding, Anthony F. and Fokkens, Harry (eds.), *The Oxford Handbook of the European Bronze Age.* 550–570. Oxford: Oxford University Press.

Fyllingen, H. (2011) *Asbestkeramikk fra bronsealderen – nye resultater fra utgravningene på Jåsund, Sola kommune.* Fra Haug ok Heiðni, tidsskrift for Rogalands arkeologiske forening, 4, 8–9.

Gjessing, G. (1942) *Yngre steinalder i Nord-Norge.* Instituttet for sammenlignende kulturforskning, Serie B Skrifter 39. Oslo:Aschehoug.

Haavaldsen, P. (1985) Sørnorske ansiktsurner – en lokal utforming av en kontinental oldsaksgruppe. In J. R. Næss (ed.), *Artikkelsamling I, AmS – Skrifter* 11. 25–32. Stavanger.

Halvorsen, L. S. (2013) *Vegetasjonshistorisk undersøkelse av sjakter på Holve. Hollve gbnr. 96/2, Granvin kommune, Hordaland.* Upublisert rapport. Bergen: De naturhistoriske samlinger, Universitetsmuseet i Bergen

Hop, H. and Lødøen, T. (2013) *Arkeologiske undersøkelser av et aktivitetsområde med kulturlag og dyrkningsspor fra senneolitikum/bronsealder. Hollve, gnr. 96/bnr. 1,2. Granvin herad, Hordaland.* Upublisert rapport. Bergen: Seksjon for Ytre Kulturminnevern, Universitetsmuseet i Bergen.

Hop, H. M. B. (2011) *Sørlig Asbestkeramikk – en presentasjon av funn, lokaliteter og teknologiske valg.* Upublisert mastergradsavhandling. Bergen: Universitetetet i Bergen.

Hulthén, B. (1991) *On Ceramic Ware in Northern Scandinavia During the Neolithic, Bronze and Early Iron Age – A Ceramic-ecological Study.* Archaeology and Environment 8. Umeå: University of Umeå.

Høgestøl, M. (1995) *Arkeologiske undersøkelser i Rennesøy kommune, Rogaland, Sørvest-Norge.* AmS-Varia 23. Stavanger: Arkeologisk museum.

Jensen, J. (1997) *Fra bronze-til jernalder – en kronologisk undersøgelse*. Nordiske fortidsminder Serie B, Bind 15. København: Det kongelige Nordiske Oldskriftselskab.

Johansen, Ø. K. (1986) *Tidlig metallkultur i Agder*. Universitetets Oldsaksamlings Skrifter. Ny rekke, 8. Oslo.

Jørgensen, R. and Olsen, B. (1988) *Asbestkeramiske grupper i Nord-Norge 2100 f. Kr.-100 e.Kr.* Tromura, kulturhistorie 13. Tromsø:Universitetet i Tromsø.

Kneisel, J. (2012) *Anthropomorphe Gefäße in Nord- und Mitteleuropa während der Bronze- und Eisenzeit: Studien zu den Gesichtsurnen:Kontaktzonen, Chronologie und sozialer Kontext*. Bonn: Rudolf Habelt.

Kutschera, E. (1995) *Kulturhistoriske registreringer, rapport. RV Hovedplan Ev.0076 Hp 07.08 Teigland-Lauareid-Håland, Etne kommune*. Upublisert rapport. Bergen: Hordaland fylkeskommune.

Lavento, M. & Hornytzkyj. S (1995) *On asbestos used as temper in Finnish subneolithic, neolithic and early metal period pottery*. Fennoscandia archaeologica, 12, 17–75.

Lomborg, E. (1973) *Die Flintdolche Dänemarks: Studien über Chronologie und Kulturbeziehungen des südskandinavischen Spätneolithikums*. Nordiske fortidsminder. Serie B, Bind 1. København: Det kongelige Nordiske Oldskriftselskab.

Løken, T. (2006). Et enestående keramikkansikt fra yngre bronsealder. In Barndon, R., Innselset, S.M, Kristoffersen, K., Lødøen, T. (eds.). *Samfunn, symboler og identitet – Festskrift til Gro Mandt på 70-års dagen*, 377–386. UBAS – Universitetet i Bergen Arkeologiske skrifter. Bergen.

Madsen, O. (1995) *Innberetning. Åkrafjordveien -RV.11 Teigland-Håland Etne kommune. Forundersøkelse -LOK. 7, 15 og 16*. Upublisert rapport. Bergen: Hordaland fylkeskommune.

Melheim, A. L. (2006) Gjennom ild og vann: graver og depoter som kilde til kosmologi i bronsealderen i Øst-Norge. In Prescott, C. (ed.), *Myter og religion i bronsealderen: studier med utgangspunkt i helleristninger, graver og depoter i Sør-Norge og Bohuslän*: Oslo arkeologiske serie 5. 7–194. Oslo.

Meling, T. (2010) *Et keramikkfunn fra slutten av yngre bronsealder ved Tornesvatnet i Haugesund – en offernedleggelse i gårdsnær utmark?* Primitive Tider, 12. 93–101.

Munch, J. S. (1962) *Boplasser med asbest-keramikk på Helgelandskysten*. Acta Borelia B. Humaniora 7, Tromsø: Tromsø museum.

Pesonen, P. (1996) *Early Asbestos Ware*. Pithouses and potmakers in Eastern Finland. Reports of the Ancient Lake Saimaa Project. Helsinki Papers in Archaeology 9. 9-39. Helsinki: University of Helsinki, Department of Archaeology.

Prescott, C. (1991) *Kulturhistoriske undersøkelser i Skrivarhelleren*. Arkeologiske rapporter 14. Bergen: Historisk Museum, Universitetet i Bergen.

Rasmussen, M. (1993a) *Bopladskeramik i ældre bronzealder*. Jysk arkeologisk Sælskab Skrifter 29. Aarhus: Selskabet.

Rasmussen, M. (1993b) *Settlement structure and Economic Variation in the Early Bronze Age*. Journal of Danish Archaeology, 11, 1992–1993, 77–107.

Shetelig, H. (1911) *To bronsealders gravrøiser i Hardanger*. Bergens Museums Aarbog, nr 5 1910, 3–11.

Sofaer, J., Bech, J., Budden, S., Choyke, A., Eriksen, B., Horvath, T., Kovacs, G., Kreiter, A., Muhlenbock, C. and Sticka, H. (2010) Technology and craft. In Earle, T. K., Kristiansen, K. (eds.) *Organizing Bronze Age Societies The Mediterranean, Central Europe & Scandinavia compared*, 185–217. Cambridge: Cambridge University Press.

Stilborg, O. (2002a) Bronsåldern. In Lindahl, A., Olausson, D., Carlie, A. (eds.) *Keramik i Sydsverige – en handbok för arkeologer*, 81-92. Monograps on Ceramics. Keramiska Forskningslaboratoriet. Lund: University of Lund.

Stilborg, O. (2002b) Ytbehandling. In Lindahl, A., Olausson, D., Carlie, A. (eds.) *Keramik i Sydsverige – en handbok för arkeologer*, 25–26. Monograps on Ceramics. Keramiska Forskningslaboratoriet. Lund: University of Lund.

Sundquist, Ø. (2000) *Funksjon, relasjon, symbol: Kjelmøykeramikk og tidlig jernbruk i Finnmark*, Tromura, Tromsø Museums Rapportserie 32. Tromsø Museum:Universitetet i Tromsø.

Thrane, H. (2008) *Nordic Bronze Age pottery and the continent – an essay on cultural interaction*. Opera ex aere. Studia z epoki brązu i wczesnej epoki żelaza dedykowane profesorowi Janowi Dąbrowskiemu przez przyjaciół, uczniów i kolegów z okazji. siedemdziesięciolecia urodzin, 245–256. Warszawa: Instytut Archeologii i Etnologii Polskiej Akademii Nauk.

Wangen, V. (2009) *Gravfeltet på Gunnarstorp i Sarpsborg, Østfold: et monument over dødsriter og kultutøvelse i yngre bronsealder og eldste jernalder*. Norske Oldfunn 27. Oslo: Kulturhistorisk museum, Universitetet i Oslo.

Østmo, E. (1973) *Innberetning om arkeologisk undersøkelse på Holmen, gnr.29, bnr.5.10, Bjerkreim kommune i tidsrommet 25/6-12/7 1973, av fortidsminner med reg. nr. 1891 A22 R4*. Unpublished rapport. Topografisk arkiv, Arkeologisk Museum Stavanger.

Ågotnes, A (1976) *Studier omkring en boplass med asbestkeramikk på Flatebakken, Ristesund, Kvamsøy*. Upublisert magistergradsavhandling. Bergen:Universitetet i Bergen.

Ågotnes, A. (1986) *Nordvestnorsk asbestkeramikk. Karform, godsstruktur, utbredelse og datering*. Arkeologiske skrifter fra Historisk Museum 3, 86-118. Bergen: Universitetet i Bergen.

To Your Health or to Your Ancestors?
A Study of Pottery in Graves from Eastern Norway in the Early Iron Age

Christian Løchsen Rødsrud

Advisor, Museum of Cultural History, Oslo

C.L.Rodsrud@khm.uio.no

Abstract: This paper aims to examine the use and social significance of pottery and other vessels found in burials from the Early Iron Age (500 BC–575 AD) in eastern Norway. Early in the period, the vessels are largely used as cremation urns, but from the beginning of the Roman Period (1 AD) complete sets of vessels for food and drink were also buried in the graves with the deceased. The scene is reminiscent of a table setting, almost as you would see in ritualised feasting. The transition from urns to sets of tableware also relates to a change of pottery shapes, temper and ornamentation, and coincides with the occurrence of Roman glass and bronze vessels. In the cremation urn, the deceased is consumed by fire, which is a passive death. However, through what appears to be a table setting, ties are created to a life that has been lived. The deceased is no longer consumed, but is himself participating in a banquet. From a high level of standardization in large cemeteries with urns, the graves are increasingly individualized by the use of mounds and a wider variety of grave goods, for instance vessels for food and drink, as a way of standing out.

Key words: Pottery; Long duree; Early Iron Age; Feasting; Grave; Eastern Norway; Lived life

Introduction

In this article I will discuss the use of pottery and, eventually, the use of glass vessels and bronze cauldrons of Roman manufacture in graves during the Early Iron Age. Early in the period, the vessels are mostly used as cremation urns, but from the beginning of the Roman Period (1 AD) complete sets of vessels for food and drink were also placed along with the deceased in the graves. The scene is reminiscent of a table setting, more or less like a ritualized feast has taken place. The article is based on the results from the Ph.D. thesis: 'I liv og død: Keramikkens sosiale kronologi i eldre jernalder[1]' (Rødsrud 2012).

I have examined the use of pottery in East Norwegian graves in a long term perspective (500 BC–575 AD) by addressing how pottery from graves can be used to understand the Iron Age man's vision of himself in life as well as in death. I discuss the ideas behind the use of urns and the change to sets of tableware buries alongside the deceased in the first century AD. Furthermore, areas of innovation will be identified through an analysis of the geographical distribution throughout the period. These considerations will be used to understand social relations and thereby to assist in understanding the establishment and renegotiation of cultural traits throughout the period.

The development of the use of pottery forms the basis for the study of a social process (chronology) that is parallelized and contrasted with general development within the community, and is explained through the functional value and aesthetic value of the pottery and the containers' symbolic value in the grave.

The association between pottery and the feast plays a central role for the understanding of the prehistoric society.

In many societies, drinking behaviour is considered important for the whole social order, and so drinking is defined and limited in accordance with fundamental motifs of the culture. Hence it is useful to ask what the form and meanings of drink in a particular group tell us about their entire culture and society (Mandelbaum 1965, p. 281).

Both the tangible vestiges and the written sources indicate that the drink had precedence at the feasts. Dispensing prodigious quantities of alcoholic drink to followers is defined as an important part of the political career of a prehistoric leader (Arnold 1999, 2001; Dietler 1990; Enright 1996; Evans 1997; Koch 2003; Pollington 2003). The archaeology is supported by written sources, not only near-contemporary classical texts such as Poseidonius (second century BC), Caesar and Tacitus, but also later texts from Ireland and Wales (e.g. Beowulf, Gododdin and Mesca Ulad) and through Snorri (e.g. Egils saga Skallagrímssonar). Scandinavia also reflects the continuation of the tradition (for a further discussion of

---

[1] Translated: "In life and death: The social chronology of pottery in the Late Iron Age."

Christian Løchsen Rødsrud

the sources see Arnold 1999; Dietler 1990; Enright 1996; Ingemark 2003; Tierney 1960).

The material

The analysed archaeological material consists of 1330 graves: 1263 containing pottery, 75 containing bronze cauldrons, 43 containing glass beakers, 12 containing drinking horns, and six containing a scoop and sieve (Rødsrud 2012). Undecorated coarse-tempered situla-shaped cooking and storage vessels (Bøe 1931, p. 12-14; Rødsrud 2012, p. 47, 204-206), mostly used as urns, were a dominant component in burials from the pre-Roman Iron Age to the Early Roman Period, but a shift occurs during the Early Roman Period when a new type of 'foreign' fine-tempered and burnished ware (Bøe 1931, p. 24-41; Resi 1986, p. 51-55; Rødsrud 2012, p. 48, 208-211), often with an ornate surface, appears. Initially, these were introduced as part of a set of vessels for food and drink which accompanied the dead, but in a transitional phase they were also used as cremation urns. In the third century AD a range of new types of smaller, black-burnished and decorated vessels (Bøe 1931; Rødsrud 2012, p. 48-55, 211-236) are included in these sets of tableware (Fig. 1).

Imports have also played an important part in the change. In the earliest occurrences, complete sets of tableware are found in the finest elite graves, accompanied by Roman glass and bronze objects. They rapidly become integrated

with local pottery, and a confluence of Roman and Germanic influences gives rise to the new vessels (for more about hybridization see Ekengren 2009).

As such, imports have been important for the occurring change, but should not be given too much value as a conveyor of foreign culture. The transformational process, which in turn is stimulated by the cultural interaction, is of equal importance where both the Roman mind-set and the local practice seem to change. In time, imported Roman glass vessels influenced local ceramic production and clay copies were produced (Bøe 1931, p. 127-129, 220 note 122; Rødsrud 2012, p. 220-222)

As Fig. 2 demonstrates, graves containing one ceramic vessel, or fragments of such, all of which are cremation burials, are dominant during the pre-Roman Period.

During the Early Roman Period, a practice of placing sets of imports or a combination of clay vessels and imports in rich inhumation graves is introduced (Fig. 3). In time, this practice also becomes interred in cremation burials, especially in the cremation patches.

These changes continued with greater impact during the Late Roman Period (Fig. 4). Complete sets of tableware, consisting of two or three vessels, became more common. However, up to six vessels have been found in one singular grave. The imports no longer appear in isolation but rather,

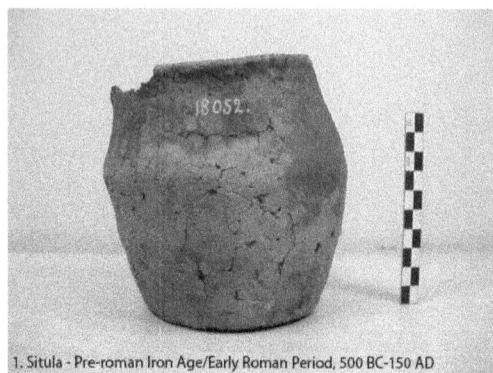

1. Situla - Pre-roman Iron Age/Early Roman Period, 500 BC-150 AD

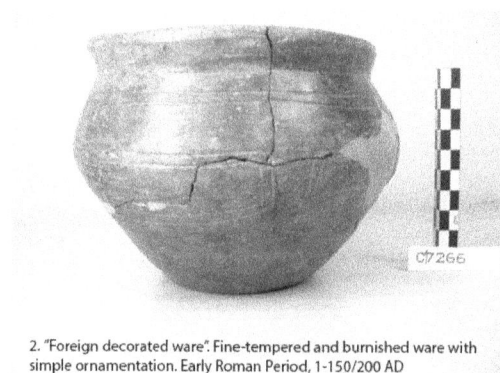

2. "Foreign decorated ware". Fine-tempered and burnished ware with simple ornamentation. Early Roman Period, 1-150/200 AD

3. Sets of black-burnished, decorated tableware. Late Roman/Migration Period, 200-575 AD

Fig. 1: Development from Situla (1), via "Foreign decorated ware" (2), to black burnished tableware (3).

14

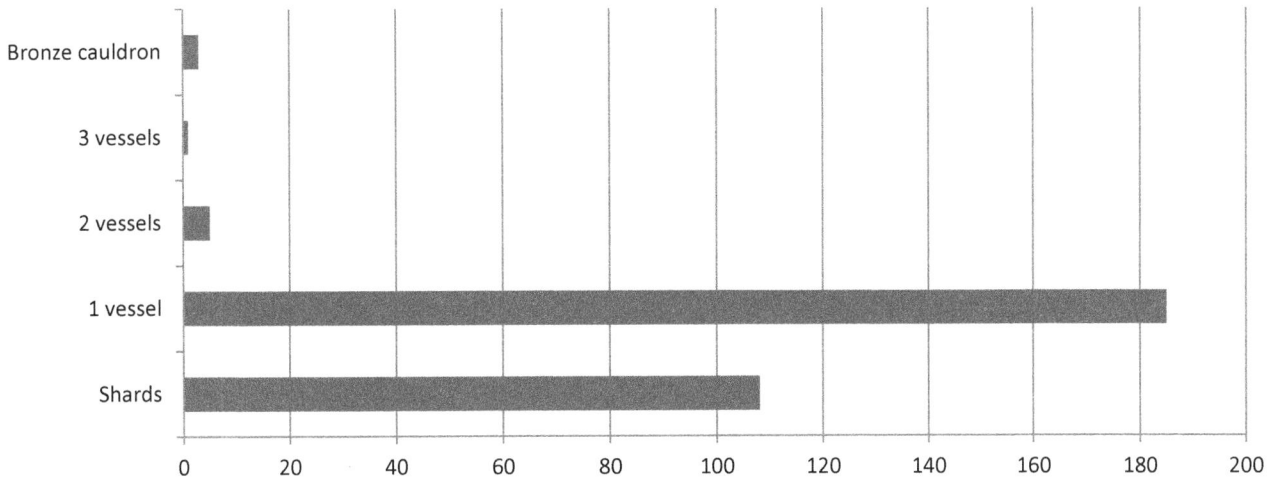

Fig. 2: Graves with pottery. Pre-Roman Iron Age, 500–1 AD.

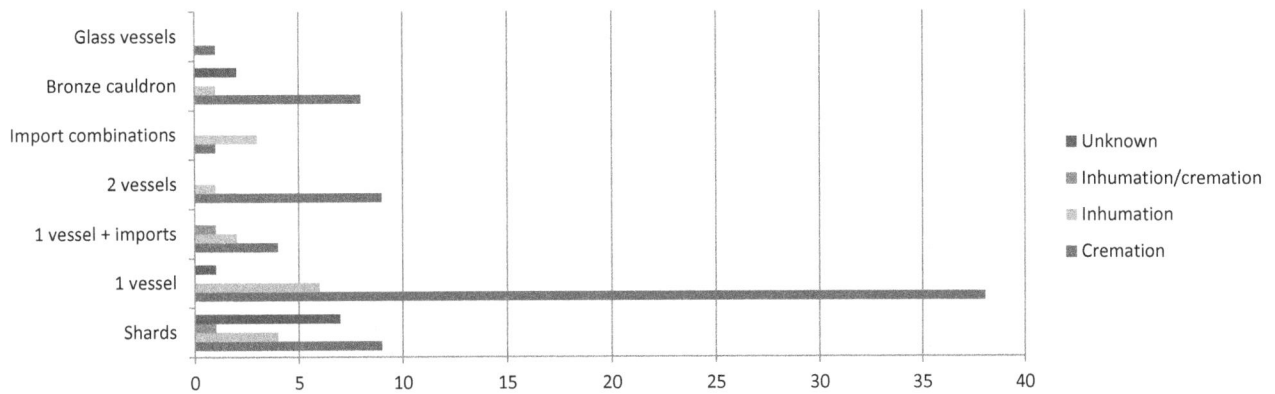

Fig. 3: Graves with pottery. Early Roman Period, 1–200 AD.

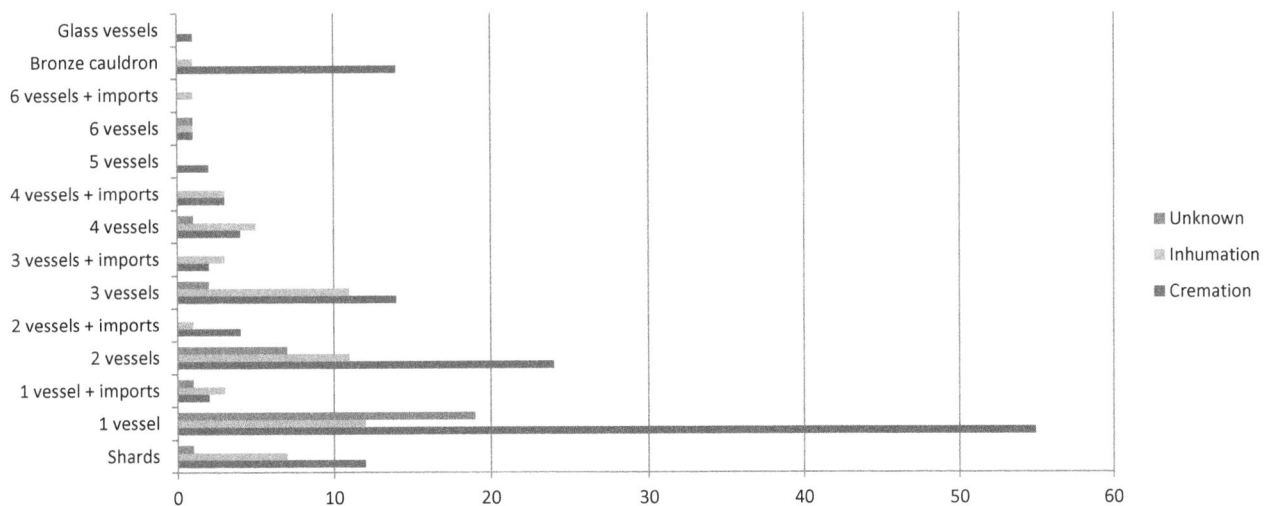

Fig. 4: Graves with pottery. Late Roman Period, 200–400 AD.

as a rule, always appear in combination with clay vessels, as if a process of hybridization is taking place.

During the Migration Period (as early as c. 400 AD in the regions of Østfold), there is a marked decrease in the practice of placing clay vessels in burials. In the Merovingian Period this practice became obsolete and ceased altogether (Fig. 5).

The second tendency is related to the geographical distribution of inhumation burials and richly furnished graves containing imports (Fig. 6). Between Phase 1 (500 BC–200 AD) and Phase 2 (200–575 AD) the number of cremation urns decrease by fifty percent in Østfold and seventy-five percent in Vestfold. This coincides well with the onset of new burial-practices, namely inhumation, which came to be dominant in Vestfold during Phase 2. The

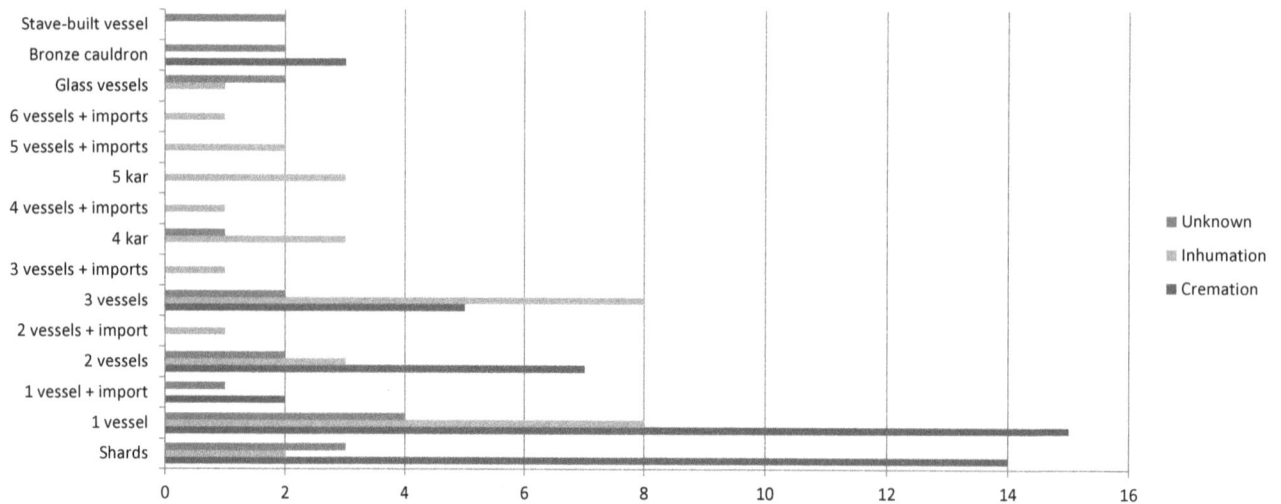

Fig. 5: Graves with pottery. Migration Period, 400–575 AD.

maps in figure 6 represent an overview of graves with sets of more than three vessels. They also reflect the region of Østfold, situated along the eastern part of the Oslo Fjord, as an area of innovation during the Early Roman Period. In time, this shifts to the western side of the fjord to include Vestfold and parts of Telemark, thus imbuing this region with traditions which endured for longer. I see this geographical distribution loosely connected to an influence from east and west Germanic areas, where richly furnished graves with imports are an eastern trait which correspond with multiple richly furnished burials in Østfold (Store Dal, Hunn, Løken og Rør), while the burial practice of inhumation which was dominant in North and Middle Jutland, is reflected through Vestfold. The greater longevity of the practice of the use of sets in Vestfold may indicate this region as a relict area, where this ritualized behaviour lives on compared to Østfold where new practices possibly were sought.

From urn to set

In 1931, Johs Bøe explicitly distinguished between two types of clay vessels: cooking vessels and tableware/ drinking vessels.

Cooking vessels are made to withstand high temperatures and avoid any tension that could result in cracks or collapse; the vessels are fairly coarse-tempered which allows the water to penetrate the vessel and thus even out the temperature it is exposed to (based onLindahl, et al. 2002, p. 18-21; Rice 1987, p. 95-98; Rye 1981, p. 31-36; Shepard 1968, p. 26-31; Skinner 1966).

Drinking vessels and tableware, however, do not need to be able to withstand temperatures higher than their initial firing. In contrast, these vessels were much denser to retain fluids and prevent leakage (Bøe 1931; Hulthén 1986, p. 77, tabell 72; Lindahl, et al. 2002, p. 30).

By analysing remnants and trace elements in thirteen vessels (Isaksson 2008) from the Oslo fjord area, it has been possible to conclude that Bøe's division of vessels for cooking/storage and drink is still valid.

The coarser vessels, often with traces of fire on the exterior, contain remnants that provide evidence that they once contained food. The smaller and more elegant vessels, with smooth, burnished exteriors and decorations, contain trace elements from carbohydrates, such as glucose and sugar. These could be the remnants of drinks based upon malt, berries or honey—typically mead or beer. We know of similar analyses from abroad, where they have found traces of fairly potent mixtures of grains, herbs, honey and berries (Moe and Oeggl 2014; Rødsrud 2012, p. 83-93 with further references).

The coarse undecorated cooking vessels contrast with the burnished decorated tableware. As with imports, fine, decorated tableware can also be tied to individual differences of status (Budden 2008: 14). This is in accordance with the general change of the society during the Roman Period, where a heightened focus is placed on the individual, both through diversity in the design of grave monuments and through an extended inventory of grave goods. The difference between decorated and undecorated vessels is consequently symbolically significant.

The symbolic value of the vessel

The functional value of the vessel adds to its symbolism in a burial context. In daily function the vessel is associated with food and drink and is thus perhaps regarded as a symbol of animating powers. This multi-vocal and ambiguous function is essential for the understanding of its place in a burial context, where initially it is associated with death (Oestigaard 2000, p. 49-50; se også Turner 1967, p. 28-29, 50-55). Through a long-term perspective, I have tried to illustrate that there is continuity between vessels that functioned as urns, and vessels that were part of a set.

The vessel as an urn

In both Celtic and Norse mythology the vessel is associated with sacrificial meals, ritualized feasting and death, most likely as a symbol of regeneration and rebirth (Davidson

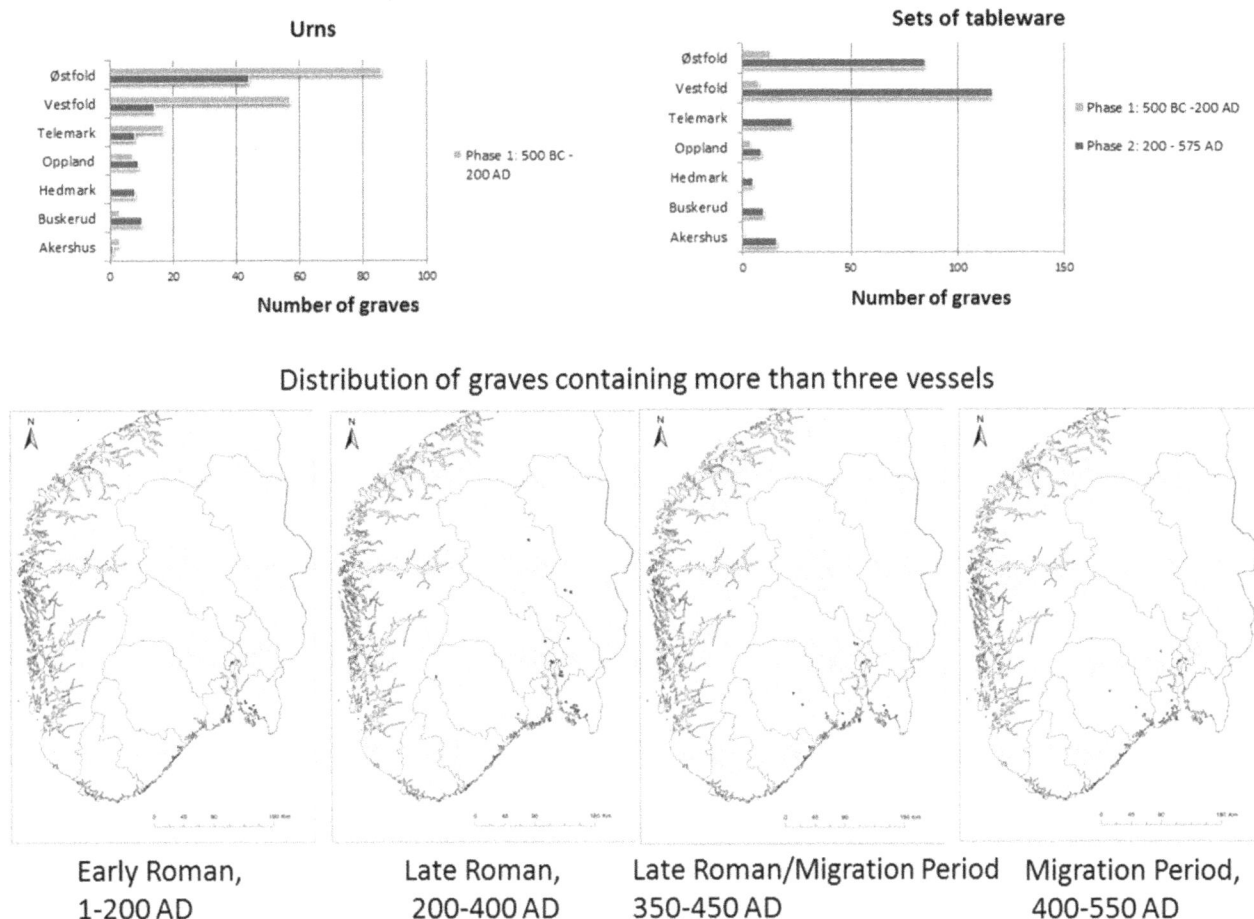

Fig. 6: Development in the use of urns and sets of tableware over time (above) and the distribution of graves containing more than three vessels (below).

1988, 1993; Drobin 1991; Green 1989, 1992, 1998; Görman 1987, 1989). On behalf of its value in a daily setting, the urn could be seen as a symbol of a consumption of the dead and consequently through the ritual, giving the deceased a new position in society.

Through the ritual of cremating the dead, the body is consumed by fire. This is further accentuated by placing the burned bones into a clay vessel in the shape of a cooking pot, thus transcending to an ancestral role (Huntington and Metcalf 1979, p. 93; Kaliff 1992, p. 140; 1993, p. 140; Rødsrud 2012, p. 114-120; Williams 2004, p. 424; Østigård 2007, p. 68). Through the ritual 'game' (Turner 1999 [1967]: 138–144), the artefacts can be tied to mythologies and structures in society. When vessels of various new forms are placed in graves in a new way—in this case, placed as sets of tableware— the practice could thus be associated with a new idea complex and a change in symbolic value.

The feast-interpretation (or hypothesis) – background

Cremation involves the deceased being consumed by fire and placed in an urn, which can be considered a passive/inactive death (no way to interpret the persons role in life), but through what appears to be a table setting, a bond to the lived life is created. The deceased is no longer consumed, but is now an active participant of the banquet. The vessels

can thus be seen as an illustration of 'the perfect host' through which an identity is upheld.

Regeneration, fertility and abundance seem to be an idea-complex of symbolism tied to vessels that can be traced back to the pre-Roman Iron Age. However, this should be understood as an enduring and continued complex, which is also applicable to the tableware sets. In mythology, drinking vessels are associated with the life-giving properties of consumption and power (Braarvig and Furuli 2008; Eliade 1958, p. 188-215; Gjærder 1975, p. 188-189; Green 1989, p. 78, fig. 32; 1992, p. 39-40, 58, 110-112, 137, 191, 227; Sopp 1921, p. 113; Steinsland 2005, p. 277). The culture of ritualized feasting, which was a part of the social life of the elite throughout the Iron Age, is an emphasis of the same longevity and power structures reflecting continuity across time and space. (Blitz 1993; Braun 1983; Bray 2003; Dietler and Hayden 2001; Enright 1996; Potter 2000). I interpret the consumption aspect as an upholder of continuity for understanding that the vessels still hold a place in the graves (see also Rødsrud 2012, p. 127-137). Concerning the tableware, however, I suggest a stronger emphasis on the power-relations that tie the vessels to the functionality of the feast in life (i.e. Enright 1996, p. 264-270; Isaksson 2003, p. 274; Onians 1951, p. 2-17; Qviller 1996, p. 56-57; 2004, p. 42; Steinsland 2005, p. 312). As such, imported vessels are imbued with a stronger symbolic significance than just being random peculiarities amongst the most richly furnished graves.

Combined analysis

There are two general tendencies that stand out in the analysis of the sets. Initially, there is a development from formal sets in the beginning of the Early Roman Period to tableware with variations over time. In early examples, some of the clay vessels—drinking-horns and glass vessels in particular—were consistently placed in pairs. This tendency decreases during the Late Roman Period until it disappears altogether. The Late Roman Period combination-sets of three and four similar vessels are also somewhat standardized in the beginning, before the sets dissolve into a variety of shapes and forms.

The second tendency is most likely related to expressions of individuality and the need to stand apart, where the symbolism seems to be reared towards feasting (see Fig. 7). The status of the deceased seems to increase with the number of vessels, and the figure shows that the occurrence of imports, precious metals or weaponry are proportional to the number of vessels in the graves. In the initial establishment of the custom in the Early Roman Period, all the graves containing complete sets of tableware also contained high-status objects. This tendency decreased over time, indicating that the custom was initially absorbed by those at the top end of the hierarchy of society (Rødsrud 2012, p. 150-173). In particular, the inhumations stand out in terms of wealth, which is an aspect that has previously been noted (Hougen 1929; Kristoffersen 2000, p. 85, 93, 127-128; Shetelig 1912). The vessels can be seen as materialized symbols of ideology that can highlight social differences. The sets of imported tableware (objects of prestige) belong to a very exclusive milieu, followed by other richly furnished graves with precious metals or weaponry, and finally the more simplistic sets of clay vessels, without any additional status objects.

Following the standardized burial practice (often with fragmented grave-goods cf. Chapman 2000) of the pre-Roman Iron Age, a break in continuity occurs during the Roman Period. At this time the burial practice becomes characterized by a re-introduction of large grave-mounds (Hougen 1924; Løken 1974). This development can be understood as a result of the tension between the collective and the individual (Herschend 1993, p. 177-184). The idea of individualization through sets of tableware mirrors the parallel development of the emergence of the great hall, a warrior aristocracy and a centralized redistributed economy (Hedeager 1992; Herschend 1993, 1997; Løken 2001; 2002). The identity focus, regardless of sex, indicates that the identification occurs through social groups, a concept which seems to correspond with the emerging elite and their idealized lifestyle.

When the feast seems to play such an important part of the burial symbolism, it is only natural to discuss its significance for society as a whole. The activity that takes place in the hall can be seen as a structuring element, both of interpersonal relations and of interaction between humans and their material culture. The metaphor in the burial contexts could thus represent or mirror 'the lived life'. The feast might, then, represent a specialized form of gift-exchange which establishes mutual relations between host and guest, as in Marcel Mauss' (2002 [1925]) theory of systems of gift-exchange. This situation would have upheld the social patterns, and reproduced and naturalized social differences or inequality (*Dietler's patron-role feasts*). In time, repeated feasting would shape social debt and incorporate a hierarchical model between the participants, while the ideology is neutralized simultaneously through repetitive rituals (Dietler 2001, p. 82-83).

In my opinion, these vessels are materialized symbols of ideology and power structure in the society (*Dietler's diacritical feasts*). They empower social differences, and influence people to adopt similar 'ways of life' (Dietler

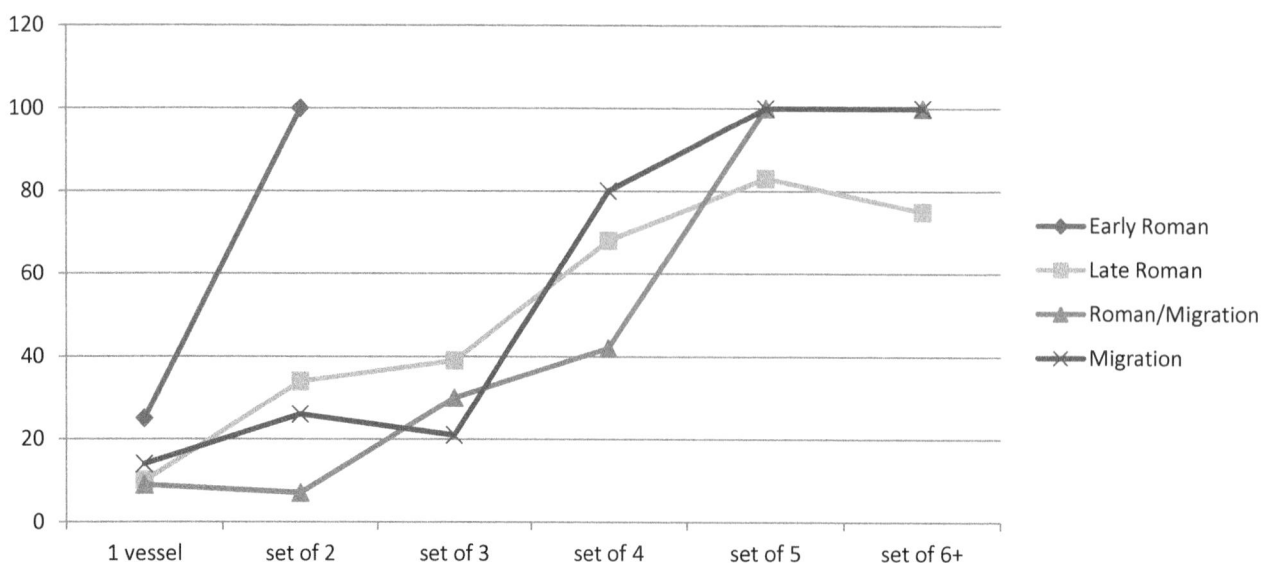

Fig. 7: The graphs show the ratio of imports, precious metals or weaponry found in graves compared to the number of vessels.

1996, p. 92-99; 2001, p. 75-88). When the elite were no longer able to differentiate themselves through the use of increasingly finer vessels, the tradition grinds to a halt and pottery disappears from the burial context altogether. This phenomenon is similar to what we see today; the wealthy find new ways of expressing their prominence, but once these expressions become absorbed into the mainstream, they must find new merits of distinction.

Bibliography

(1941) Mesca Ulad. In J. C. Watson (ed.), *Mesca Ulad*. Mediaeval and modern Irish series. vol. 13. The Dublin institute for advanced studies, Dublin.

(1976) Beowulf. In J. W. Dietrichson (ed.), *Beowulf-kvadet*. Aschehoug i samarbeid med Fondet for Thorleif Dahls kulturbibliotek, Oslo.

(1994) Egils saga Skallagrímssonar. In M. Heggstad (ed.), *Egilssoga*. Samlaget, Oslo.

Aneirin (1978 [1969]) The Gododdin. In K. H. Jackson (ed.), *The Gododdin: the oldest Scottish poem*. Edinburgh University Press, Edinburgh.

Arnold, B. (1999) "Drinking the Feast": Alcohol and the legitimation of power in Celtic Europe. *Cambridge Archaeological Journal* 9(1), 71-93.

Arnold, B. (2001) Power drinking in Iron Age Europe. *British Archaeology* 57, 13-19.

Blitz, J. (1993) Big Pots for Big Shots: Feasting and storage in a Missisippian Community. *American Antiquity* 58, 80-96.

Braarvig, J. and R. Furuli (2008) *Baal: gudenes konge i Ugarit*. Oslo: Bokklubben.

Braun, D. (1983) Pots as Tools. In J. A. Moore and A. S. Keene (eds.), *Archaeological Hammers and Theories*, 107-134. New York: Academic Press.

Bray, T. L. (2003) *The Archaeology and politics of food and feasting in early states and empires*. New York: Kluwer Academic/Plenum.

Bøe, J. (1931) *Jernalderens keramikk i Norge*. Bergen museums skrifter Nr. 141. Bergen: A/S John Griegs boktrykkeri.

Caesar, G. J. (1951) Bellum Gallicum. In S. A. Handford (ed.), *The conquest of Gaul (Bellum Gallicum)*. Penguin Books, Harmondsworth.

Chapman, J. (2000) *Fragmentation in archaeology: people, places and broken objects in the prehistory of south-eastern Europe*. London: Routledge.

Davidson, H. R. E. (1988) *Myths and symbols in pagan Europe: early Scandinavian and Celtic religions*. Manchester: Manchester University Press.

Davidon, H. R. E. (1993) *The lost beliefs of Northern Europe*. London: Routledge.

Dietler, M. (1990) Driven by drink. The role of drinking in the political economy and the case of early iron age France. *Journal of anthropological archaeology* 9, 352-406.

Dietler, M. (1996) Feasts and commensal politics in the political economy. Food, power and status in prehistoric Europe. In P. Wiessner and W. Schiefenhövel (eds.), *Food and the status quest : an interdisciplinary perspective*, 87-125. Providence, R.I. : Berghahn Books.

Dietler, M. (2001) Theorizing the feast: Rituals of consumption, commensal politics and power in African contexts. In M. Dietler and B. Hayden (eds.), *Feasts. Archaeological and Ethnographic Perspectives on Food, Politics and Power*, 65-114. Washington D. C.: Smithsonian Institution Press.

Dietler, M. and B. Hayden (eds.) (2001) *Feasts: archaeological and ethnographic perspectives on food, politics, and power*. Smithsonian Institution Press, Washington, D.C.

Drobin, U. (1991) Mjödet och offersymboliken i fornnordisk religion. In U. Drobin, P.-A. Berglie and L. Bäckman (eds.), *Studier i religionshistoria: tillägnade Åke Hultkrantz, professor emeritus den 1 juli1986*, 97-142. Löberöd: Plus Ultra.

Ekengren, F. (2009) *Ritualization – hybridization – fragmentation: the mutability of roman vessels in Germania Magna AD 1-400*. Acta archaeologica Lundensia, Series in 4° Lund: Institutionen för arkeologi och antikens historia, Lunds universitet.

Eliade, M. (1958) *Patterns in comparative religion*. London: Sheed and Ward.

Enright, M. J. (1996) *Lady with a mead cup: ritual, prophecy and lordship in the European warband from La Tène to the Viking Age*. Dublin: Four Corts Press.

Evans, S. S. (1997) *The lords of battle: image and reality of the comitatus in Dark-Age Britain*. Woodbridge: Boydell Press.

Gjærder, P. (1975) *Norske drikkekar av tre*. Bergen: Universitetsforlaget.

Green, M. J. (1989) *Symbol and image in Celtic religious art*. London: Routledge.

Green, M. J. (1992)*Dictionary of Celtic myth and legend*. London: Thames and Hudson.

Green, M. J. (1998) Vessels of Death: sacred cauldrons in archaeology and myth. *Antiquaries Journal* 78, 63-84.

Görman, M. (1987) *Nordiskt och keltiskt: sydskandinavisk religion under yngre bronsålder och keltisk järnålder*. Lund: M. Görman.

Görman, M. (1989) Hur kan man använda arkeologiskt material i religionshistorisk forskning? Nogra metodiska övervägnaden och tolkningsforsök. In L. Larsson and B. e. Wyszomirska (eds.), *Arkeologi och religion: rapport från arkeologidagarna 16-18 januari 1989*, 31-42. Lund: University of Lund, Institute of archaeology.

Hedeager, L. (1992) *Danmarks jernalder: mellem stamme og stat*. Århus: Aarhus Universitetsforlag.

Herschend, F. (1993) The origin of the hall in the Southern Scandinavia. *Tor, Tidskrift för arkeologi* 25, 175-199.

Herschend, F. (1997) *Livet i hallen: tre fallstudier i den yngre järnålderns aristokrati*. Occasional papers in archaeology 14. Uppsala: Institutionen för arkeologi och antik historia, Uppsala universitet.

Hougen, B. (1924) *Grav og gravplass: eldre jernalders gravskikk i Østfold og Vestfold* 1924:6. Kristiania: i kommission hos J. Dybwad.

Hougen, B. (1929) Trekk av østnorsk romertid, *Universitetets oldsaksamlings skrifter II*. vol. II, 75-126. Oslo.

Hulthén, B. (1986) En keramisk "industrianlägging" från romersk järnålder på Augland, Kristiansand, Vest-Agder fylke i Syd-Norge. Keramikproduktionen. *Universitetets Oldsaksamling Årbok* 1984/1985, 59-86.

Huntington, R. and P. Metcalf (1979) *Celebrations of death: the anthropology of mortuary ritual*. Cambridge: Cambridge University Press.

Ingemark, D. (2003) Glass, alcohol and power in Roman Iron Age Scotland: a study of the Roman vessel glass from non-Roman/native sites in north Northumberland and Scotland, Lund university, Department of Archaeology and Ancient History, Lund.

Isaksson, S. (2003) Vild vikings vivre. Om en tidligmedeltida matkultur. *Fornvännen. Journal of Swedish Antiquarian Research* 98, 271-288.

Isaksson, S. (2008) *Analys av organiska lämningar i keramik från Oslofjordsområdet, Norge.* Upublisert rapport fra Arkeologiska forskningslaboratoriet, Stockholms Universitet.

Kaliff, A. (1992) *Brandgravskick och föreställningsvärld: en religionsarkeologisk diskussion.* Occasional papers in archaeology 4. Uppsala: Societas Archaeologica Upsaliensis.

Kaliff, A. (1993) Världsbild och dödsuppfatning. En essä med exempel. *Tor, Tidskrift för arkeologi* 25/1993, 125-144.

Koch, E. (2003) Mead, chiefs and feasts in later prehistoric Europe. In M. Parker Pearson (ed.), *Food, culture and identity in the Neolithic and Bronze Age*, 125-143. Oxford: BAR Publishing.

Kristoffersen, S. (2000) S*verd og spenne: dyreornamentikk og sosial kontekst.* Studia humanitatis Bergensia 13. Kristiansand: Høyskoleforl.

Lindahl, A., D. S. Olausson, A. Carlie and O. Stilborg (2002) *Keramik i Sydsverige: en handbok för arkeologer.* Lund: University of Lund. Institute of Archaeology.

Løken, T. (1974) Gravminner i Østfold og Vestfold: et forsøk på en typologisk – kronologisk analyse og en religionshistorisk tolkning, Upublisert hovedfagsoppgave ved Universitetet i Oslo, Oslo.

Løken, T. (2001) Oppkomsten av den germanske hallen – Hall og sal i eldre jernalder i Rogaland. *Viking* LXIV, 49-87.

Mandelbaum, D. G. (1965) Alcohol and culture. *Current anthropology* 6, 281-293.

Mauss, M. (2002) [1925] *The gift: the form and reason for exchange in archaic societies.* London: Routledge.

Moe, D. and K. Oeggl (2014) Palynological evidence of mead: a prehistoric drink dating back to the 3rd millennium B.C. *Vegetation History and Archaeobotany* 23, 515–526.

Myhre, B. (2002) Landbruk, landskap og samfunn 4000 f.kr. – 800 e.kr. In B. Myhre and I. Øye (eds.), *Norges landbrukshistorie, bind I. Jorda blir levevei: 4000 f.kr. – 1350 e.kr.,* 11-213. Oslo: Det Norske Samlaget.

Oestigaard, T. (2000) Sacrifices of Raw, Cooked and Burnt Humans. *Norwegian Archaeological Review* 33, 41-58.

Onians, R. B. (1951) *The origins of European thought: about the body, the mind, the soul, the world, time, and fate : new interpretations of Greek, Roman and kindred evidence, also of some basic Jewish and Christian beliefs.* Cambridge: University Press.

Pollington, S. (2003) *The Mead Hall. The Feasting Tradition in Anglo-Saxon England*: Anglo-Saxon Books.

Potter, J. (2000) Pots, Parties and Politics. Communal feasting in the American Southwest. *American Antiquity* 65, 471-492.

Qviller, B. (1996) *Rusens historie.* Oslo: Samlaget.

Qviller, B. (2004) *Bottles and battles: the rise and fall of the dionysian mode of cultural production. A study in political anthropology and institutions in Greece and Western Europe.* Oslo: Hermes Publishing.

Resi, H. G. (1986) *Gravplassen Hunn i Østfold.* Norske Oldfunn XII. Oslo: Universitetets Oldsaksamling.

Rice, P. M. (1987) *Pottery analysis: a sourcebook.* Chicago: University of Chicago Press.

Rye, O. S. (1981) *Pottery technology: principles and reconstruction.* Washington, D.C.: Taraxacum.

Rødsrud, C. L. (2012) *I liv og død: keramikkens sosiale kronologi i eldre jernalder.* Oslo: Kulturhistorisk museum, Universitetet i Oslo.

Shepard, A. O. (1968) *Ceramics for the archaeologist.* Washington: Carnegie Institution.

Shetelig, H. (1912) *Vestlandske graver fra jernalderen.* Bergens Museums Skrifter. Ny række B. 2, No. 1. Bergen: Bergens Museum.

Skinner, B. J. (1966) Thermal expansion. In S. P. Clark (ed.), *Handbook of physical constants*, 75-96. New York: Geological Society of America.

Snorri, S. (1990) Heimskringla. In E. Monsen and A. H. Smith (eds.), *Heimskringla, or The lives of the Norse kings*, XXXVII, 770 s. Dover, New York.

Sopp, D. O. J. (1921) Lidt av øllets historie. In N. Vogt (ed.), *Schous bryggeri: mindeskrift til hundreaarsjubilæet 1921,* 104-125. Kristiania: Schous bryggeri.

Steinsland, G. (2005) *Norrøn religion: myter, riter, samfunn.* Oslo: Pax.

Tacitus, C. (1997) Germania. In T. Width (ed.), *Agricola og Germania*, 117 s. Aschehoug i samarbeid med Fondet for Thorleif Dahls kulturbibliotek og Det norske akademi for sprog og litteratur, Oslo.

Tierney, J. J. (1960) The Celtic Ethnography of Posoidonius. *Proceedings of the Royal Irish Academy. Section C* 5, 189-275.

Turner, V. W. (1967) *The forest of symbols: aspects of Ndembu ritual.* Ithaca, N.Y.: Cornell University Press.

Williams, H. (2004) Potted Histories – Cremation, Ceramics and Social Memory in Early Roman Britain. *Oxford Journal of Archaeology* 23(4), 41-427.

Østigård, T. (2007) *Transformatøren: ildens mester i jernaldern. Rituelle spesialiteter i bronse- og jernalderen II.* GOTARC SERIE C. Arkeologiska skrifter 65. 2 vols. Göteborg: Göteborg universitet, Institutionen för arkeologi och antikens kultur.

Use Traces on Crucibles and Tuyères? An Archaeological Experiment in Ancient Metallurgy

Katarina Botwid[1] and Paul Eklöv Pettersson[2]

Department of Archaeology and Ancient History, Lund University

[1] Katarina.Botwid@ark.lu.se

[2] Paul.Eklov.Pettersson@ark.lu.se

Abstract: To what extent can we identify sites where metallurgy has been conducted by studying the ceramic residue found at the site? Ceramic tools used for metal casting, such as crucibles, clay moulds and tuyères—so called 'technical ceramics'—are often used as indicators of metalcrafts. Their often vitrified and sintered appearance is, on many occasions, used as traits of identification. This article discusses a crucible and a tuyère that show no clear traces of vitrification, and whether or not the objects should be disregarded as technical ceramics. By building reconstructions of these two objects and testing them in an archaeological experiment, we have been able to study the traces of use on the reconstruction and compare them to the two artefacts. In this article we argue that signs of use, such as vitrification and sintering, are not always present on used tuyères and crucibles and that we should also try to look for other signs of use when classifying archaeological materials as technical ceramics.

Key words: Technical cearmics; Tuyére; Crucible; Bronze casting; Experimental archaeology; Ceramic artefacts

An archaeological experiment in ancient metallurgy

Metalcraft is intriguing, beautiful and complex, but tracing it in the archaeological material can be difficult. Ceramic artefacts used as tools within metallurgy (so called 'technical ceramics') are often regarded as important when determining that metalcraft really took place at a site. A tuyère (bellow nozzle) and a melting crucible that show *no* clear traces of use from metalcraft are discussed in this article. Should they be disregarded as technical ceramics? In extension, what activities took place at these sites?

Aim and objectives

The aim of this article is to present and discuss the results of an experiment made on ceramic tools used for bronze casting in Scandinavia during the Late Bronze Age (LBA). The experiment was conducted at Lund University and the open air museum *Vikingatider*, Sweden. Two artefacts were in focus for this study: a ceramic decorated pipe-shaped object from the site Pryssgården dated to the LBA period V (ca 900–700 BC) and several sherds of what was assumed to be debris of crucibles from the site Brogården dated to the LBA period V–VI. In this study the authors tested two theories: that the artefact from Pryssgården was a tuyère (as earlier proposed by Thrane 2006, Goldhahn 2007 and Botwid 2015; conference paper, Lund) and that the sherds from Brogården derived from crucibles (as presented by Petré 1959, p. 53) used for melting Cu-alloys. The possibility that these artefacts are not technical ceramics but instead derive from another type of ceramic object is the background to the experiment described in this article. The artefact from Pryssgården (find 5918) has been interpreted as a figurine (Stålbom 1998, p. 130–132) but during an investigation of the shape, traces of forming processes and evidence of use were established using the method *artisanal interpretation* (Botwid 2013a; conference paper 2013b, 2014, Lund). Consequently, the object was re-interpreted to be a tuyère (bellow-nozzle) by the author (Botwid). The sherds from Brogården might derive from another type of ceramic object since they show no clear traces of use that are usually connected to Cu-alloy melting crucibles such as vitrification, sintering or a red patina from the Cu-alloy (Eklöv Pettersson 2011).

The sites

Brogården

Brogården consists of a burial site and a settlement with activity areas. It was excavated in connection with the building of a housing area in the city of Bromölla in Skåne, south Sweden (Fig. 1) (Petré 1959). The settlement as well as the burial site was typologically dated to the LBA Montelius period V–VI (900–500 BC). The excavation uncovered artefacts and constructions indicating that various crafts such as ceramic manufacture, building of kilns and hearths, and metal casting had been conducted at the site. The latter was indicated by clay and stone moulds and sherds from melting crucibles of the type that are common in the area during the LBA (Fig. 2). Alongside these artefacts and features, the archaeologist also uncovered what appeared to be sherds from an unusual

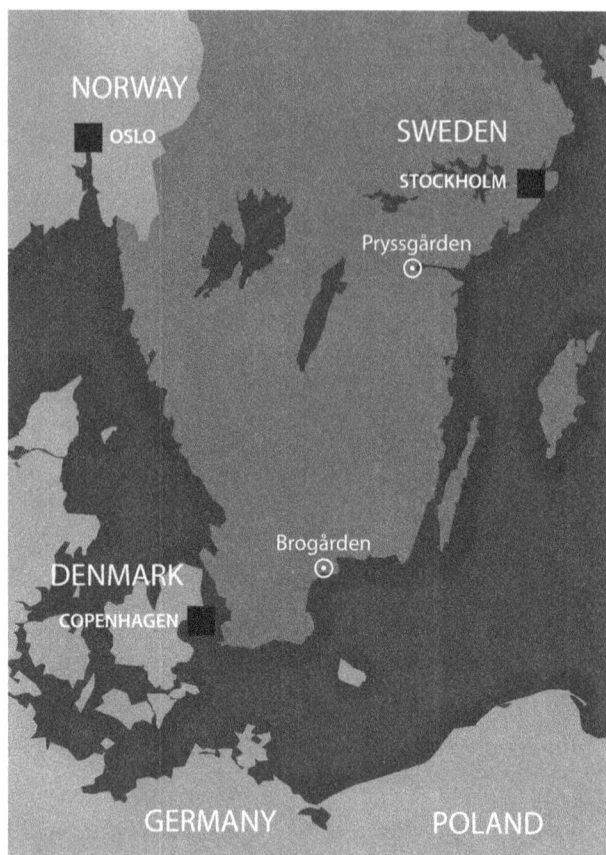

Fig. 1: The location of the sites Pryssgården and Brogården. Illustration Henning Cedmar Brandstedt 2015.

Fig. 2: Artefacts connected to bronze casting found at the site Brogården. Top left: clay mould; top right: crucible sherd; bottom: stone mould (photo Eklöv Pettersson).

Fig. 3: Refitted pieces of what seems to be, for Scandinavia, unusually large crucibles dated to the Late Bronze Age. Photo Eklöv Pettersson. Scale 10 cm.

type of crucible which was larger and differently shaped than earlier crucibles registered in the area (Fig. 3).

Pryssgården

Pryssgården is a well-known archaeological site in Sweden. It is situated near the modern city of Norrköping in the southeast part of the country (Fig. 1). The location, between the Baltic Sea and the big lake of Vättern, makes this site special as the landscape and the water road makes a 'scar' through fields and landmarks. The inlet towards Norrköping, called Bråviken, makes its way towards the natural channel Motala ström before finally reaching the lake of Vättern, and consequently into western parts of Sweden.

During the Bronze Age the cultivation of land and farming spread eastwards from the inland area towards the coast region. The 1660 rock carvings at Himmelstalund are examples of the increasing activity in the area. Close to Himmelstalund lies Pryssgården, a site which has been active on and off from the Neolithic to the Early Middle Ages. Pryssgården was excavated in 1993–94 and became a well known Swedish Bronze Age site (Stålbom 1998).

The archaeological material, description and earlier theories of use

A melting crucible (in this text simply referred to as a crucible) is the vessel which contains the metal during

the melting process of metal casting. The most common type of crucible during the LBA is known from several sites in Scandinavia. It is a rather small container which can be used several times, and when viewed from above it has an oval/pear shape (see for example Janzen 2008). In comparison to their successors during the Late Iron Age, they are relatively shallow and were often used repeatedly (Bayley and Rehren 2007). Sometimes another layer was added between usages, and is thus interpreted as a 'mending layer' (Oldeberg 1976, p. 75). The crucible material from Brogården consists of sherds from crucibles of the more commonly known type, as described, but also from crucibles of a more debatable type. During excavations in the 1950s some of the sherds from Brogården were interpreted as deriving from crucibles despite having no clear traces of sintering or metal residue. There are few parallels in Scandinavia to compare these finds to. These sherds are in focus in this study and carry none of the above described features. If deriving from crucibles, these seem to have been circular in shape with a diameter of approximately 20 cm and a depth of 5–7 cm. They consisted of two layers lacking evidence of usage in between. Most importantly, they carry no traces of use such as vitrification and sintering of the ware, or a red Cu-alloy

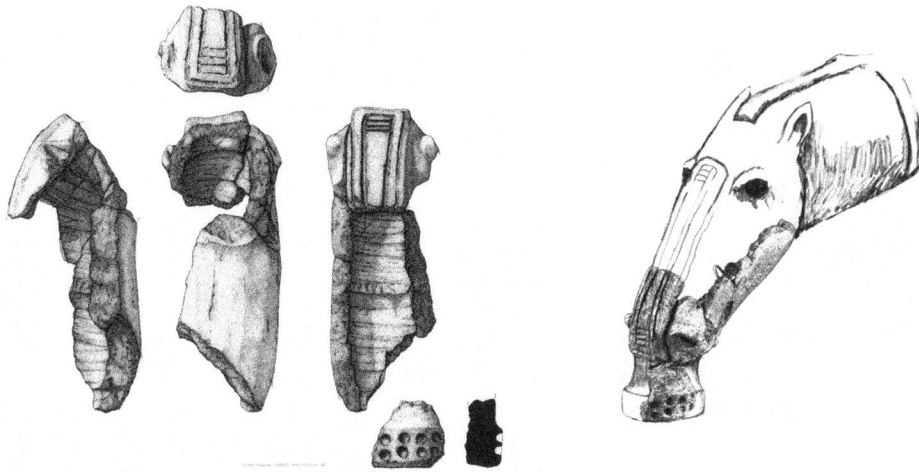

Fig. 4: The object from Pryssgården intrepreted by Botwid (2013b) and Trane (2006) as a tuyère and by Stålbom 1998 as a figurine (left). Reconstruction suggestion made by Botwid (2013b) (right).

patina on their inside surface (Fig. 3). If the sherds do come from a crucible, this crucible would hold up to a litre of melted bronze and might explain what type of crucibles were used when making the larger bronze objects that were casted in Scandinavia at this time. The dating of the sherds has been discussed with the archaeologist Dr. Rolf Petré who led the excavation, and he confirms that the sherds were found in the same contexts as material dating to the Late Bronze Age Monetlius period V (ca 900–700 BC) (Petré 1959). This has led one of the authors of this article (Eklöv Pettersson) to propose that the sherds may derive from another artefact, rather than from a crucible. In 2008 archaeologists at Viborg Museum, Denmark, uncovered a similar type of crucible which now may support the interpretation made at the excavation of Brogården in 1958 (Petré 1959; Larsen 2013).

A tuyère is a funnel or pipe -shaped object made of clay which is used to divert the airflow from a bellow or other air source into an oven or hearth (Thrane 2006, p. 271; Stilborg 2002 p. 150; Tylecote 1976, p. 22, 190; Jantzen 2008). There are several types of tuyères and in this article we use the term to refer to an elbow-shaped (Tylecote 1976, p. 22) ceramic pipe. This elbow-shaped tuyère would conduct the airstream from a pair of bellows into the hearth from above (Rehren and Bayley 2007; Fig. 8 this article). The most famous artefact discovered at Pryssgården was the so-called Pryssgård figurine which was interpreted as a unique find of a goddess figurine (Stålbom 1997, p. 112). Later this artefact has been re-interpreted as a possible tuyère by Thrane (2006) and Goldhahn (2007). At the conference *Prehistoric pottery across the Baltic* in Lund 2013, the author presented the artefact as a zoomorphic pipe-shaped object with features of a horse (Botwid 2013b) (Fig. 4).

Making the replicas

The crucible sherds from Brogården derive from an original object consisting of two layers of clay (Fig. 5), both of which, by ocular assessment, seem to have been

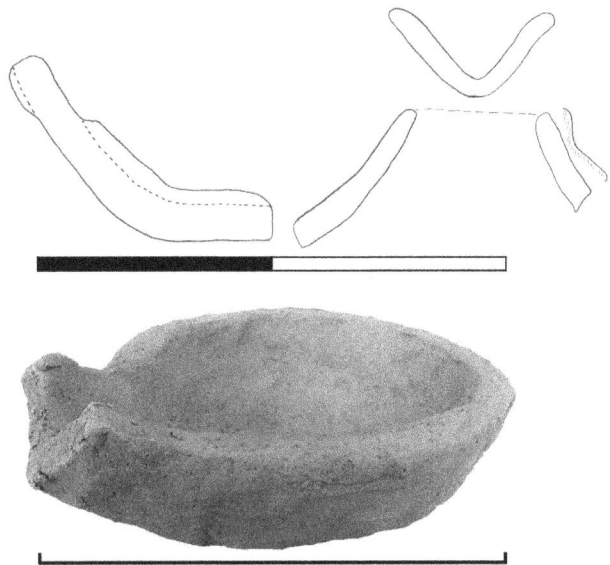

Fig. 5: The reconstructed crucible (bottom) and the drawing (top) made from studying the archaeological material (photo Eklöv Pettersson; scale 20 cm).

tempered with sand. The replica was made in a ceramic workshop together with the tuyère (described below). The material used was sand-tempered brick clay. The replica was made through pinching and the morphology copied from sketches and measurements of the sherd material (Fig. 5). The crucible was then left to dry until leather hard, after which the inside of the crucible was rugged and a circular, thinner clay cake was made and attached to the inside of the crucible. The complete two-layered crucible was then left to dry and biscuit-fired to 900°C before use.

To make the replica of the tuyère a clay pipe was used as a starting point. The photos below show the technique used to make a pipe-formed object in the clay with a special tucking technique. The tool used for this kind of tucking is made from a stick, onto which bast or straw is tied. The stick is then covered with clay. The photos below (Fig. 6) show how the pipe is tucked from the inside (Botwid 2015). After tucking, the pipe needs to dry a while before

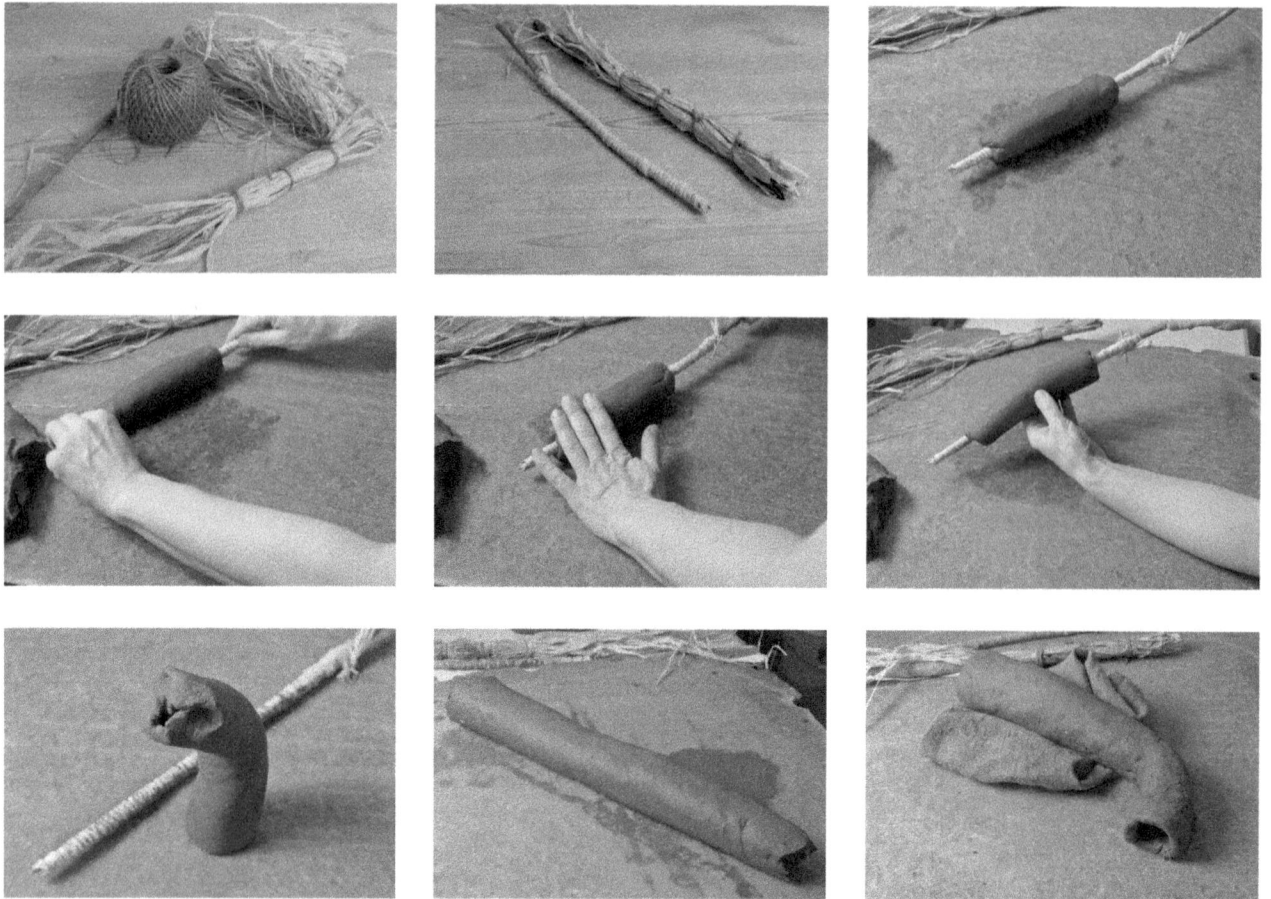

Fig. 6: The special tucking technique for making pipes. Pipes can be manufactured in different sizes depending on the length of the stick. This makes the manufacturing of pipes easier than with other described ceramic-forming techniques such as coiling or pinching (photo: Botwid).

forming it to the desired shape—in this case a tuyère. After drying to a leather hard consistency it is possible to design eventual features. The tuyère must be completely dry before it is fired together with other ceramic objects in a ceramic bonfire. Three such replicas were made for the study to evaluate their technical performance and appearance.

The archaeological experiment

The Tuyère was tested together with several types of crucibles in a reconstructed workshop at the open air museum Vikingatider in Löddeköpinge, Skåne, along with the replica of the crucible from Brogården. The workshop consisted of a pit-hearth covered with clay and surrounded by bricks which represented the use of stones for reducing the heat loss from IR-radiation. To this a pair of bellows was applied together with the tuyère which was fitted in a way that it would direct the airflow from the bellows into the hearth from above. The pit was then pre-heated with wood after which charcoal was used as fuel. The crucible presented in this article was moved and placed using wooden pliers. In this setup it is vital to know that just a few centimetres under the exit hole of the tuyère the highest temperature of the hearth will be reached (B in Fig. 8) due to the position having the best access to constantly flowing oxygen. The tuyère itself (A in Fig. 8), however, will never be exposed to these temperatures since it is placed some centimetres above and cool air is constantly

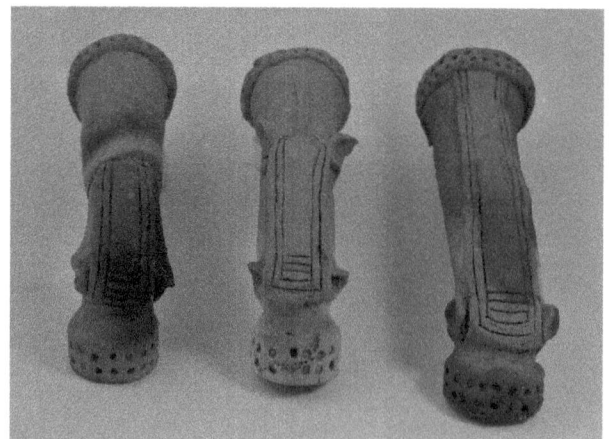

Fig. 7: The reconstructed tuyères after being used in the experiments (photo: Botwid).

being pumped through it, working as a cooling effect. The open shallow crucible type that is common during this period in Scandinavia works perfectly with this setup as it allows the metal inside (C in Fig. 9) to be exposed to the highest temperatures while the ceramic ware (hatched in Fig. 8) is placed some centimetres away from or under the molten metal, and is thus less exposed.

In this experiment the reconstructed crucible was filled with 1 kg of a 10% tin-bronze (10% Sn and 90 % Cu). It was placed on top of gloving charcoal directly under

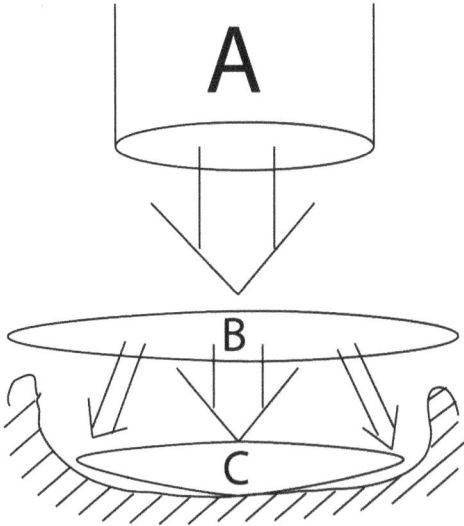

Fig. 8: The theoretical idea behind the workshop. The tuyère (A) will direct the airflow from the bellows into the hearth from above resulting in a airstream of un-warmed/cold air into the fuel (B) in which the air heats up to temperatures above 1000 degrees C or more. The airstream then continues down through the fuel into the crucible (hatched) and hits the metal (C) (illustration by Eklöv Pettersson).

Fig. 9: The workshop in practice (photo: Eklöv Pettersson).

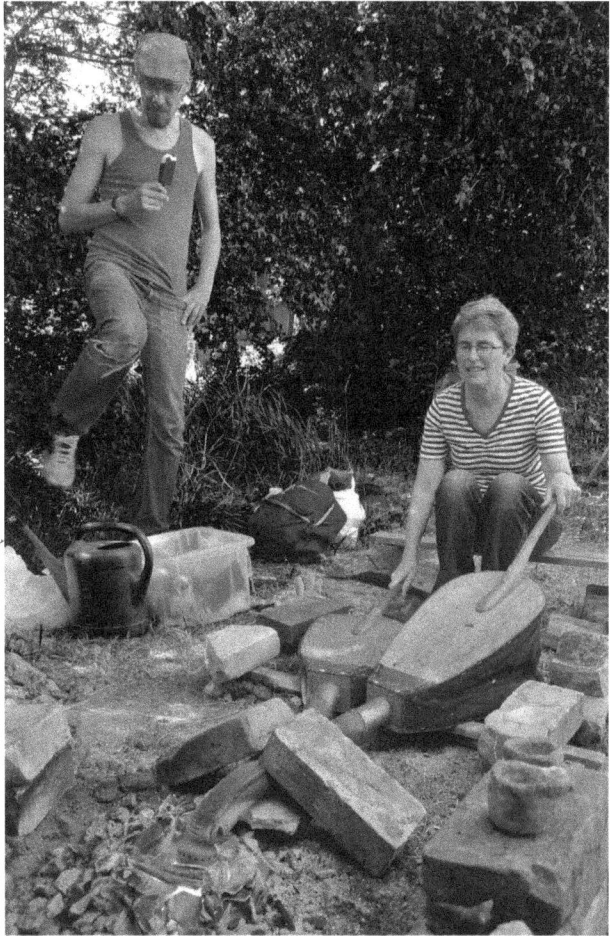

Fig. 10: Professor Deborah Olausson and PhD student Andreas Nilsson, Lund University, trying the bellows (photo: Botwid).

Fig. 11: High temperature is reached according to visual experience. The clear white-yellow shine is visible at 1000–1100°C (Munsell's visual temperature scale (http://munsell.com/about-munsell-color/) (photo Eklöv Pettersson).

the airstream conducted by the tuyère and was covered with additional charcoal. In order to prevent the rim of the crucible from sintering and melting whilst at the same time allowing enough heat to reach the bottom of the crucible and metal, the crucible was placed relatively high and in close connection to the airflow but was also centralized in relation to it so that the rims were at the greatest possible distance from the tuyère (Figures 8 and 9). During the experiment additional charcoal was added when it was necessary, to keep the crucible covered and surrounded with fuel. However, while doing so we accidentally moved the crucible from its original position and it got placed with one part of the rim to close to the tuyère, this meant that the rim was partially sintered. The height of the crucible did not fluctuate that much as the access to oxygen under the crucible is low since the crucible works as isolation material restricting the access to oxygen directly under it. After two hours the mass of metal was clearly getting softer and by three hours the metal had melted. By that time the crucible was removed from the hearth using wooden pliers and the metal poured out of the crucible. After that the crucible was shortly studied in field and then left to cool off in the open hearth with the inner surface exposed to oxygen. As well as this casting event the three tuyères were used for several castings over three days using a multitude of different crucibles. We did this in order to observe the traces of use made on the tuyères after long and diverse use.

Two conclusions could be drawn from the experiment:
- The artefact described by Stålbom (1998) as a figurine was usable as a tuyère.
- The artefact described as a crucible could be used as a melting crucible for Cu-alloy.

However, the possibilities of using an object in a particular way do not necessarily prove that it was used to do that activity. In order to find further proof, the traces of use were studied on the artefacts and compared with the replicas used in the experiments.

Comparison of use traces on the archaeological material and the reconstructions

The crucible sherds from Bromölla originally derive from more than one crucible. The sherds all share the same features by which they have been recognized: they are made of a sand-tempered clay built in two or more layers and show no clear evidence of vitrification, sintering or a red patina from the Cu-alloy, not on the inner surface nor in between the layers (as mentioned above). This had led the authors to a conclusion that these sherds may not derive from crucibles but from some other ceramic object. However, the sherds do show that the assumed inner surface has been (re-)burned or cooled off in a reduced atmosphere, something that can be achieved by leaving the hot crucible upside down in the hearth as it is slowly burning out. Except for this, the traces of use are very few on the archaeological material, almost as if it had never been used.

When looking at the crucible used in the experiments it is clear that the rim sintered from being too close to the tuyère where it was exposed to high temperatures and heavy reduction. However, it is possible and likely that a skilled craftsperson would have been able to avoid this situation by simply keeping the crucible in its original position related to the tuyère. With this exception, the ware

seems more or less unaffected by the heat and the heavy reduction. By leaving the crucible to cool off in the hearth by putting it with the upside/inside exposed to oxygen while the underside/outside was not, this triggered a reduction of the ceramic ware during the cooling process, giving it a specific grey coloured surface (Figures 12 and 13). When comparing this to the archaeological material it seems like those crucibles (assuming they were used) were cooled off upside down, resulting in the grey-coloured surface seen on the sherds (Figures 12 and 13). In conclusion, the traces of how the crucible was used in the stages after the casting were similar but not identical for the two materials. However, this does not contradict that they were used in the same way during the casting process.

When discussing archaeological signs of tuyères there are hypotheses about the mouth (of the pipe) reaching the vitrification point and sintering (Heeb 2014, pp. 42). Findings of vitrified pieces at excavated sites indicate the presence of metalcraft. The object from Pryssgården (presented as a tuyère in this article) showed no such signs of vitrification. Furthermore, when looking at the technique

Fig. 12: The mouth/spout of the crucible. On the right side the ware has been too close to the nozzle of the tuyère and consequently sintered, while the left part is clearly less affected and is similar to the appearance of the archaeological material (photo: Eklöv Pettersson).

Fig. 13: To the left, the outside of the reconstructed crucible (after use) compared with one of the crucible sherds from Brogården. To the right, the inside of the same reconstructed crucible compared with the same sherd from Brogården (photo: Eklöv Pettersson).

used to manufacture such an object, it seems very likely that this pipe-shaped artefact was made using a tucking technique as shown in this article or equivalent.

Looking at the replica of the tuyère used in the experiments presented above, it is clear that the traces of the manufacturing technique are strikingly similar, suggesting that the same method has been use to make both objects (Botwid 2015, in press). In other words, it seem like the pipe had been formed with a tucking technique. Putting clay around a stick clad with bast and then tucking it onto a flat surface enables the artisan to form long pipes that can be shaped into all kinds of artefacts—a known technique in ceramic craft.

When studying the traces of vitrification it was clear in this experiment that when the charcoal was kept below the tuyère during the whole casing process there were no signs of sintering on the tuyère, only a little soot and, in one case, oxidized metal (Fig. 14, Fig. 15: I, III). When the charcoal was pushed up on the sides and covered the outfall (mouth) of the tuyère it underwent a reduction and the material weakened and started to sinter (Fig. 15: II). In such a scenario the metal oxides will also come closer and will help to vitrify the material. In other words, sintering depends on how you use the tuyère, and therefore it is possible that tuyères can be hidden in the archaeological material as parts of pipes with the features of tucking technique on the inside (Botwid 2015, in press). Consequently, the fact that the artefact from Pryssgården

discussed in this article does not have any clear traces of sintering does not exclude the possibility that these sherds derive from a tuyère.

Discussion and conclusions

The experiment shows us that the vitrification and sintering of crucibles (due to heavy reduction and high temperatures) as an indicator of whether the objects have been used or not should be used with caution. If metal is melted using a technique where it is placed in an open crucible and heated from above, the crucible is not necessarily exposed to the same temperatures as the metal. Consequently, crucibles used for melting bronze may not carry any signs of sintering, vitrification or other indications of being exposed to high temperatures, especially if they are only used once or a small number of times. The reason that Scandinavian melting crucibles usually carry clear traces of sintering mostly around the rim is that they are smaller than the ones from Brogården (as described earlier) and therefore their rims are closer to the intensive heat (and heavy reduction) nearby the mouth of the tuyère (see Fig. 8). In that case sintering of the crucible seems to be inevitable, especially after it has been used for several castings (Eklöv Pettersson 2011, p. 34, 2012, p. 38).

As in the case of the large crucibles, sintering of the tuyère nozzle is not a necessary outcome of metalcraft. We have proved through archaeological experiment that signs of sintering say more about the handling of the tuyère and

Fig. 14: The tuyère in use (left) and the traces from the use on the nozzle (right) (photo: Botwid).

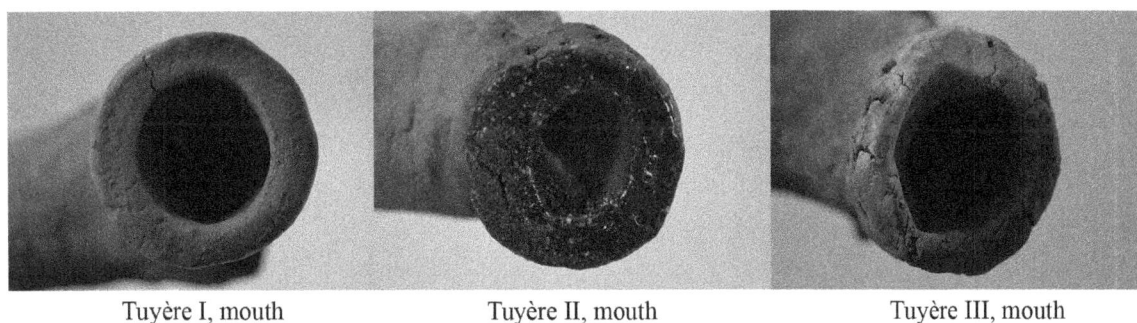

| Tuyère I, mouth | Tuyère II, mouth | Tuyère III, mouth |

Fig. 15: The three different use traces (photo: Botwid).

other technical ceramics than they say about metalcraft. Figure 15 shows the differences in use traces upon the reconstructed tuyères, focusing on the exposed mouth which is closest to the most intensive heat (see Fig. 11). Tuyère I was used for 10 hours and displayed no signs of vitrification. Tuyère II was used for 2 hours and was totally vitrified, while tuyère III was used for 2 hours and only displayed a shade of oxide from the metal at the mouth. All of the reconstructed tuyères worked well and one of them melted a kilo of bronze in three hours.

We argue that the prehistoric artisans who used tuyères showing clear signs of sintering were probably beginners or had a low degree of skill (artisanal knowledge). An artisan who knows their craft would not risk so-called 'potters-tears' (drops of melted clay) in the valuable metal (good artisanal knowledge) (Botwid 2013a), and further, would not risk damage to the tuyère while in the process of melting metal. This technical mistake is avoided by treating the coal and the reduction processes in the right way. Pushing coal over the mouth will start the vitrification process as shown (Fig. 15 middle). We propose that pipe-formed objects with traces of the tucking technique can indicate metalcraft.

In conclusion, it is possible to regard the studied artefacts as evidence of ancient metallurgy even though no traces of vitrification or usage are visible. This implies that we must consider not only traits as sintering or copper alloy residue when studying artefacts in search for technical ceramics, but also put more emphasis on the morphology and shape as direct indicators of this type of artefacts.

Acknowledgements

Thanks to Rolf Petré for your help with the material and for interesting discussions. Acknowledgement goes also to Andreas Nilsson and Simon Rosborg together with whom we conducted the experiments.

Bibliography

Bayley, J. and Rehren, T. (2007) Towards a functional and typological classification of crucibles. In La Niece, S; Hook, D; Craddock, P. (eds.) *Metals and mines. Studies in Archaeometallurgy.* pp. 46–55. The British Museum, London.

Botwid, K. (2015). Manuscript dissertation thesis paper 4.

Botwid, K. (2013a) *Evaluation of ceramics: Professional artisanship as a tool for archaeological interpretation.* In Journal of Nordic Archaeological Science. No. 18 pp. 31–44. The Archaeological Research Laboratory, Stockholm.

Botwid, K. (2013b) *Archaeological ceramics in a new light – early results from artisanal interpretations of ceramics from Pryssgården, Östergötland in Sweden.* Conference paper, presentation at the conference: *Prehistoric Pottery Across the Baltic – regions, influences and methods.* Laboratory of Ceramic Research. Lund University. 2013-03-08.

Botwid, K. (2014). *From Figurine to tuyère.* Conference paper, presentation at the workshop: *Teknisk keramik,*

bronshantverk och innovationsspridning i Skandinavisk förhistoria. Laboratory of Ceramic Research. Lund University. 2014-06-02.

Eklöv Pettersson (2011) *En hållbar utveckling? – hållbarheten för bronsålders keramiska deglar.* Master essay in archaeology, Lund University.

Eklöv Pettersson (2012) *Social status through crucibles.* In Lund Archaeological Review vol. 18 2012. Lund University, Lund.

Goldhahn, J. (2007) Döden hand –en essä om Brons och hällsmeden. In Goldhahn, J. and Oestigaard, T. (eds.) *Rituelle spesialister i bronse- og jernalderen.* GOTARC ser. C Arkeologiska Skrifter no. 65, Göteborgs Universitet, Göteborg.

Heeb, J. (2014) *Copper shaft-hole axes and early metallurgy in south-eastern Europe.* Archaeopress.

Jantzen, D. (2008) *Quellen zur Metallverarbeitung im Nordishen Kreis der Bronzezeit.* Akademie der Wissenschaften und der Literatur, Mainz.

Larsen, L-A. (2013) *VSM 09398 Løgstrup SØ II – etape I, Fiskbæk sogn, Nørlyng herred, Viborg amt 130805-162, -166, -167.* Archaeoloogical report. Viborg Museum, Viborg.

Oldeberg, A. (1976) *Die ältere Metallzeit in Schweden II.* Kungliga Vittergets, Historie och Antikvitets Akademien, Stockholm.

Petré (1959) *En bronsåldersby I Bromölla.* Skånes hembygdsförbunds årsbok 1959. Skånes Hembygdsförbund.

Stilborg, O. (2002) Blästermunstycke. In (eds.) Lindahl, A; Olausson, D; Carlie, A. *Keramik i Sydsverige* pp.150. Institute for Archaeology and Ancient History: report Ser. No. 81. Institute for Archaeology and Ancient History, Lund University.

Stålbom, U. (1998). In: Borna-Ahlkvist, Hélène (1998). *Pryssgården: från stenålder till medeltid: arkeologisk slutundersökning RAÄ 166 och 167, Östra Eneby socken, Norrköpings kommun, Östergötland.* Riksantikvarieämbetet, Byrån för arkeologiska undersökningar. Linköping

Thrane, H. (2006) *Figurinen fra Pryssgården –et alternativt tolkningsforslag.* In Fornvännen – Journal of Swedish antiquarian research. No.101, 2006 pp. 268–273. Kungl. Vitterhets Historie och Antikvitets Akademien, Stockholm.

Tylecote, R.F. (1976). *A history of metallurgy.* Second edition (1992). Maney Publishing, London.

http://munsell.com/about-munsell-color/. *Munsell (temperature definition by) Colour.* [accessed 22-10-2015]

Ertebølle and Pitted Ware Culture? The Late Mesolithic and Neolithic Sites of Hamburg Boberg

Laura Thielen[1] and Britta Ramminger[2]

Archäologisches Institut, Hamburg University

[1] *Laura.thielen@uni-hamburg.de*

[2] *Britta.Ramminger@uni-hamburg.de*

Abstract: The archaeological sites of Hamburg Boberg seem to play a significant part in the transition between Ertebølle and Funnel Beaker culture. In this context, special attention is paid to ceramics which differ in decoration and manufacturing from the local pottery and have been designated as imports. In discussions so far, there is considerable disagreement on the chronological setting of the sites as well as the provenances of the supposed imports. These interpretations consider only a limited part of the pottery excavated in the 1950s and 1960s and do not reflect the whole assemblage. Also, reconstructions and typo-chronological classifications of specific vessels are open to discussion. The diverse suggestions concerning the pottery show that a re-evaluation of the Hamburg Boberg sites, based on the whole assemblage of excavated pottery, is necessary. The study of typological criteria and manufacturing technique, in combination with archaeometrical analysis, will help to answer the question of whether the interactions indicated by imported pottery actually influenced local ceramic production.

Key words: Hamburg Boberg; Ertebølle culture; Funnel Beaker culture; Imported pottery; Chronology

Introduction

The Late Mesolithic and Neolithic sites of Hamburg Boberg (ca. 4500–3500 BC) are of special interest concerning the interaction and communication structures between foragers and farmers. The most prominent find, a globular beaker (*Kugelbecher*) (Fig. 1) originating from the Rössen culture, illustrates contacts between societies with different economies. In addition, further ceramics were identified as being of foreign manufacture compared to the local pottery.

In sum, all intended imports were assigned to cultural groups distributed in the south. The south-north route became of major interest when questioning how the 'Neolithic way of life' reached northernmost Germany. Finally, the archaeological sites of Hamburg Boberg are seen as key sites for the Mesolithic-Neolithic transition, including the adoption of agriculture and the Funnel Beaker pottery spectrum. This process is reflected in various ways and the focus is held on the indicated interactions between the Late Mesolithic foragers and Neolithic southern farmers. The communication axis in the northern direction is highlighted in connection with the Pitted Ware culture.

The Hamburg Boberg sites might help to shed some light on the ongoing discussion on the transition between hunter-gatherers and farmers. However, after early excavations in the 1950s and 1960s, there is still no comprehensive documentation and analysis of the archaeological remains. The project *The Neolithisation process of northernmost Germany – with particular reference to the Late Mesolithic and Neolithic sites of Hamburg Boberg*, funded by the German Research Foundation (DFG), aims to put the entire assemblage of the excavated pottery in perspective. The discussions concerning the chronology and function of the sites, as well as the imported ceramics that have been identified, need to be reviewed with respect to the pottery spectrum as a whole.

Location of the sites and palaeoenvironmental setting

The archaeological sites of Hamburg Boberg are located south-east of the city of Hamburg, in northernmost

Fig. 1: Boberg 20, globular beaker, not to scale (photo: Archaeological Museum of Hamburg).

Fig. 2: Location of the Hamburg Boberg sites. Location 15, 15east and 20, light grey: inland dunes, black: water, grey: preboreal sandy elevations, dark grey: excavation areas (drawing: B. Ramminger).

Germany (Fig. 2). The sites under investigation, Hamburg Boberg 15, 15east and 20, were situated on small Preboreal sandy elevations in the Elbe-Urstrom-Valley, north of large ancient inland dunes. Today, the landscape north of the foreland of the dunes is characterized by the Elbe wetlands (*Elbmarsch*). In contrast, the Geest with its higher elevations extended to the south of the dunes.

The palaeomorphological formation of the Elbe-Urstrom-Valley is mainly the result of glacial formation processes of the Saale and Weichsel Glacial. During the last Saale Glacial the ice shield expanded from an easterly direction. With the retreat of the glaciers, at the end of the Saale Glacial the melt-water drained off in a westerly direction and formed the Elbe-Urstom-Valley by abrasion of the earlier sediments. Although the Weichsel Glacial did not cover the area of modern-day Hamburg, the latter's geomorphological formation was strongly affected by its location close to the glacier edge. The run-off of the melt-water after deglaciation was mainly channelled through to the Urstrom-Valley, which was developed at the end of the Saale Glacial. Finally, the corresponding abrasion of earlier sediments influenced the natural formation of the Elbe-Urstrom-Valley, with a valley bottom up to 20–30 m below NN and the Geest with a higher elevation, which extends from southeast to northwest.

As a result of the preceding melting of the Weichsel Glacial, during the early Holocene the research area was characterised by a branched river-system and well-sorted sands were deposited by water transport. In the further course of the Holocene, the exposed fluviatile sediments

were redistributed by aeolian processes. This resulted in the formation of the inland dunes as well as the small sandy elevation in front of the dunes, where the Late Mesolithic and Neolithic sites of Hamburg Boberg are situated (Ehlers 1994, p. 183–206; 2011, p. 136; Miehlich 1986, p. 100–102; 1999; p. 199–202).

Excavations in the 1950s and 1960s

The Hamburg Boberg sites 15, 15east and 20 have been most extensively excavated by F. Lienau, on behalf of R. Schindler, director of the state office for the preservation of monuments of the city of Hamburg. Lienau was very familiar with the research area due to collections of surface finds since the late 1930s.

The Hamburg-Boberg sites were mainly excavated in the 1950s and 1960s with partial financial assistance from the DFG.[1] Altogether, the excavations of the final Mesolithic and Neolithic sites lasted 13 years. The site of Hamburg Boberg 15 was first investigated in 1951 by opening a test-trench. As Neolithic finds came to light, further excavations were carried out in 1952, 1953, 1954 and 1960. An additional investigation in 1959 took place to prove the extent of the site and resulted in the discovery of the separate prehistoric site of Hamburg Boberg 15east. The independence of location 15east was finally acknowledged

---

[1] Recent excavations have been conducted at site 20 in 1991 in the course of the DFG-funded project The Neolithisation of Schleswig-Holstein (Lübke 1992, p. 49; 2000, p. 326f.). These investigations are excluded in the following text.

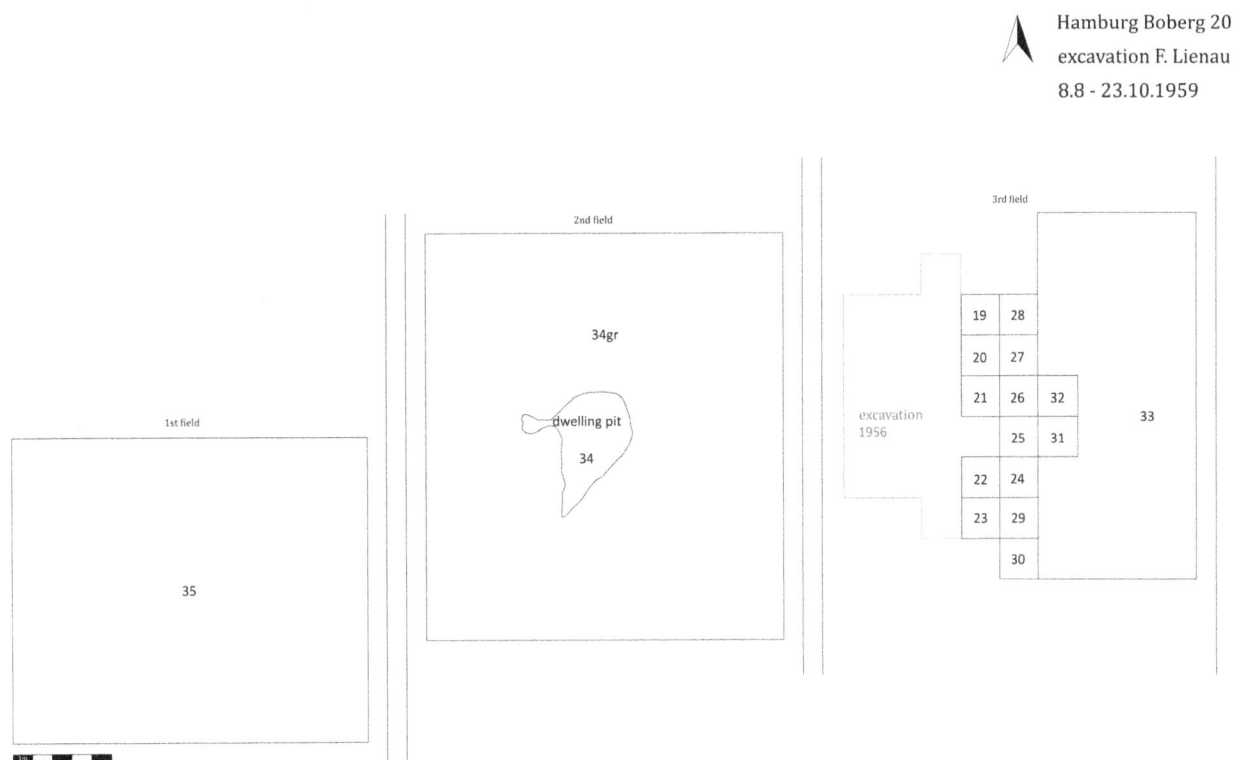

Fig. 3: Boberg 20, site excavation map (after Lienau 1959).

due to sediment-drillings by O. Friedrichsen (Friedrichsen 1960; Schindler 1961, p. 11).

Motivated by the results of the early excavations of location 15, further investigations were carried out at the site of Hamburg Boberg 20. A first trench opened in 1956 led to follow-up excavations in 1959 and 1964.

During the excavations all sites were divided into quadrants (4m² up to 360 m²) (Fig. 3). The cultural layers are described as uniform according to the excavation reports. The black-greyish colour of the find horizon is separated from the surrounding soils—sand below and gley above (Fig. 5). The cultural layers were between 10 cm and 40 cm thick. The thick horizons in particular give the impression that they represent a large time period and therefore a long settlement history. However, Lienau was sure about a relatively short-term occupation of the sites and highlighted the 'homogenous character' of the occupation layers in his excavation reports (Lienau 1952, 1953, 1956, 1959a, 1959b).

Dolmen age and Pitted Ware culture?

A selection of the archaeological finds from Hamburg Boberg 15, 15east and 20 has been presented in various articles. All papers have in common that they only provide information on a selection of the artefacts excavated at the Boberg locations (see Laux 1986; Schindler 1953, 1960, 1961, 1962), with the exception of the flint inventory of Boberg 15east fully studied by H. Lübke (2000). On the basis of the limited inventory published so far, the interpretations concerning the chronological setting do not provide a coherent picture.

Location Hamburg Boberg 15 was first published by Schindler (1953). He emphasised the homogenous character of the flint and pottery artefacts in his preliminary report. With reference to O. Montelius (1891) and S. Müller (1897) who established the Early Neolithic chronology of Dolmen-, Passage Grave and Cist, Schindler (1953, p. 7–9) dated the settlement inventory into the Dolmen Age. Both the beginning and end of the occupation are marked by the absence of specific flint artefacts. Whereas the lack of microliths is decisive for dating the lower time horizon, missing thick-butted axes determine when the settlement had been abandoned. Although Schindler (1953, p. 10) mentioned pottery with pointed bases and clay lamps, he did not consider a potential Late Mesolithic settlement.

Later on, Schindler (1961; 1962) returned to the Boberg 15 material and also discussed the chronological setting of Hamburg Boberg 20. The typo-chronological dating of the prehistoric sites was now based on H. Schwabedissen's (1957−1958) chronology, generated after excavations at the Satrup-Holmer Moor, distr. Schleswig. Given this new chronological sequence, Schindler (1961, p. 23f.) revised his conclusions concerning the dating of Hamburg Boberg 15 and postulated a continuous occupation from Ertebølle-Ellerbek[2] to the Early Neolithic and late Early Neolithic, with Boberg 20 dating to Ertebølle-Ellerbek and to the Early Neolithic. According to Schwabedissen (1957−1958, p. 17f.), Ertebølle-Ellerbek is seen as a specific characteristic in northernmost Germany which is defined by its semi-

---

[2] The term Ertebølle-Ellerbek was introduced by H. Schwabedissen (1957−1958) aiming to differ between a coastal Ertebølle tradition and an Ellerbek tradition in the inland of northernmost Germany. In this article, terms are used as in the original papers.

farming subsistence and therefore suggested as the earliest stage of the Neolithic.

Schindler's (1961) article does not provide a direct chronological comparison of diagnostic artefacts. A comparison between the criteria identified by Schwabedissen (1957–1958, p. 7) and the published artefacts from locations Boberg 15 and 20 lead to the assumption that pointed bases from both sites and clay lamps of Boberg 15 are associated with Ertebølle-Ellerbek. Funnel beakers with vertical body decoration (*Bauchfransenverzierung*) and round, slightly flattened bases (*Wackelboden*) were assigned to the Early Neolithic period. Collared flasks and decorated sherds with applied moulding (*plastische Leisten*) which are suggested as indicators for the late Early Neolithic occupation, are therefore only represented at Boberg 15 (see Schindler 1953, 1961, see also 1960, 1962).

In the first preliminary report Schindler (1953, 8) suggested that Hamburg Boberg 15 was a permanent settlement. This seems to be mainly a result of the typo-chronological dating of the site into the Dolmen Age as well as of the perceived homogeneity of the archaeological artefacts. In his revised paper, Schindler (1961, p. 21f.) rejected his former conclusions. With reference to the ongoing excavations, he characterized the sites of Boberg 15 and 20 as temporary hunting stations. The corresponding base camps were believed to be located on the higher ground of the Geest, although to date no such sites have been identified.

A re-evaluation of the duration of occupation of the Hamburg Boberg sites was carried out by F. Laux (1986), Schindlers' successor as director of the state office for the preservation of monuments of the city of Hamburg. The typo-chronological classification is mainly based on the archaeological artefacts illustrated by Schindler (1953, 1961, 1962), interpreted in accordance with the chronology established by J. Lichardus (1976). Based on the excavation reports, Laux (1986) provides selective surface-mapping of diagnostic flint and pottery artefacts as well as tables dealing with the quantity of recovered flint artefacts.

According to Laux (1986, p. 15), Boberg 20 is connected to the Ertebølle Culture and was settled for one single summer. He assumed that the pottery belongs to 'more or less pointed vessels'. The horizontal stratigraphy by Lienau (1959a) appears to support a limited period of occupation. This led to the identification of separate, but contemporary work spaces. For example, the spatial distribution of core and flake axes in the southwest area of the excavation is interpreted as a production area for dug-outs (Laux 1986, p. 15; Figures 7 and 8).

The same conclusions were reached for the site of Hamburg Boberg 15east, firstly treated as an individual site. However, of the excavated pottery and flint remains only a selection was published. A sample of sherds with incisions or pits and slanting grooves are presented, as well as three pointed bases. Finally, Laux (1986) suggests that Boberg 15east was settled during the Ertebølle-Ellerbek period, also for one

single summer (Laux 1986, p. 18, 32; see also Figures 10 and 11). Like Schindler (1961, p. 21f.), he assumed that the Boberg sites had a functional character and were related to base camps situated on the Geest (Laux 1993).

The detailed investigation of the flint inventory by Lübke (2000) proves that Hamburg Boberg 15east was occupied at the transition between the Late Mesolithic and the Earliest Neolithic. A large quantity of soft-hammered blades and blade tools with parallel edges are connected to the knapping technique of the Ertebølle culture, whereas hard-hammered flakes and flaketools seem to belong primarily to the beginning of the Earliest Neolithic. Nonetheless, a clear separation of the flint assemblage of each settlement period was not possible, as the site was not excavated stratigraphically (Lübke 2000, p. 339f, 374).

An Ertebølle settlement is also suggested for site Hamburg Boberg 15, given the pointed bases and clay lamps. The relative date of Hamburg Boberg 15 covers a large time span. In contrast to Schindler (1961, p. 23f.), Laux (1986, p. 21–23) did not agree with a continuous occupation until the late Early Neolithic. He rather argued for a reoccupation of the site in the late Early Neolithic. Collared flasks and lugged flasks, as well as funnel beakers with roundish and slightly straightened profile, are cited as diagnostic ceramics, alongside vertical body decoration and applied stripes (*plastische Leisten*). Subsequent settlements of the Late Neolithic single grave culture, influenced by Bell Beakers, are mentioned, but without further comment.

The typo-chronological consideration of specific decorated funnel-necked vessels with small flat bases, excavated at Hamburg Boberg 15 (Fig. 4), is somewhat difficult. The pottery in question is characterised by fingernail or fingertip impressions covering the whole body of a vessel or placed in double rows at the neck and belly (Schindler 1953, p. 11). According to Schindler (1953, p. 11), they show a continuous development from the pointed Erebølle jars. Due to their shape and size these ceramics were called *Urbecher* (primeval beaker) and dated to somewhere within the transition period between Ertebølle-Ellerbek and Early Neolithic (Schindler 1953, p. 15). Without further comment, in his later report Schindler (1961, p. 18) mentioned the funnel-necked vessels in the same section as collared bottles, which implies a late Early Neolithic dating.

E. Sprockhoff (1954) traced a relationship between the Boberg examples and premegalithic Danish Domestic Ware as well as Finnish Comb Ware. Because the ornamentations are not clearly comparable it is suggested that the pottery with fingernail impressions represents a local variation (Sprockhoff 1954, p. 15f. See also Struve 1955, p. 122).

Lichardus (1976) discussed a chronological relationship with Rössen III (after Lichardus 1976) or Funnel Beaker A (after Becker 1947, modified after Lichardus 1976). The impulse for the decoration pattern was seen in connection with comparable finds in Poland, but without

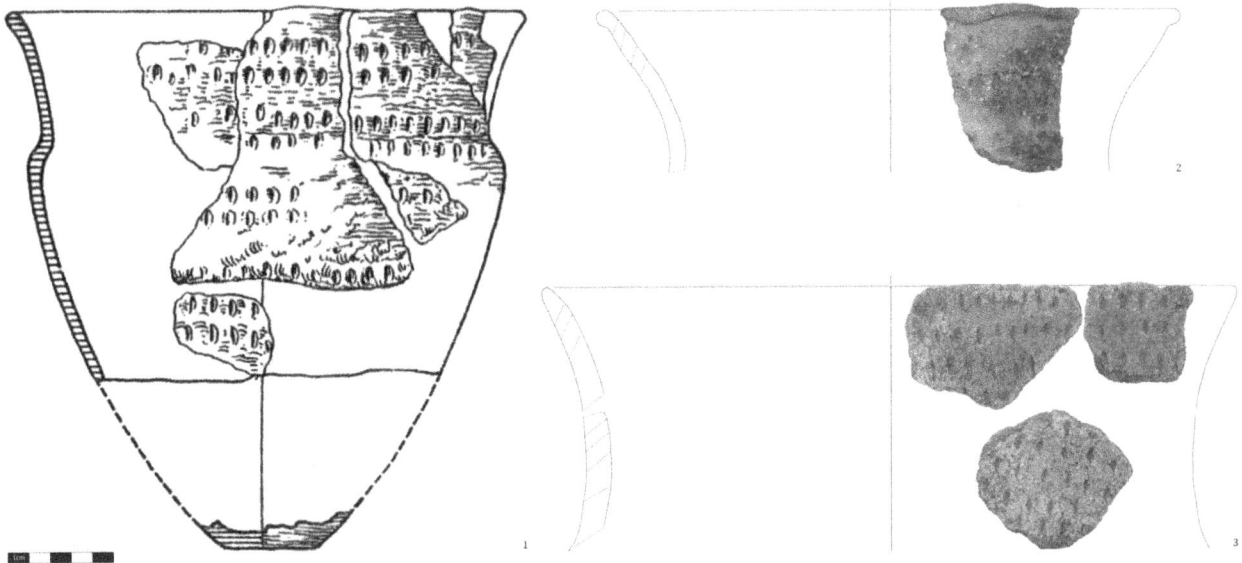

Fig. 4: Boberg 15, Pottery with fingernail impressions, ((1) after Schindler 1953, Taf. IX.5; drawing: Archaeological Museum of Hamburg).

explicit specifications (Lichardus 1976, p. 173; com. 335). Furthermore, analogies were pointed out in a north-western direction between the Boberg pottery and the Swifterbant culture (de Roever 1979, p. 23; van der Waals 1972, p. 167; contra Raemaekers 1999, p. 165) and Hazendonk-I (Louwe-Kooijmans 1976, p. 269).

The typological evolution from pointed vessels is also suggested by Laux (1986, p. 29). In sum, these ceramics are connected to the Pitted Ware culture. The absence of diagnostic flint artefacts of the latter is explained by an early Pitted Ware culture that is present at the site and used a Late Mesolithic flint tradition. Impulses for the decoration technique are also seen in the Ertebølle culture, initially influenced by the Rössen culture. Influences by the Stroke Ornamented Pottery finally resulted in the ornamentation of the whole vessel body (Laux 1986, p. 23–29).

Comparable pottery has been excavated at Friesack 4, dist. Havelland/Brandenburg (Schneider 1932, Figure 50; see also Beran 2012, Figure 5.1–8). J. Beran (2012) draws the conclusion that this special decorated ware represents a Late Mesolithic-Proto Neolithic pottery manufacture, which is common in the inland areas of northernmost Germany. Finds comparable to Schöningen and Salzmünde indicate interactions between both traditions (Beran 2012, p. 513, 523; see also Beran 1993). Recently, G. Wetzel defined the 'Friesack-Boberg Group' as a local facies under consideration of the specific decorated pottery from Friesack 4 and Hamburg Boberg 15. In addition, similar ornamentations appear on the ceramics from site Rhinow 30, dist. Havelland/Brandenburg[3] (Wetzel, manuscript Greifswald 2012).[4]

Mesolithic dwelling pit and imported pottery?

The sites of Hamburg Boberg have become of special interest because of many imports that have been identified, and these ceramics were discussed in various ways. Their assignations to particular archaeological cultures and proveniences are not coherent. These differing interpretations have been collated sufficiently by L. Klassen (2004) and B. Ramminger (2012), and so another summary is not necessary here. Instead, the focus will be on a feature observed at Hamburg Boberg 20 in 1959.

During the excavations at the Hamburg Boberg sites, Lienau was constantly trying to detect soil colourations, indicating ancient pit dwelling or houses. These efforts finally seemed to pay off in 1959. By opening a big quadrant (Q 34 = 360m²) he recovered a pea-shaped slightly dark-greyish soil colouration contrasting from the surrounding cultural layer (Figs. 3 and 5). It covered approximately 16m² and was 79 cm deep. A hearth with two fist-sized stones was revealed in its centre, and the discolouration was interpreted as a pit dwelling (Laux 1986, p. 13; Lienau 1959a; not explicitly in Schindler 1961; der. 1962).

Of special importance was a relatively well-preserved pottery fragment excavated from this feature (Fig. 6). Because both the shape and the preparation of the clay differed from the local ware, Schindler (1961, p. 14; 1962, p. 253) drew an analogy to Rössen pottery. The cultural context was expanded by Lichardus (1976, p. 172) to a generally Danubian shape.

Laux (1986) also supported a Rössen provenience, although he presented a slightly different reconstruction (Laux 1986, Figure 9.5, see also Klassen 2004, p. 77; Ramminger 2012, p. 307). In this context, he highlighted a typological parallel with a vessel excavated at the settlement of Wahlitz, dist. Burg, in the Middle-Elbe-Saale region (Laux 1986, p. 15, com. 18; see Behrens 1973, Figure 19c). Schwabedissen

---

[3] The pottery of all three sites (Hamburg Boberg 15, Friesack 4 and Rhinow 30) gives the same impression and is highly comparable. Special thanks go to G. Wetzel who made the pottery of the Brandenburg site accessible.

[4] Special thanks go to G. Wetzel for providing his manuscript.

Hamburg Boberg 20
Quadrant 34, Profile A
excavation Lienau 8.8.-23.10.1959

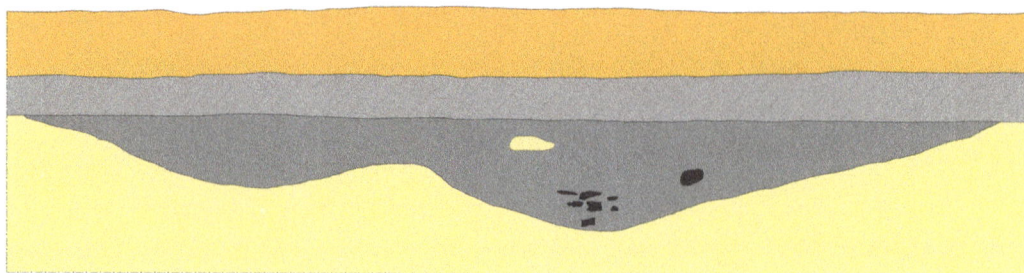

Hamburg Boberg 20
Quadrant 34, Profile B
excavation Lienau 8.8.-23.10.1959

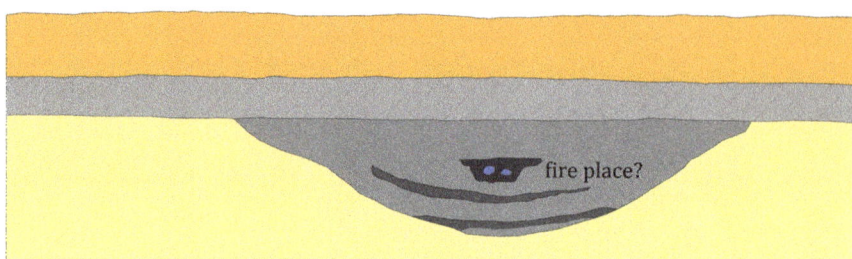

fire place?

gley cultural layer
sand soil discolouration

1m

Fig. 5: Boberg 20, Profile of soil discolouration in Quadrant 34 (Q 34gr) (after Lienau 1959).

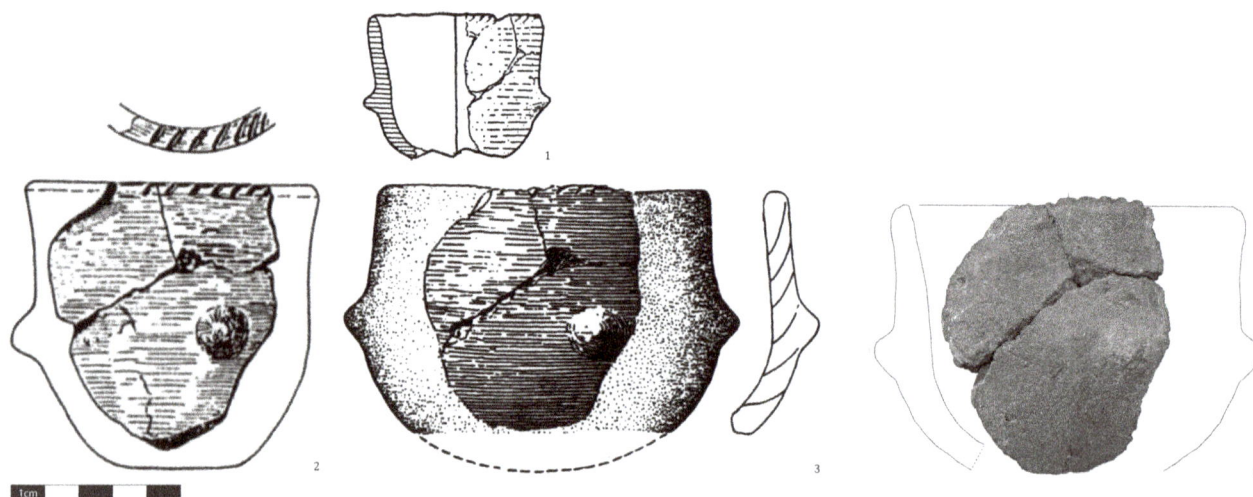

1cm

Fig. 6: Boberg 20, Pottery from soil discolouration ((1) after Schindler 1961, Fig. 4.1, (2) after Laux 1986, Fig. 9.5 (Archaeological Museum of Hamburg), (4) after Schwabedissen 1994, Taf. 19.4).

(1994) suggested a cultural connection to the Linear Pottery culture and reconstructed a deep bowl. Both Laux's (1986) and Schwabedissen's (1994, p. 377) typological reasonings were critically reviewed by Klassen (2004, p. 77).

In addition, Schindler (1961, p. 14; 1962, p. 253) provided a list of the excavated flint artefacts comprising of flake axes (n=2) and core axes (n=3), as well as 96 flakes and 38

blades and blade fragments, alongside three rim sherds. These were identified as funnel-necked vessels, each different in shape. There is one straight and one slanting rim as well as one wavy-rimmed sherd with a slightly curved profile (Fig. 7.2, 4–5). However, the explanations within the text are in contradiction to the illustrations provided. The caption of Figure 3 in Schindler (1962) suggests that the ceramics are assigned to the discolouration because

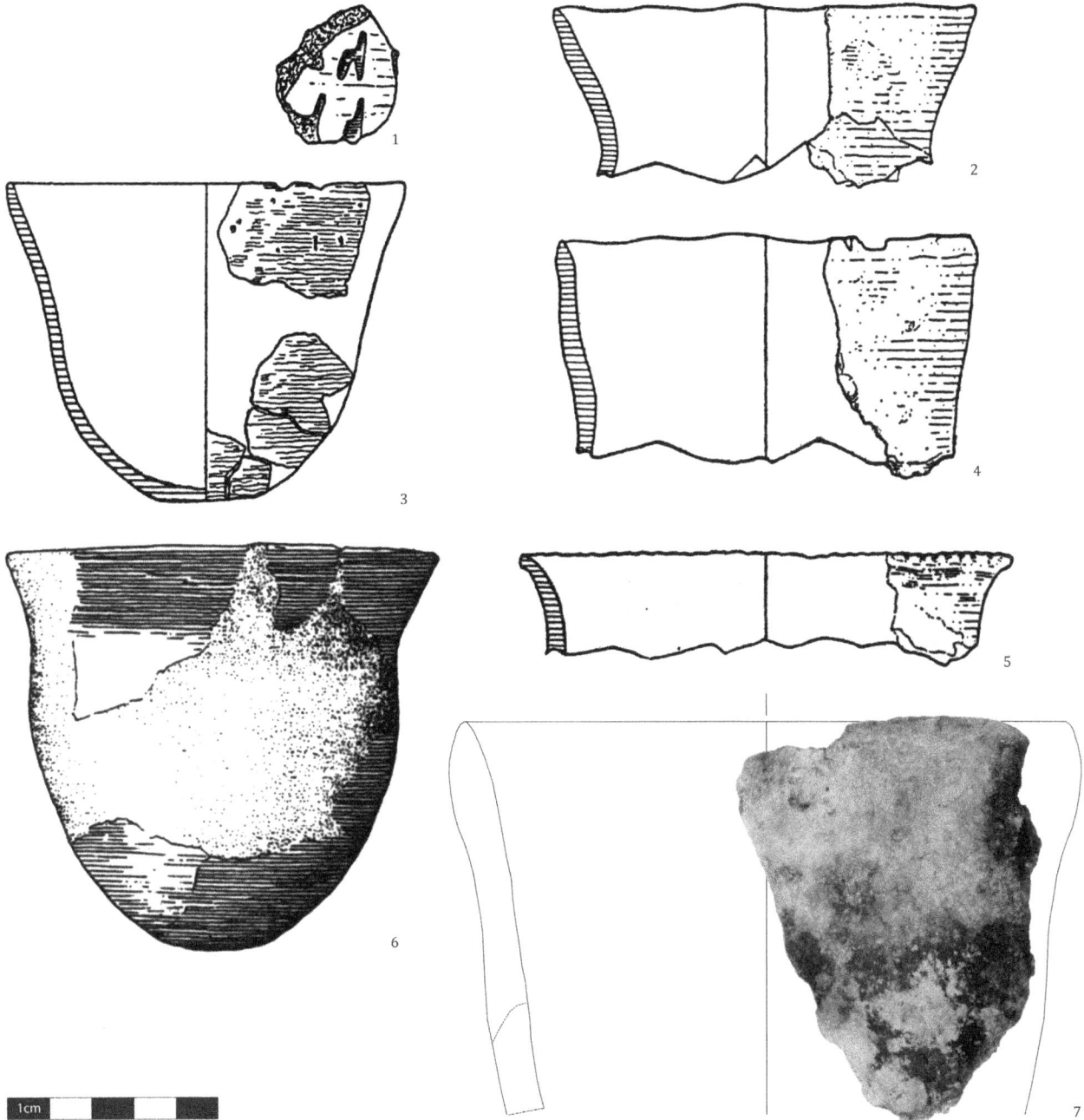

Fig. 7: Pottery discussed in connection with soil discolouration, Boberg 20 ((1-5) after Schindler 1961, Fig 3.1; 4.2-3,5, drawing: Archaeological Museum of Hamburg (6) after Schwabedissen 1966, Fig. 24c).

they are described as 'closed find originating from a pit' (*Geschlossener Fund aus einer Grube*) (Fig. 7.1-4). This might be crucial for the further discussion on this pottery, because the illustrated rim sherds were attributed to the soil discolouration. Lichardus (1976, Taf. 84, A.1-2, 4) interpreted these ceramics as imports and connects them with a Danubian Neolithic, without any specification of the provenience. In contrast, Klassen (2004) suggests an origin from the Michelsberg culture. In particular, the complete reconstructed vessel seems to represent a 'reliable identified import of the Michelsberg culture' (type 14, after Lüning 1968). However, there are some misleading references. According to written description, Klassen (2004) refers to Schindler (1962, Figure 3.4), but the illustration provided there actually shows a reconstructed vessel from Hamburg Boberg 15 (Fig.

7.6), taken from Schwabedissen (1994, Taf. 20.3; first published id. 1966, Figure 24c).

Apart from the fact that the undecorated rim sherds have collectively been the object of some confusion, neither the excavation report nor the inventory list quotes this pottery. According to Lienau (1959a), only one undecorated rim sherd (Fig. 7.7) and the lug decorated vessel fragment with carved rim (Fig. 6) was found. The majority of the pottery was still covered with thick sandy crusts but after cleaning and recording, a few very small and fragmented rim sherds could be added which do not represent the ceramics in question. Therefore, it is apt to conclude that not all discussed imported ceramics can be linked to the feature, except the two samples mentioned by Lienau (1959a).

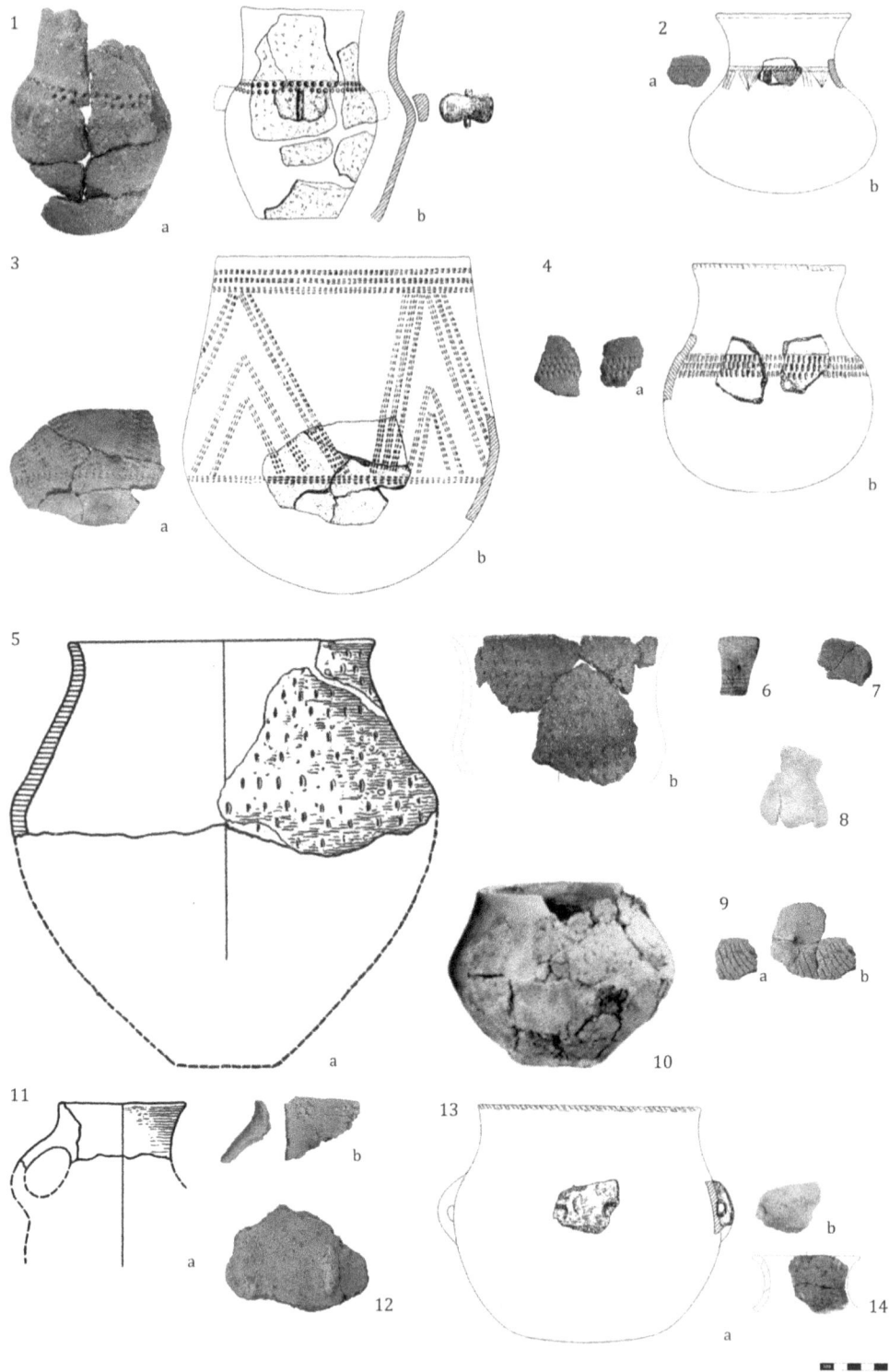

Fig. 8: Discussed imports. (1) Boberg 15, Rössen culture, after Struve 1955; Gartersleben culture, after Klassen 2004, Laux 1986; (2, 7) Boberg 15, Rössen culture, after Laux 1986, Lichardus 1976, Schindler 1961, id. 1962; Bell Beaker culture, after Klassen 2004; (3) Boberg 15, Rössen culture, after Laux 1986 contra Klassen 2004; (4) Boberg 15, Rössen culture, after Laux 1986; Lichardus 1976; (5a) Boberg 15, Rössen culture, after Struve 1955; (5b) reconstruction after fitting; (6) Boberg 15, Linear Pottery culture, after Schindler 1953; Stroke Ornament Pottery culture, after Klassen 2004, Laux 1986, Lichardus 1976, Raddatz 1956, Schindler 1961, id. 1962, Struve 1955; (8) Boberg 15, imitation of Rössen Pottery, after Schindler 1961; Gartersleben culture, after Laux 1986; (9a) Boberg 15, Rössen culture, after Laux 1986, Lichardus 1976, Schindler 1962; (9b) reconstruction after fitting; (10) Boberg 15, Rössen Culture, after Lichardus 1976, Schindler 1961, id. 1962; Gartersleben culture, after Klassen 2004, Laux 1986; (11) Boberg 15, Baalberge culture, after Laux 1986; (12) Boberg 15, Rössen Culturer, after Laux 1986; (13) Boberg 15east, Baalberge culture, after Laux 1986 (see Klassen 2004) (published in connection with Boberg 20, in Schindler 1961; published in connection with Boberg 15, in Laux 1986); (14) Boberg 15east, Linear Pottery culture, after Schwabedissen 1994 (published in connection with Boberg 15); ((1b, 2b, 3b, 4b, 13a) after Laux 1986, Fig. 19.1-5 drawing: Archaeological Museum of Hamburg, (5a, 10, 6, 11a) after Schindler 1953, Taf. VII.4; VIII.17; IX.9; XI.12, drawing: Archaeological Museum of Hamburg, (1a, 2a, 3a, 4a, 5b, 7, 9a-b, 11b, 12) photo: Th. Weise, Archaeological Museum of Hamburg.

The Late Mesolithic and Neolithic sites of Hamburg Boberg – research objective and strategy

The various interpretations of the chronological setting and function of the sites result from the limited publication and therefore restricted information on excavated artefacts. A representative selection of the excavated archaeological remains has not been analysed until now, and the investigations carried out in the 1960s are not taken into account in any paper. The very different ideas concerning the supposed 'imported' ceramics are closely related to these problems. All in all, around 15 ceramics have been discussed as imports (Fig. 8). Various chronological classifications, as well as differing origins and cultural connections complete the discussion on the sites of Hamburg Boberg. In addition, disagreements in the literature and incorrect data with respect to the archaeological remains, as highlighted in the example above, make the situation even worse.

A re-evaluation of the Late Mesolithic and Neolithic sites of Hamburg Boberg (locations 15, 15east and 20) is planned within the DFG funded project *The Neolithisation process of northernmost Germany – with particular reference to the Late Mesolithic and Neolithic sites of Hamburg Boberg*, with special regard to the specific function of the sites at the transition between hunter-gatherer/forager and farming societies. In terms of this question, it is an essential precondition to consider the excavated pottery as a whole, in order to make adequate propositions about chronological setting and function of the sites. Alongside typo-chronological criteria, manufacturing aspects also play a significant part. In this context, the archaeological recording will be supplemented by archaeometrical analysis, which contributes a deeper insight into the technological production of the pottery. The study aims to analyse the potters' craft regarding clay preparation, as well as the raw clays used. These investigations will help to detect specific manufacturing traditions. Furthermore, the designated imports suggest interactions between different craft traditions, so it could be possible to identify influences on the local ceramic production. By taking into account both typological and technological criteria, the study of the Late Mesolithic and Neolithic sites of Hamburg Boberg will shed light on the Neolithisation process of northernmost Germany, as it will not only consider the adoption of specific vessel types, but also reflect on changes in manufacturing traditions.

Bibliography

Becker, C. J. (1947). *Mosefundne Lekar Fra Yngre Stenalder. Studier Over Tragtbægerkulturen I Danmark.* Aarbøger for nordisk Oldkyndighed og Historie, 40. København: Gyldendal.

Behrens, H. (1973). *Die Jungsteinzeit im Mittelelbe-Saale-Gebiet.* Berlin: Veröffentlichungen des Landesmuseums für Vor- und Frühgeschichte in Halle, 27. Berlin: Lit.

Beran, J. (1993). *Untersuchungen zur Stellung der Salzmünder Kultur im Jungneolithikum des Saalegebietes.* Beiträge zur Ur- und Frühgeschichte Mitteleuropas, 2. Wilkau-Haßlau: Beier & Beran.

Beran, J. (2012). *Spitzhauen, Schöningen und Swifterbant – Überlegungen zu Endmesolithikum und beginnendem Jungneolithikum im Nordostdeutschen Binnenland.* In Gleser, R., Becker, V. (eds.), *Mitteleuropa im 5. Jahrtausend vor Christus. Beiträge zur Internationalen Konferenz in Münster 2010* 509–527. Berlin: Lit.

Friedrichsen, O. (1960). *Bohrergebnisse.* Schreibmaschinenmanuskript über die Bohrergebnisse im Ortsaktenarchiv des Helms-Museums, Abteilung Bodendenkmalpflege.

Ehlers, J. (1994). *Allgemeine und historische Quartärgeologie.* Stuttgart: Enke.

Ehlers, J. (2011). *Das Eiszeitalter.* Heidelberg: Spektrum Akademischer Verlag.

Klassen, L. (2004). *Jade und Kupfer. Untersuchungen zum Neolithisierungsprozess im westlichen Ostseeraum unter besonderer Berücksichtigung der Kulturentwicklung Europas 5500–3500 BC.* Jutland Archaeological Society, 47. Aarhus: Aarhus University Press

Laux, F. (1986). *Die mesolithischen und frühneolithischen Fundplätze auf den Boberger Dünen bei Hamburg.* Hammaburg, N. F. 7. Vor- und Frühgeschichte aus dem niederelbischen Raum, 1984–1985, 9–38.

F. Laux (1993), *Frühneolithische Äxte aus der Elbe bei Hamburg. Ein Beitrag zum Beginn des Neolithikums an der Niederelbe.* Hammaburg, N. F. 10. Vor- und Frühgeschichte aus dem niederelbischen Raum, 83–98.

Lichardus, J. (1976). *Rössen – Garterleben – Baalberge. Ein Beitrag zur Chronologie des mitteldeutschen Neolithikums und zur Entstehung der Trichterbecher-Kulturen.* Saarbrücker Beiträge zur Altertumskunde, 17. Bonn: Habelt.

Lienau, F. (1952). *Grabungsbericht Boberg 15.* Ortsaktenarchiv des Helms-Museums, Abteilung Bodendenkmalpflege.

Lienau, F. (1953). *Grabungsbericht Boberg 15.* Ortsaktenarchiv des Helms-Museums, Abteilung Bodendenkmalpflege.

Lienau, F. (1954). *Grabungsbericht Boberg 20.* Ortsaktenarchiv des Helms-Museums, Abteilung Bodendenkmalpflege.

Lienau, F. (1959a). *Grabungsbericht Boberg 20.* Ortsaktenarchiv des Helms-Museums, Abteilung Bodendenkmalpflege.

Lienau, F. (1959b). *Grabungsbericht Boberg 15ost.* Ortsaktenarchiv des Helms-Museums, Abteilung Bodendenkmalpflege.

Louwe Kooijmans, L. P. (1976). *Local Developments in a Borderland. A Survey of the Neolithic at the Lower Rhine.* Oudgeidkundige Mededelingen. Uit het Rijksmuseum van Oudheden te Leiden LVII, 1976 (1977), 227–297.

Lübke, H. (1992). *Neue Ausgrabungen in Boberg.* Archäologie in Deutschland, 1, 49.

Lübke, H. (2000). *Die steinzeitlichen Fundplätze Bebensee LA 26 und LA 76, Kreis Segeberg. Die Steinartefakte. Technologisch-ergologische Studien zum Nordischen Frühneolithikum.* Untersuchungen und Materialien zur Steinzeit in Schleswig-Holstein, 3. Neumünster: Wachholtz.

Miehlich, G. (1986). *Tour I. Freshwater-marsh of the Elbe river*. Guidebook for a tour of landscapes, soils and land use in the Federal Republic of Germany. 13th Congress International Society of Soil Science Hamburg, Germany August 1986. In Mitteilungen der Deutschen Bodenkundlichen Gesellschaft, 51, 99–128.

Miehlich, G. (1999). *Böden und Bodenkultur der Vier- und Marschlande – Segen und Last einer Flußmarschenlandschaft*. Hamburger Geographische Studien, 48, 199–224.

Montelius, O. (1891). *Zur Chronologie der jüngeren Steinzeit in Skandinavien*. Correspondenz-Blatt der deutschen Gesellschaft für Anthropologie, Ethnologie und Urgeschichte, 22, 99–105.

Müller, S. (1897). *Nordische Altertumskunde 1. Steinzeit – Bronzezeit*. Straßburg: Trübner.

Raddatz, K. (1956). *Ein Gefäß der Rössener Kultur aus der Uckermark*. Berichte und Mitteilungen aus dem Schleswig-Holsteinischen Landesmuseum für Vor- und Frühgeschichte in Schleswig und dem Institut für Ur- und Frühgeschichte an der Universität Kiel, 15, 1958, 25–30.

Raemaekers, D. C. M. (1999). *The Articulation of a 'New Neolithic'. The meaning of the Swifterbant Culture for the process of neolithisation in the western part of the North European Plain (4900-3400 BC)*. Archaeological Studies Leiden University, 3. Leiden: Faculty of Archaeology, University of Leiden.

Ramminger, B. (2012). *Multiple Grenzen: Das Beispiel Boberger Dünen*. In Doppler. Th., Ramminger, B., Schimmelpfennig, D. (eds.), *Grenzen und Grenzräume? Beispiele aus Neolithikum und Bronzezeit*. Fokus Jungsteinzeit. Berichte der AG Neolithikum, 2, 297–319. Kerpen-Loogh: Welt und Erde.

de Roever, J. P. (1979). *The Pottery from Swifterband – Dutch Ertebølle*? Helenium, XIX, 13–36.

Schindler, R. (1953). *Die Entdeckung zweier jungsteinzeitlicher Wohnplätze unter dem Marschenschlick im Vorgelände der Boberger Dünen und ihre Bedeutung für die Steinzeitforschung Nordwestdeutschlands*. Hammaburg, 4(9), 1-17.

Schindler, R. (1960). *Die Bodenaltertümer der freien und Hansestadt Hamburg*. Veröffentlichungen des Museums für Hamburgische Geschichte. Hamurg: Christians

Schindler, R. (1961). *Rössener Elemente im Frühneolithikum von Boberg*, Hammaburg, 7(13), 9–29.

Schindler, R. (1962). *Rössener Elemente im Boberger Neolithikum*. Germania. Anzeiger der römisch-germanischen Kommission des deutschen Archäologischen Instituts, 40, 245–255.

Schneider, M. (1932). *Die Urkeramiker. Entstehung eines mesolithischen Volkes und seiner Kultur*. Leipzig: Kabitzsch.

Schwabedissen, H. (1957–1958). *Die Ausgrabungen im Satruper Moor. Zur Frage nach Ursprung und frühester Entwicklung des nordischen Neolithikums*. Offa. Berichte und Mitteilungen aus dem Schleswig-Holsteinischen Landesmuseum für Vor- und Frühgeschichte in Schleswig und dem Institut für Ur- und Frühgeschichte an der Universität Kiel, 16, 1957–1958 (1960), 5–28.

Schwabedissen, H. (1966). *Ein horizontrierter „Breitkeil" aus Satrup und die mannigfachen Kulturverbindungen des beginnenden Neolithikums in Norden und Nordwesten*. In *Neolithic Studies in Atlantic Europe. Proceedings of the Second Altantic Colloquium*. Groningen, 6–11 April 1964 Palaeohistoria. Acta Communicationes Instituti Bio-Archeologici Universitatis Groninganae, 12, 1966 (1967), 409–468.

Schwabedissen, H. (1994). *Die Ellerbek-Kultur in Schleswig-Holstein und das Vordringen des Neolithikums über die Elbe nach Norden*. In Hoika, J., Meurers-Balke, J. (eds.), *Beiträge zur frühneolithischen Trichterbecherkultur im westlichen Ostseegebiet*. 1. Internationales Trichterbechersymposium in Schleswig vom 4. bis 7. März 1985. Untersuchungen und Materialien zur Steinzeit in Schleswig-Holstein, 1, 361–401. Neumünster: Wachholz.

Sprockhoff, E. (1954). *Kammerlose Hünenbetten im Sachsenwald*. Offa. Berichte und Mitteilungen aus dem Schleswig-Holsteinischen Landesmuseum für Vor- und Frühgeschichte in Schleswig und dem Institut für Ur- und Frühgeschichte an der Universität Kiel, 13, 1954 (1955), 1–16.

Struve, K. W. (1955). *Die Einzelgrabkultur in Schleswig-Holstein und ihre kontinentalen Beziehungen*. Vor- und frühgeschichtliche Untersuchungen aus dem Schleswig-Holsteinischen Landesmuseum für Vor- und Frühgeschichte der Universität Kiel N. F. 11. Offa-Bücher. Neumünster: Wachholz..

van der Waals, J. D. (1972). *Die durchlochten Rössener Keile und das frühe Neolithikum in Belgien und in den Niederlanden*. Die Anfänge des Neolithikums vom Orient bis Nordeuropa. Fundamenta, A 3, 153–184.

Wetzel, G. *Manuscript Greifswald* 12.2012.

Containers of Meaning

Alise Šulte

Department of Archaeology, Institute of Latvian History, Latvia University

Alise.Sulte@gmail.com

Abstract: This paper is a short introduction to one of the Couronian burial tradition aspects: miniature pottery. Miniature pottery was widely used in Couronian culture between the fifth and ninth centuries AD but on occasion the pots can still be found up to the end of the tenth century. The focus of this paper is the theoretical possibility to understand this material in relation to symbolic understanding of afterlife and the person's transition into it. Miniature pots appear as part of Couronian burial traditions with the forming of Couronian culture in the fifth century. The shift from cremation burials to inhumation burials prompts a change in the burial urns. As the burial urns have no more practical use they can be resized to become symbolic vessels for the soul's passage into the afterlife. The miniature pots seem to have no practical meaning and are made specifically for placement in graves. In later centuries when miniature ceramics become less used it can be seen that the original meaning of miniature pottery has changed, influencing the whole burial symbolism. Miniaturized objects are no longer connected with vessels to the afterlife but with the symbolic representation of the objects that are to be transported.

Key words: Grave goods; Household pottery; Miniature pots; Burial pottery; Couronian bural traditions; Cremation burials; Symbolic representation

While researching ceramic material from western Latvia and experimenting with different possible social interpretations, my attention was captured by a unique grave ceramics tradition in this area. Among typical grave goods placed in inhumation graves one can find miniature pots with seemingly no practical use. Although it did not touch my primary research I took an interest in this phenomenon and examined the available material. My analysis of these miniature pots was presented in the format of a poster at the 2013 conference 'Prehistoric Pottery Across the Baltic'. As a whole year has passed from the conference until this publication, I have revised and updated some of my perspectives. However, the time that has passed has not changed my original understanding of these artefacts and their function in the burial tradition. In the following text I will give a short summary of this phenomenon and a hypothetical explanation of the symbolical meaning of this tradition and its changes over time.

To start at the assumed beginning, the Couronian tradition of adding miniaturized vessels as grave goods appears in the fifth century in southwestern Lithuania and western Latvia (Fig. 1). As part of the emerging Couronian culture miniature pottery in burials was continued from the pre-existing tradition of Stone circle burial culture (ed. Griciuvienė 2008, p. 53). In the seventh–ninth century's burials with miniature clay pots formed one third of Couronian inhumation burials (Tautavičius 1996, p. 268–270). From the ninth century, however, the tradition fades before completely disappearing at the end of the tenth century (Nakatite 1964, p. 66-68; Ozere 1986, p. 48-58).

Miniature pots, with some rare exceptions (e.g. Mežīte hillfort), are found only at burial sites and never at living sites (Šulte 2013, p. 55). The tradition of adding miniature pottery to inhumation burials (usually by the head) is widespread across all of the regions where Couronian culture was present. Miniature pottery has been found in burials of different genders and burials that vary in 'richness'. Some have also been found in the graves of children. With a few isolated exceptions (two miniature pots were found in Laiviai cemetery at grave 124 and at

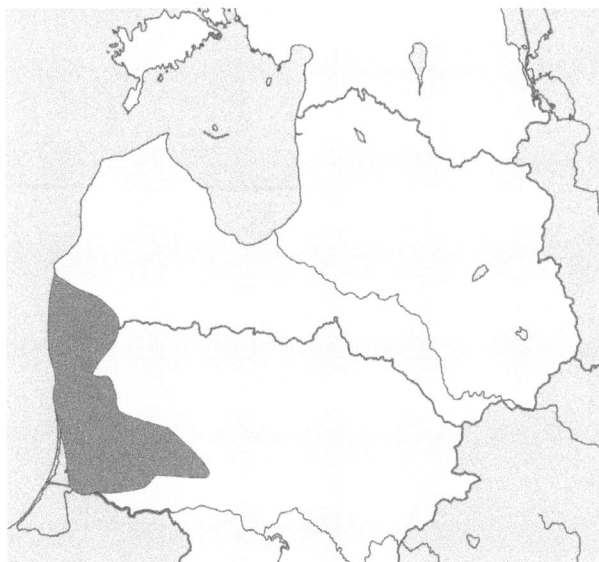

Fig. 1: Map of Latvia and Lithuania. Approximate territory of Stone circle burials first to seventh century marked with red. © Creative Commons, NordNordWest ; License CC-BY-SA 3.0.

Palanga cemetery at graves 118 and 150) there is only one miniature pot per burial (Bliujiene 2005, p. 149.). Although miniature pots are not found in all graves it has been suggested that many have been unpreserved in the soil due to poor firing (ed. Stasulane 2008, p. 45). However, this question needs further investigation as any unfired pots would leave few visible traces, making it hard to argue for one case or the other. Among the preserved pots it can be seen that the quality does seem to vary greatly, both in the precision of their shape and in the composition of the material. However, it must be taken into account that the poor state in which miniature pots come into archaeologist's hands is not always to be attributed to their original state but also to post-depositional influences.

Although the function of these objects as 'pots' may seem clear—to serve as containers of other objects—this does not seem to be their primary purpose. The miniature pots present in graves mostly appear to have been empty. It has only been in isolated occasions that miniature pots have contained some pieces of amber or a few small pieces of jewellery. This is further accentuated by the fact that some miniature pots have themselves been placed in other vessels (ed. Stasulane 2008, p. 45, 98).

In looking at the miniature pots themselves it can be seen that from the fifth century until the eight century miniature pots varied little in height (4–10 cm) or in shoulder diameter (5–10 cm) (ed. Stasulane 2008, p. 98). However, the shape of miniature pots seems to have great variability. It is possible to split these pots into approximately seven types (Fig. 2) (Ozere 1986, p. 48–58). The shape of some pots

has been made with great care and precision in contrast to others that may seem quite simplistic.

Although the household ceramic material from this period is scarce, some comparisons can be made by using closely related pottery material. The household pottery data available is both from the previous and from a slightly later period, and indicates a continuous use of existing shapes. Although it is not the ideal situation for pottery shape comparison, it is hard to imagine a sudden shift in pottery tradition in a period of just a few hundred years which would leave no trace in the preceding or subsequent pottery.

If compared with the available household pottery most types of miniature pots are not simply miniaturized copies. The existing curves are notably deeper and angles are sharper (Fig. 3). The original shape of miniature pottery seems to be exaggerated to such a degree that it becomes a hyperbolic representation of the household pot. The first and second types of shapes refrain from doing so only to the degree that the originals contain no curves to be exaggerated. A need for exaggeration of everyday shapes suggests a need to emphasize the symbolic link with the pottery being emulated. One possibility of explaining the phenomenon of miniature pottery is by linking it with the previous cremation burial tradition and the use of burial urns (ed. Stasulane 2008, p. 45).

Burial urns placed in earlier cremation graves served not only as 'containers' but also as 'vessels'. In the first case the term 'containers' is based on the root 'contain',

Fig. 2: Seven types of miniature pot shapes (by I.Ozere-Virse). Examples from LNVM: 1. Mazkatuzi A 9954:1; 2. Osenieki VI 290:4; 3. Mazkatuzi A 9936:1; 4. Geistauti A 9926:13; 5. Mazkatuzi A 9949:2; 6. Mazkatuzi A 9939:3; 7. Geistauti A 9920:5. Scale 3 cm.

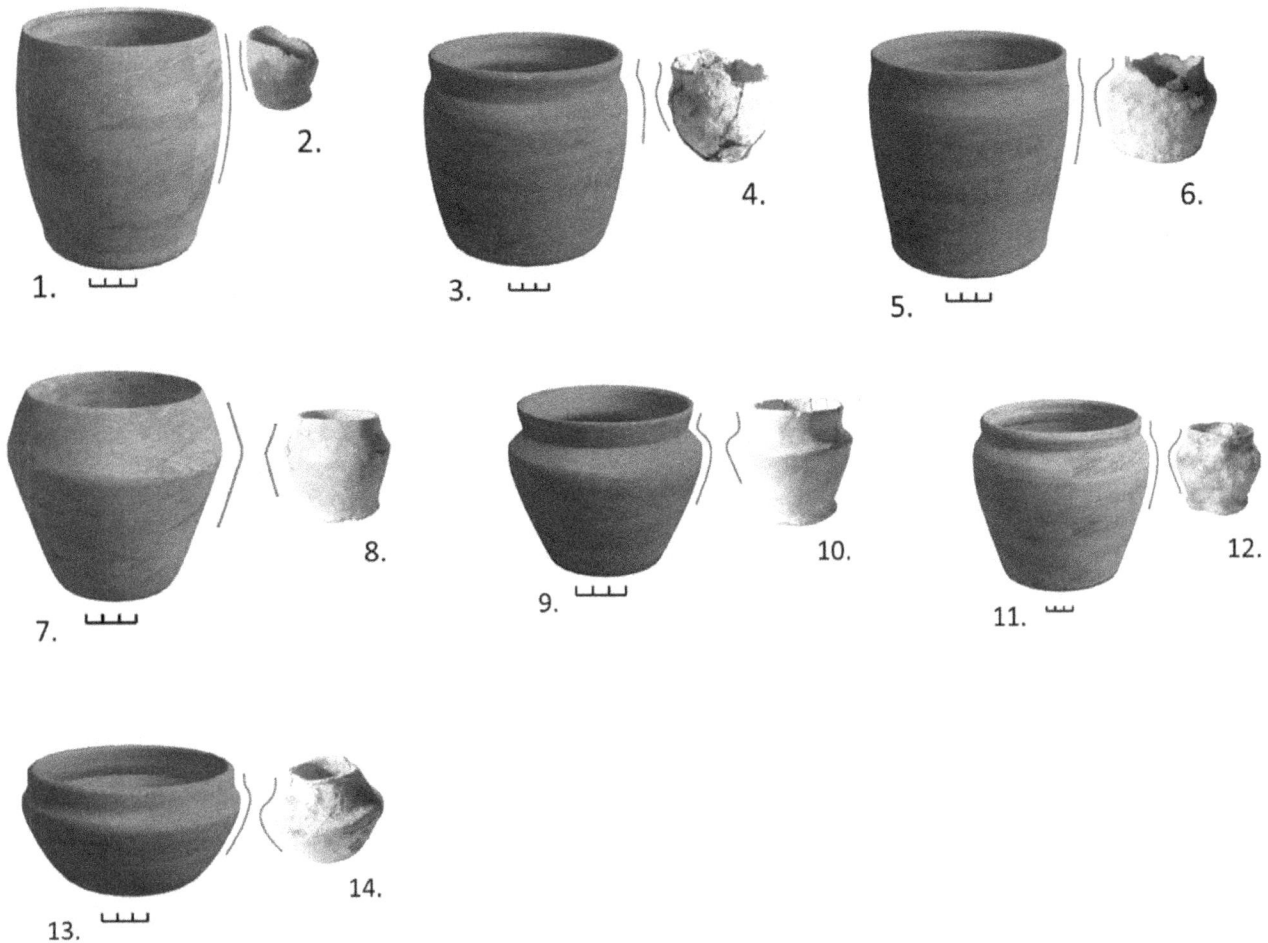

Fig. 3: Digital reproductions of household pots (left) compared with miniature pots (right). Mežite hillfort: 1. (A 12800:110); Padure hillfort: 5. (A 13517:150); Talsi settlement: 3. (A 12940:21), 7. (A 1143:2897), 9. (A 1143:2986), 13. (A 12940:18); Strazdi settlement: 11. (A 12467:16); Osenieki burials: 2. (IV 290:156), 6. (IV 290:15), 12. (IV 290:128); Geistauti burials: 8. (A 9926:13), 10. (A9926:14); Mazkatuzi burials: 4. (A 9936:1), 14. (A 9939:3). All provided examples of household pots are digital reproductions based on potsherds using OpenDocument Drawing software (by A.Šulte). Scale 3 cm.

indicating that it encompasses or holds. The second term 'vessel' is synonymous with a ship or a device for travel. Consequently, the burial urns serve firstly as 'containers' that hold the cremated remains and secondly as 'vessels' that transport the deceased to the afterlife. In other words, the burial urn both physically contains the remains and symbolically transports the individual to the next life. It is not my aim to postulate that the English language uncovers the dual function of burial pottery because the same words can have different meanings across different times and to different people. Similar to the linguistic approach of analysing archaeological data used by Hodder, this peculiar coincidence allows us to illustrate the dual function of burial urns in the described case (Hodder 1990, p. 44–46).

This dual function of burial pottery is put under strain with the appearance of many contrasting burial traditions (Vasks 2000, p. 49). In a gradual shift to inhumation graves the burial urns lost their practical function as containers but the need for symbolic vessels of travel remained. This can also be ascribed to 'mimesis' of memory practice which Katina T. Lillios describes as 'material behaviours that cite or reference imagery from the natural or cultural landscape in new media' (Lillios 2008, p. 245). With the practical function of burial urns disappearing, they are left only with

their symbolic purpose and hence do not need to retain the practical aspects. As the pot no longer needs to physically hold remains of the deceased its size becomes irrelevant. Instead the focus is put on it as a symbol for a pot/vessel. To emphasize that this clay object is a vessel the most visible aspect of pottery was enhanced—its shape.

A tradition of miniature vessels or pots that are added to burials exists for several hundred years. With the passing of time the perception of this tradition seems to have changed. In the ninth century the amount of miniature pots in graves dramatically decreases and their appearance becomes more uniform and loses the exaggerated shape. The miniature pots that still remain in use shrink to 1–2 cm high and start resembling small cruets or thimbles (Fig. 4). This has been classified in type eight (Ozere 1986, p. 56). However, at the same time as changes in miniature pottery occur, other miniaturized objects begin to be used as grave goods (ed. Stasulane 2008, p. 98). A variety of everyday objects (tools, weapons and household objects) are made in miniature and placed in the graves instead of the actual object.

It seems that the symbol of a pot as a 'vessel' loses its meaning but the idea that it is not the physical pot

41

Fig. 4: The eight miniature pot shape type (by I.Ozere-Virse). Example from Kapenieku grave no.21, A 7627:52. Scale 3 cm.

that is carried on to the next life but its metaphysical representation gains a wider application. It is probably most fruitful to think of this in terms of the journey from this world to the other. Instead of a person's body, his soul is transported to afterlife; similarly, it is not the actual grave goods but the 'soul' that travels to the afterlife. The physical objects in grave goods are not as important as what they represent. The shift of symbolic thinking is evident also when considering the evolvement of new cremation burial traditions in the tenth century which do not involve specific burial urns (Bliujiene 2005, p. 147–151). Both the individual's body and his grave goods are to be physically destroyed in order to be sent to the afterlife. It will be the metaphysical representation or 'soul' of the objects that are sent and the 'soul' does not have to be proportional to the physical object. Consequently, the use of miniaturized pottery may well be both the cause and the consequence of a general shift of a culture's relation to the afterlife and, most importantly, their travel to this afterlife.

Bibliography

Bliujiene, A. (2005). Pottery in couronian cremation burials. Some aspects of interaction across the Baltic sea in the late Viking age and early Medieval period. In: V.Lang, ed. Culture and Material Culture. Papers from the first theoretical seminar of the Baltic archaeologists (BASE) held at the University of Tartu, Estonia, October 17th-19th, 2003. (Interarchaeologia, 1). Tartu, Riga, Vilnius, 2005, 147-165.

Griciuvienė, E. (ed.), (2008). Kuršiai : genties kultūra laidosenos duomenimis. Vilnius: Lietuvos nacionalinis muziejus.

Hodder, I. (1990). *The Domestication of Europe.* Oxford: Brasil Blackwell.

Lillios, K.T. (2008). Heraldry for the Dead: Memory, Identity, and the Engraved Stone Plaques of Neolithic Iberia. Austin: University of Texas Press.

Nakaite, L. (1964). Miniatiūrinės IX-XIII amžiaus ikapes Lietuvoje. Lietuvos TSR mokslų akademijos darbai, A serija, 2(27), 38–47.

Stasulane, I. (ed.), (2008). Kurši senatnē. Couronians in antiquity. Rīga: National History museum of Latvia.

Šulte, A. (2014). Vēlā dzelzs laikmeta keramika Rietumlatvijā. Rīga: Maģistra darbs.

Tautavičius, A. (1996). *Vidurinysis geležies amžius Lietuvoje (V-IX a.); Zusammenfassung: Die Mittlere Eisenzeit in Litauen (V.-IX. Jh.).* Vilnius: Pilių Tyrimų Centras Lietuvos Pilys.

Vasks, A. (2000). Daži agrā un vidējā dzelzs laikmeta uzkalniņu kapulauku sociālās interpretācijas jautājumi. In Gorenko, I. (ed.), *Cauri Gadsimtiem,* 45–49. Riga: NIMS.

Озере, И.А. (1986). *Миниатюрные глиняные сосуды в куршских погребениях V – IV веков.* LPST Zinātņu akadēmijas vēstis, 1(462), 48–58.

Pottery Firing without a Kiln – Hand-Built Pottery in the Territory of Present-Day Latvia in the Middle and Late Iron Age (5th–12th centuries AD)

Baiba Dumpe[1], Agnese Stunda-Zujeva[2] and Jana Vecstaudža[2]

[1] *National History Museum of Latvia*

[2] *Institute of General Chemical Engineering, Riga Technical University*

Baibadumpe@inbox.lv

Abstract: The presented research focuses on hand-built pottery produced in Latvia in the Middle and Late Iron Age (5th–12th centuries AD). The colour of vessel surface and the appearance of the sherd fracture surface are among the indicators of the conditions during firing. However, these primary features may have changed both in the course of the pottery use and after the respective vessel life ended and its sherds found their way into the occupation layer. Through experiments and with the help of X-ray powder diffraction analysis (XRPD) the authors seek to establish how the pottery firing process was organised, with special focus on determining the firing temperature interval. In the course of research 43 pottery samples from archaeological settlements and burial sites were analysed. Concurrently series of samples from several clay deposits of Latvia were taken. These samples were open-fired imitating the hypothetical pottery firing regime. This was the first time that XRPD analysis was used in the research of archaeological pottery of Latvia. The results of the analysis indicated that the samples had been fired at a maximum temperature not lower than 600°C, but not higher than 900°C. The experiments allow the defining of the ancient pottery firing temperature maximum interval to fall within the range of 600–700°C.

Key words: Experimental archaeology; Laboratory analysis; XRPD-analysis; Iron Age Latvia; Firing methods; Firing temperature; Reconstruction; Pottery

Introduction: archaeological context

Throughout the Late Iron Age (5th–12th centuries AD) ceramic vessels in Latvia were made by hand with a coiling technique with the exception of the second half of the Late Iron Age (the 11th and 12th centuries), when the production of wheel-shaped pottery began alongside the production of hand-built pottery. From the 12th century and forward the production of hand-built pottery gradually ended (for example Stubavs 1976; Šnore 1961).

In Latvian archaeology hand-built pottery is traditionally classified according to the surface finish of vessels. From the beginning of the Middle Iron Age (400–800 AD) rusticated pottery (Fig. 2:1, 3) dominated in most of the territory of present-day Latvia although smooth-walled (Fig. 2:2), polished (Fig. 2:4, 6), and pinched (Fig. 2:5) vessel types were also used.

The earliest pottery kilns in Latvia are known from the time when early wheel-thrown pottery appeared during the 11th–13th centuries AD (Šnore 1957, p.14-15; Šnore 1961, p.109-110; Urtāns 1967, p.42; Urtāns 1974, p.75; Dumpe 2009). However, to this date no pottery firing structures that could be linked to the production of hand-built pottery have been found. This prompted a search for a possible firing method of this kind of pottery.

Research focuses

This article revolves around several questions connected to the firing of hand-built pottery during the Middle and Late Iron Age in the territory of Latvia:

- What was the firing temperature preferred by the Iron Age potters?
- Was any of the sampled pottery fired in a different temperature than the other samples?
- How long was the firing process?
- How was the pottery placed and what impact did the positioning have upon the appearance of the ceramic, its fabric composition, and other physical changes throughout firing?

To try to answer these questions the following methods were used:

- Studies of visual characteristics of the archaeological material.
- XRPD analysis of Iron Age pottery samples.
- Ceramic firing experiments of clay samples.

Pottery: the studied samples

Archaeological excavations in Latvia have yielded only

a few whole vessels or partial vessels that could be fully reconstructed from the period in focus. The bulk of pottery collection consists of potsherds; moreover, often thousands of sherds come from a single settlement. For example, during the excavation at Ķente hill fort (Fig. 1:1) 29350 units of pottery were registered (Stubavs 1959), of which 28087 units were related to the Middle Iron Age (400–800 AD) (Stubavs 1976, p.99). Excavation in the Abora I settlement (Fig. 1:2) yielded more than 18000 pottery units, of which approximately 1000 units were related to Iron Age households (Loze 1979, p.204).

In this article we will present the analysis of 43 ceramic samples: 28 sherds from Ķente hill fort, 10 sherds from the Abora I settlement, and 1 sample each from burial grounds at Boķi (Fig. 1:3) and Zariņi (Fig. 1:4) (see Fig. 3, 8, 9, 10, 11). The sampled sherds were selected to ensure that each pottery type (rusticated, smooth-walled, polished, and pinched) from the studied period was represented. Furthermore, 3 pottery samples from the Late Neolithic Age (2900–1800 BC), the Bronze Age (1800–500 BC), and the Early Iron Age (1–400 AD) were added to the group in order to determine whether

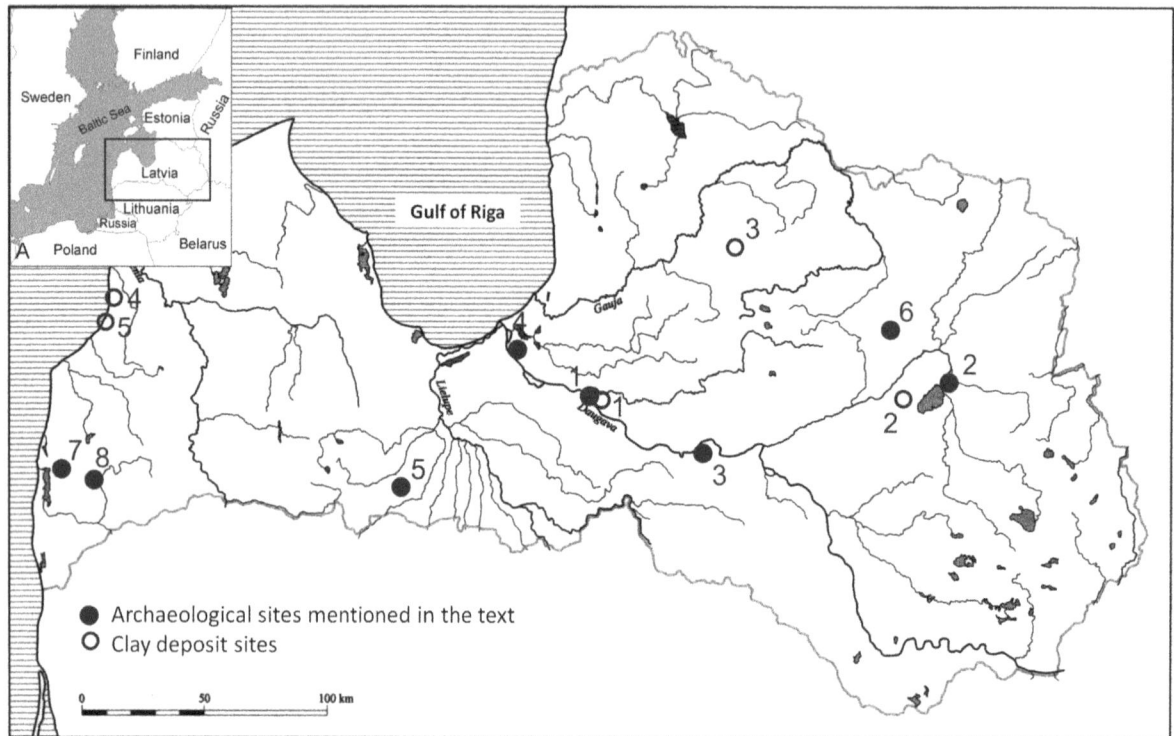

Fig. 1: Archaeological sites mentioned in the text: 1 – Ķente hill fort and settlement; 2 – Abora I settlement; 3 – Boķi burial ground; 4 – Zariņi burial ground; 5 – Tērvete hill fort and settlement; 6 – Ušuru Lake fort; 7 – Grobiņa hill fort and settlement; 8 – Vārtaja hill fort and settlement. Clay deposit sites: 1 – Ogre; 2 – Barkava; 3 – Rauna; 4 – Sārnate; 5 – Jūrkalne.

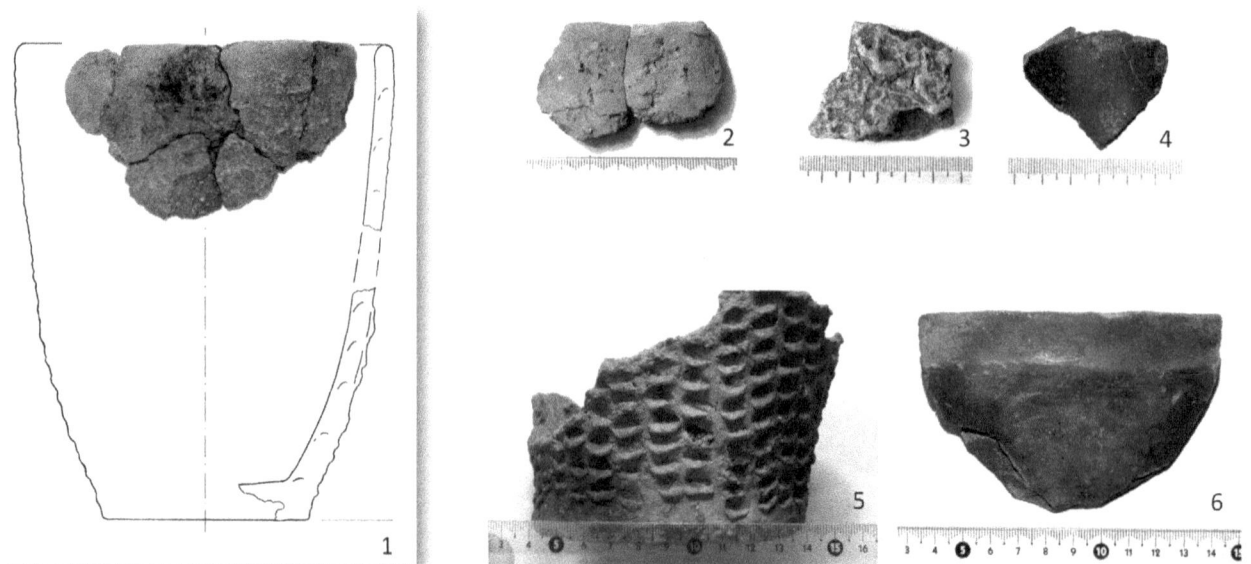

Fig. 2: Ceramic samples from the Tervete hill-fort (1, 2), Abora I settlement (3, 4) and Ušuru lake fort (5, 6).

the Middle and Late Iron Age pottery firing temperature differed from earlier periods.

In this research we tried to see a variety of features of the samples and the possibilities to correlate them to each other. In this way, vessels with different surface finishing were separated into groups by their fabric composition (coarse- and fine-grained pottery). It was observed that most of the coarse-grained pottery, both rusticated (Fig. 2:1, 3) and smooth-walled (Fig. 2:2), as well as that covered with nail impressions (Fig. 2:5), is light in colour: reddish-brown or reddish-yellow. Fine ware, on the other hand, especially smoothed and polished pottery, is usually dark-gray or even markedly black (Fig. 2:4, 6).

Pottery features: observations and discussion

The surface colour of the vessel is largely dependent on the conditions in which it was fired, especially the finishing part of the firing process. After the maximum temperature has been achieved the atmosphere in which the vessel is allowed to cool down is most important. These conditions are usually described as oxidizing or reductive depending on the supply of oxygen during the firing.

Oxidizing conditions of firing are when there is enough oxygen for the organic fuel to completely burn up. When the vessels are cooling, the chemical processes in the pottery fabric stop and the vessels maintain the atmospheric characteristics gained at the end of the firing. If the firing is done in an open fire then a fully oxidised surface is achieved by taking the vessels out of the ashes and coals before they have cooled. If the vessels are left in the smouldering fire the remaining ashes and coals decrease the access of oxygen which results in dark, partly reduced patches.

Reduction is a process when the access of oxygen is restricted during the firing process. Such an environment creates carbon (C) and carbonic oxide (CO) which at an elevated temperature is chemically active. Carbon attracts oxygen found in clays in an oxide form which results in the reduction of metal oxides to metals, or lower value oxides.

C – carbon
CO – carbon monoxide
CO_2 – carbon dioxide
iron oxides: FeO – black
　　　　　　Fe_3O_4 – black (magnetite)
　　　　　　Fe_2O_3 – red (hematite)

$$3Fe_2O_3 + CO \rightarrow 2Fe_3O_4 + CO_2$$

$$Fe_3O_4 + CO \rightarrow 3FeO + CO_2$$

The clay from Latvia contains a large amount of iron oxide. Therefore neutral or oxidizing firing conditions give vessels a reddish-brown or reddish-yellow colouring. On the other hand, in a reductive environment the vessel colour becomes grey, blue-grey, or black.

It is also notable that in a confined environment with airless conditions reduction also happens to unfired clay. This occurs if the clay is saturated with organic substances. Over an extended period of time the decomposition of organic material uses up the oxygen found in iron oxide in the clay itself. For example, secondary or so-called gleyed clays have collected organic matter. Their blue-gray colouring is caused by partially decomposed organic matter and iron compounds (Hamer and Hamer 2004, p.62).

Historically, reductive firing technologies have been linked to cultures who had known specialized pottery ovens, for example, Etruscan or the famous Greek red-figure and black-figure style pottery. However, it is possible to partially reduce vessels also in relatively simple open fire conditions (Rice 1987, p.154). This can be achieved by covering the vessels in coal and smothering the burning with soil or turf. It is also possible to cover the still-hot vessels in leaves or grass (Barley 1997).

Occasionally, potters and ceramic researchers reactualize the debate on whether or not the vessels made in simple firing conditions (e.g. open fire) are to be considered as reduced. The main argument in this dispute is the fact that reduction—it being understood as reduction of coloured metal oxides (mainly iron)—in ceramics occurs only at 800-900°C. Such a high temperature is not always achievable in an open fire. At lower temperatures the dark colouring in vessels is created by free carbon which saturates the outer layer of the pottery fabric (The Prehistoric Ceramics Research Group 2010, p.28). However, some authors do believe that iron oxide in ceramics can be reduced already at a temperature of 700°C (Hamer and Hamer 2004, p.300). Taking into account the different points of view, the term 'reduction' should be used with caution. In this paper the terms 'reduced environment' and 'reduction process' are used to describe a restricted supply of air which hinders the burning of organic material (both fuel for fairing and admixtures in the fabric), not chemical changes of iron in the clay.

As can be seen the surface colour of the vessel is one of the features of ceramics that allows us to draw conclusions about the firing regime. The light yellow, red, or brown colouring of fabric is an indication of open-firing with a free supply of air, while the dark grey or black colouring indicates that the vessel had been exposed to a reduction environment at the end of the firing process. However, the fracture surface of the sherds reveals a great and rather puzzling diversity (Fig. 3 & 11). Part of the researched pottery is evenly light-coloured all the way through the ware, since they have been exposed to an oxidisation process during first or later firings. Traces of excessive burning or a total absence of any traces of use (cooking) lead us to the conclusion that the respective vessel had undergone repeated firing (Fig. 3:1): the settlement had been razed by fire, the vessel has been part of a cremation burial, or the sherd had simply got into the hearth and there lost the traces of the original firing.

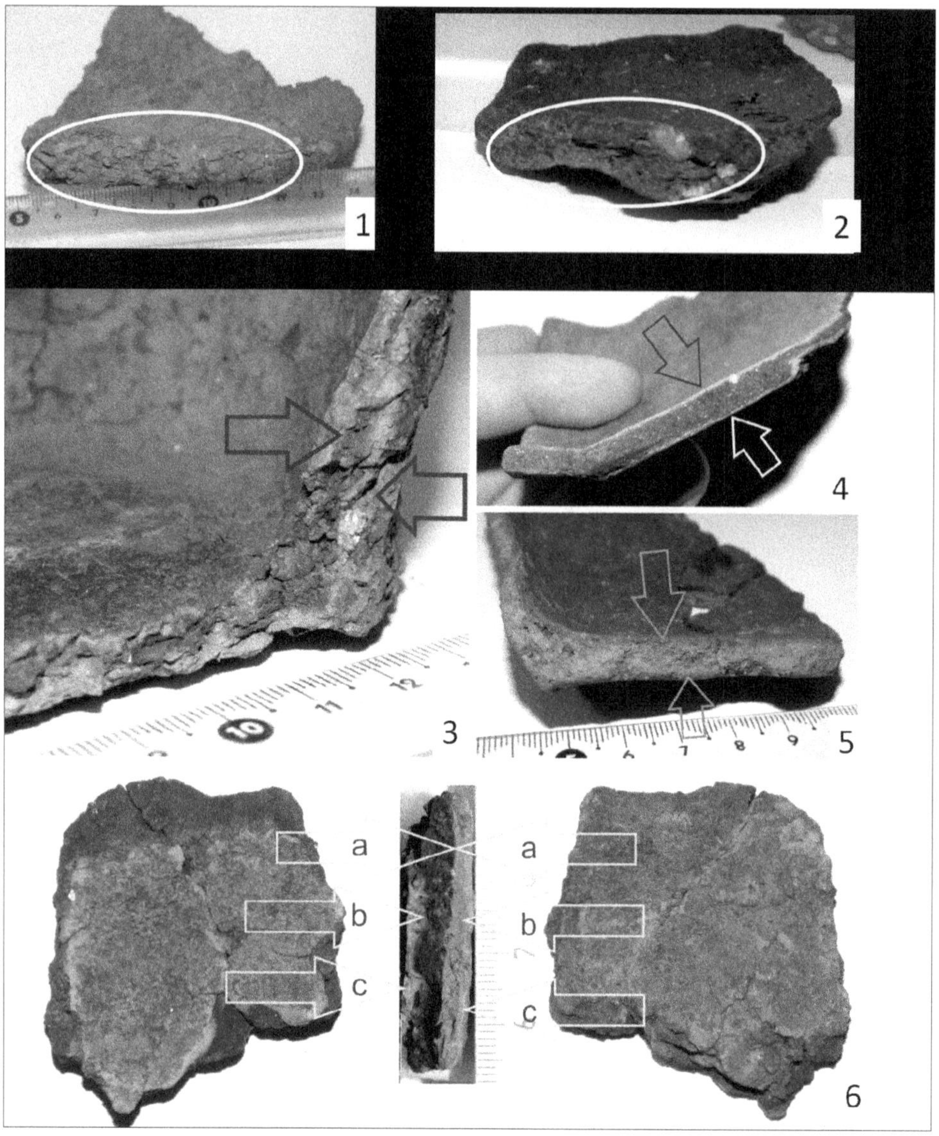

Baiba Dumpe, Agnese Stunda-Zujeva and Jana Vecstaudža

Fig. 3: Traces of firing, use an erosion in the fabric of pottery (1 – Tērvete settlement, VI 22; 2 – Vartaja hil fort, LM 16294; 3, 4, 5 – Ušuru lake fort, VI 48; 6 – Ķente hill fort, VI 31): 1 – pot sherd with traces of excessive burning; 2 – traces of atmosphere reduction throughout the fabric; 3 – traces of use: boiling products have adsorped into the fabric on the inside, but ash and soot from the heart – on the outside of the vessel; 4 – eroded inside and outside surface of vessel; 5 – traces of atmosphere reduction on the inside and outside surfaces of vessel; 6 – sample No. 27 – a potsherd with traces of: a) firing, b) use (cooking) and c) erosion visible on the fracture surface.

An evenly black fabric (Fig. 3:2, 4) or a darker zone on the sherd (Fig. 3:3, 5, 6a) suggests that reduction process had taken place during the firing of the vessel. As discussed above, and as we know from previous experience in pottery making, the dark colour of the pottery is dependent on various factors, including the mass composition.

A layer of light inexpressive colour on the other hand is a result of the erosion process as the sherd had undergone an extended exposure to water and air (Fig. 3:4, 6c). Most sherds emerge from the latter process rather plain-looking with an unrevealing texture. Parts of the sherds reveal clear traces of use on their fracture surface: the products that had been boiled in the respective vessel had been absorbed into the fabric on the inside while ash and soot from the hearth were present on the outside (Fig. 3:3). It is this part of the fabric—the one which had undergone wear—that is most affected by erosion (Fig. 3:6b). Only after identifying and

separating the features that have developed in the course of the wear of the vessels, or while the sherds had lain in the occupation layer, can one start trying to establish the traces of pottery firing.

The methods of hard sciences in the research of archaeological pottery in Latvia

In Latvia the first attempts at comprehensive analysis of pottery fabric were undertaken in the 1960s, when archaeologist Ieva Cimermane submitted 84 potsherds from different periods for study at the Central Laboratory of the Latvian SSR Board of Geology and Mineral Resources (Birzniece et al. 1964; Vītiņš and Šķiņķis 1963; Vītols and Vītiņš 1962). The laboratory performed a macroscopic and microscopic investigation of the fabric, which included: mineralogical analysis by petrographic microscope, determination of granulometric composition,

46

chemical analysis of some elements, and analysis of several physical parameters (water absorption, density, and loss on ignition). Previous studies of the earliest pottery in Latvia have established that vessels were made of Quaternary clays with good plastic properties (Vītols and Vītiņš 1962). The raw materials were sourced from layers of gleyed (eroded and reworked) clays, which have a low optimum firing temperature: 800–900° C.

Regretfully, the application of the above-described methods in the interpretation of archaeological finds was rather fragmented. In the subsequent decades the study of fabric was limited to visual observation performed by archaeologists themselves (in some cases with the help of a microscope).

In 2005, through the activities of Latvian archaeologist Valdis Bērziņš, and thanks to his co-operation with Swedish archaeologist Ole Stilborg, analysis of Latvian Early Neolithic pottery was performed in the Laboratory for Ceramic Research at Lund University (Dumpe et al. 2011). It consisted of the microscopic analysis of eight samples to determine mineral and organic inclusions in the mass of clay.

One of the fastest and thus one of the most popular methods of mineralogical analysis of ceramic materials is X-ray powder diffraction analysis (XRPD). XRPD determines the type of mineral phases in the sample. In Latvia this method has not been used in archaeological research to date. In archaeological research in Western Europe and the United States XRPD has already been used extensively from the 1950s (Shepard 1959, p.146–147). Since then the method has been developed and applied in combination with other methods such as thermal analysis, thin-section microscopic analysis, scanning electron microscopy, etc.

By studying the composition of pottery samples with the XRPD method, archaeological research seeks answers to questions concerning the origin of pottery (or its raw materials) and its firing temperatures. The origin can be deduced from inclusions of minerals that are not typical for the respective site but which are typical for another area. The degree of decomposition of these minerals or their recrystallization into different minerals assists us in establishing the firing regime. One of the major advantages of XRPD compared to thin-sections is the possibility to analyse the potsherd (if it is 1–5 cm wide and relatively smooth) without leaving an impact on it; in other words, XRPD is a non-destructive method which is of particular importance in archaeology in cases of unique samples. Still, it must be taken into consideration that X-rays penetrate into the sample only a few micrometers deep and thus XRPD is to be considered a surface analysis method. To analyse the middle layer the sample must be fully ground into a homogeneous powder (analysis area 3–20 mm, optimal 10 mm).

The most important shortcoming of the XRPD method is that X-ray diffraction patterns (diffractograms) of the

similar crystal structures belonging to different minerals may overlap and thus the identification of minerals is not always unambiguous. Identification is considerably easier if the chemical composition is known, for example, as established by electron dispersive X-ray spectroscopy (usually available together with scanning electron microscopy). It should also be taken into consideration that amorphous and very weakly crystalline compounds, such as organic rests and soot, cannot be identified: such compounds may raise the background line in the form of a wide peak, which in turn makes it more difficult to identify the other components.

Temperatures of mineral phase decomposition or formation depend on the overall composition of the respective sample and its firing conditions, such as oxidizing or the reductive environment, and the rate of temperature increase. Decomposition of the clay mineral illite occurs between 700°C and 1000°C; Iordanidis et al. (2009) concluded that illite did not decompose at firing temperatures lower than 850°C. Maritan et al. (2004) pointed out that the decomposition of illite in an inert atmosphere (N_2) containing dolomite and calcite takes place when the temperature reaches approximately 870°C, while a sample containing calcite decomposes only at around 820°C.

Results of X-ray powder diffraction analysis (XRPD)

The sample was prepared by rubbing off or breaking off a small piece of a potsherd and grinding it. In the process of grinding, the hardest bits (gravel), which looked to be consisting mostly of quartz, were picked out and the remaining parts of the sample were finely ground and analysed by XRPD. Such an approach was selected because it was not so important to compare the average composition of samples as it was to determine the degree of decomposition/ recrystallization of temperature changing minerals, as well as to identify the possible mineral inclusions of non-local origin.

In figure 4, the selection of most different diffractograms is shown. They are quite similar, however, because the mineral composition of samples is rather homogenous—they contain illite, quartz and minerals of the feldspar group: orthoclase and anorthite, or albite. There was no trace of calcite or dolomite in the samples. Whole sherds with a higher and lower degree of wear did not differ from each other as to the mineral composition determined by XRPD. Illite is the only identified clay mineral and its amount differs from sample to sample (see Fig. 4 where intensities of marked peaks were compared). Sample No. 12 contained barely any illite and had the lowest peak intensity indicating crystalline phases. It is thus the most amorphous of the samples, which means that it had been fired at a higher temperature than the other analysed samples from Ķente.

In the present status of research the data from the mineralogical analysis can be interpreted as follows: samples possess high mechanical endurance thus they

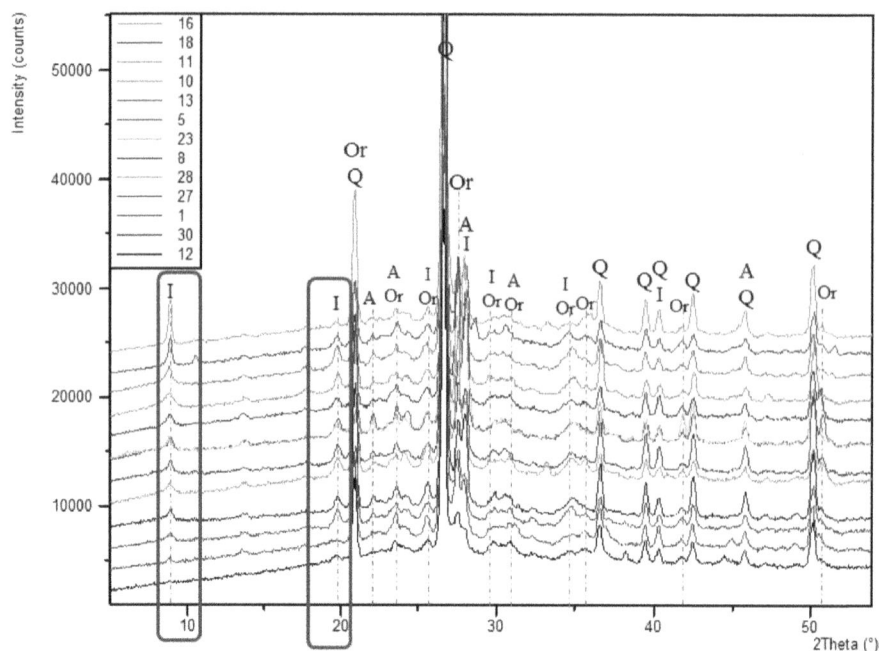

Fig. 4: Diffractogram of some pottery from Ķente hill fort. I – Illite, Q – Quartz, Or – Orthoclase (K-feldspar), A – albite or anorthite (plagioclase group; Na- and Ca-feldspar).

had been fired at temperatures of at least 600°C, and since illite is not fully decomposed, the firing temperature did not exceeded ~900°C. Although the prevalence of illite in the clay greenbody is unknown, the comparison of the diffractograms allows us to draw the conclusion that the firing temperatures were probably lower than 800°C; in most of the samples the peaks corresponding to illite are intense and illite has decomposed very little, if at all. Sample No. 12 had been fired at a higher temperature than the other analyzed samples. The illite in this sample had almost completely decomposed, yet the temperature had not been much higher than 900°C as the high-temperature minerals had not yet crystallized within it.

The mineral composition of pottery from the Abora settlement (Fig. 5) is mostly similar to that of the samples from Ķente, however deviation from the average was detected in the following samples:

- No. 43 contains calcite (shells visible to a naked eye);
- No. 33 contains unidentified inclusions;
- No. 32 and No. 35 contain aluminium oxide (corundum), which had formed as a result of the decomposition of illite at approximately 600–800°C (Sedmalis et al. 2002).

The prevalence of illite varies from sample to sample (as with the samples from Ķente hill fort), however all samples contain illite which allows us to draw the conclusion that these samples, too, had been fired at temperatures lower than 900°C.

Firing experiments

Based on the experience of ten earlier experimental firings of pottery the following procedure of firing has been

developed and was used for the eleventh, twelfth, and thirteenth experiments presented in this article:

1. Pottery products are stacked in the place where the centre of the fire will be. Surrounding the stacked vessels several small bonfires are lit a close distance away (Fig. 6:1);
2. The fire is gradually moved closer to the vessels by combining the separate small bonfires into a singular circle of fire around the stack of vessels (Fig. 6:2);
3. The fire is moved very close to the vessels, at the same time observing changes taking place on their surface (organic substances contained in clay start smouldering) (Fig. 6:3);
4. The fire is maintained very close to the vessels and above them with the aim of reaching the desirable firing temperature (Fig. 6:4);
5. After the desirable temperature has been reached, the bonfire is left to burn out slowly (Fig. 6:5).

Such a gradual process of pre-heating before firing allows for the control of the rise of temperature and avoids cracking the pottery. However, within the researched context it is only a hypothetical firing method of archaeological pottery, and for the present it is not possible to prove whether this method had indeed been used.

The experiments were conducted in order to examine how the ceramic fabric changes during firing. For this purpose a series of samples from several clay deposits in Latvia were taken: clays used in the experiments were taken from Barkava and Sārnate clay deposits, Jūrkalne coastal detritions, the Ogre river detritions, as well as clays that ceramic workshop 'Raunas ceplis' had taken from the Rauna clay deposit (see Fig. 1, 8, 9 & 10). To fire experimental samples in a controlled temperature regime,

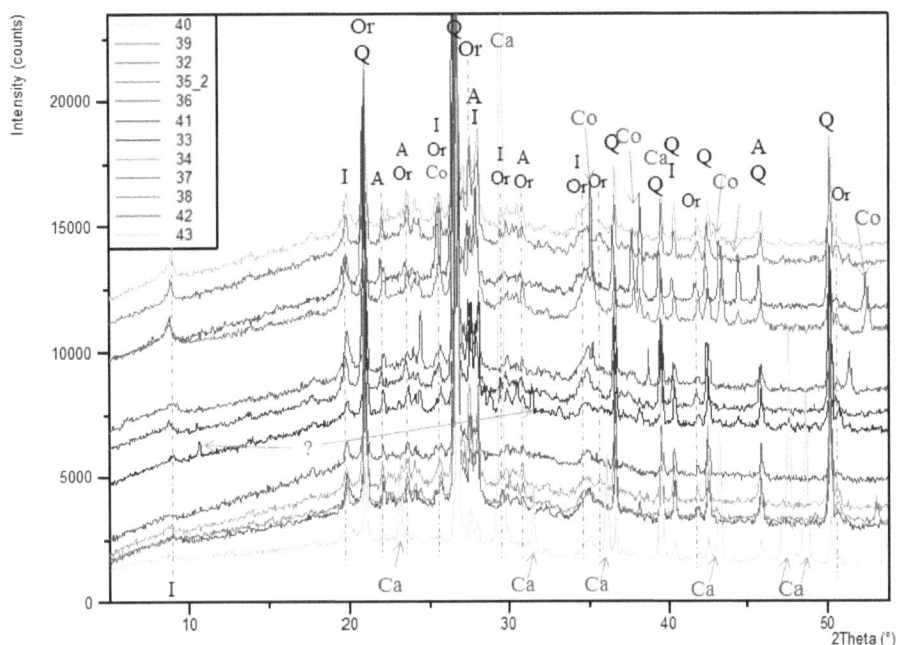

Fig. 5: Diffractograms of pottery from Abora I settlement. I – Illite, Q – Quartz, Or – Orthoclase (K-feldspar), A – albite or anorthite (plagioclase group; Na- and Ca-feldspar), Ca – calcite, Co – corundum, ? – not identified phase.

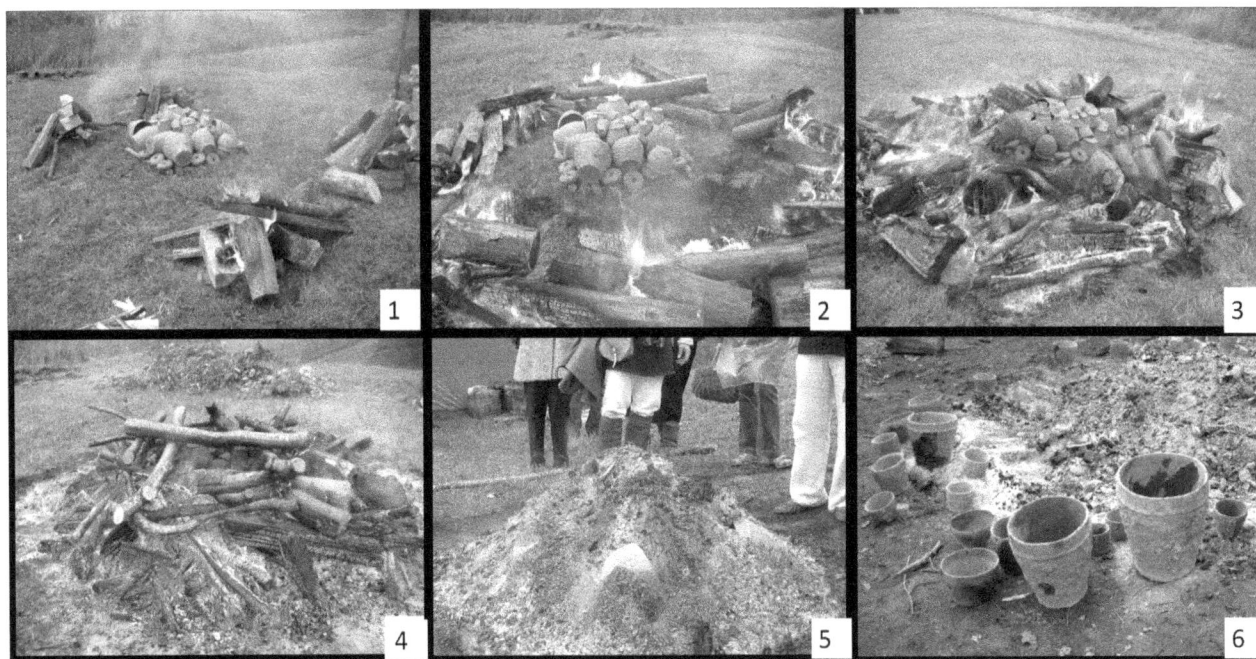

Fig. 6: Burning with a slow heating. Slow rise of temperature was achieved by moving fire step by step closer to vessels. Photos of firing 8, 2008.

three bonfire firings as described above—tests 11, 12 and 13—were conducted. Unlike the above-described firing course, the samples did not cool down in coal, but upon reaching the required temperature they were removed from the fire. Temperature control during bonfire firing was done using thermocouple MASTECH MY64.

Bonfire firing test No. 11 lasted for 4 hours, reaching the temperature of 940°C. The thermocouple was not adequately protected from flame during this test, which made it difficult to register the exact temperature. In the

subsequent firing tests this shortcoming was rectified. The temperature dynamics during bonfire firing tests No. 12 and No. 13 are shown as diagrams (Fig. 7). The points at which experimental samples were removed are indicated on the curves.

In the course of experiments it was established that the temperature of 600–700°C can be easily reached by burning tree branches and brushwood in all weather conditions. Open-firing also allows the temperature to reach 800 to 900°C.

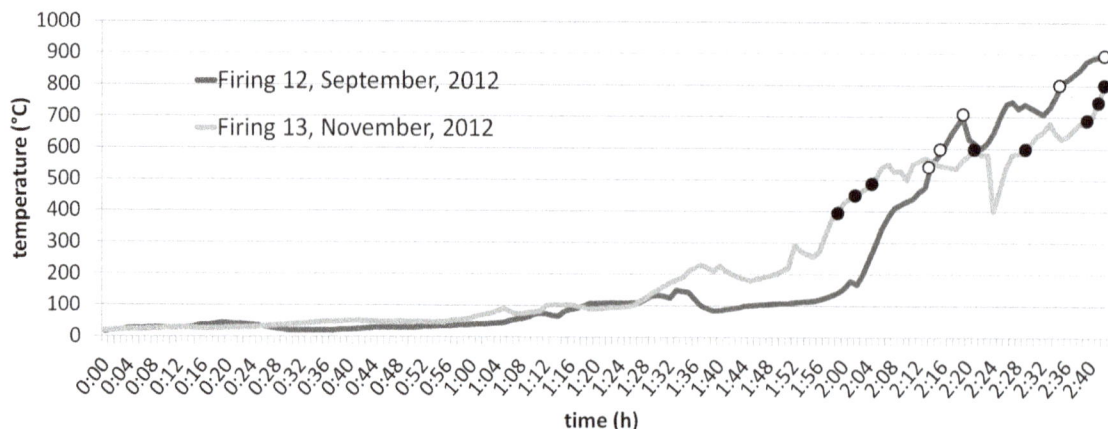

Fig. 7: Temperature dynamics during bonfire firing.

Visual comparison of samples: results

The results yielded by firing experiments are very illustrative when sample series are organized as in Fig. 8-11. The fracture surface of the samples displays different zones of the ware that have occurred in the course of firing. The samples from the series displayed in Fig. 8 (firing test No. 12) contained no artificial temper, however, there were various natural inclusions in it: organic substances in the form of tiny plant particles and microorganisms and a little of fine sand. In the outer part of the fabric organic substances burn away quickly, and the outer layer is turned red orange due to the oxidation of iron in the clay. In the core of the fabrics of tested samples charred remains of organic substances create a dark coloration. The colour of the charred organic substances is most intense within the firing temperature interval of 550 to 700°C. By the time the temperature reaches 800°C the organic substances have burned away, triggering reduction processes in the middle part of the fabric that turns slate-blue as a result. Fig. 9 shows the sample series of firing test No. 13 which involved a larger number of samples than the previous tests, but yielded similar results.

Figure 10 shows the sample series of firing test No. 11. It is obvious that a large proportion of organic inclusions create an intense dark colouring that endures until the temperature of 700°C is reached, however, mineral inclusions expedite their burning away. Irrespective of whether we use the term 'reduction' to describe the ceramic firing process at low temperatures, the presence of organic matter in the pottery fabric is a key precondition for the creation of a dark area in the core of the sherds (see Fig. 10, first and second column, and for more about organic inclusions in Middle and Late Iron Age pottery fabrics in present-day Latvia, see Dumpe and Stivrins 2015).

These samples also demonstrate another process which is important when untreated clay sediments are used in pottery. Clays from Ogre contain a large proportion of sand and limestone pebbles. The largest pebbles could be picked out in the process of pugging the clay, but the finest particles remained in the fabric. Since clay is relatively plastic—fat—the natural mineral inclusions serve as a lean material and help to heat the fabric evenly. It is known that when temperatures exceed 750°C, the calcium carbonate ($CaCO_3$) contained in clay turns into calcium oxide

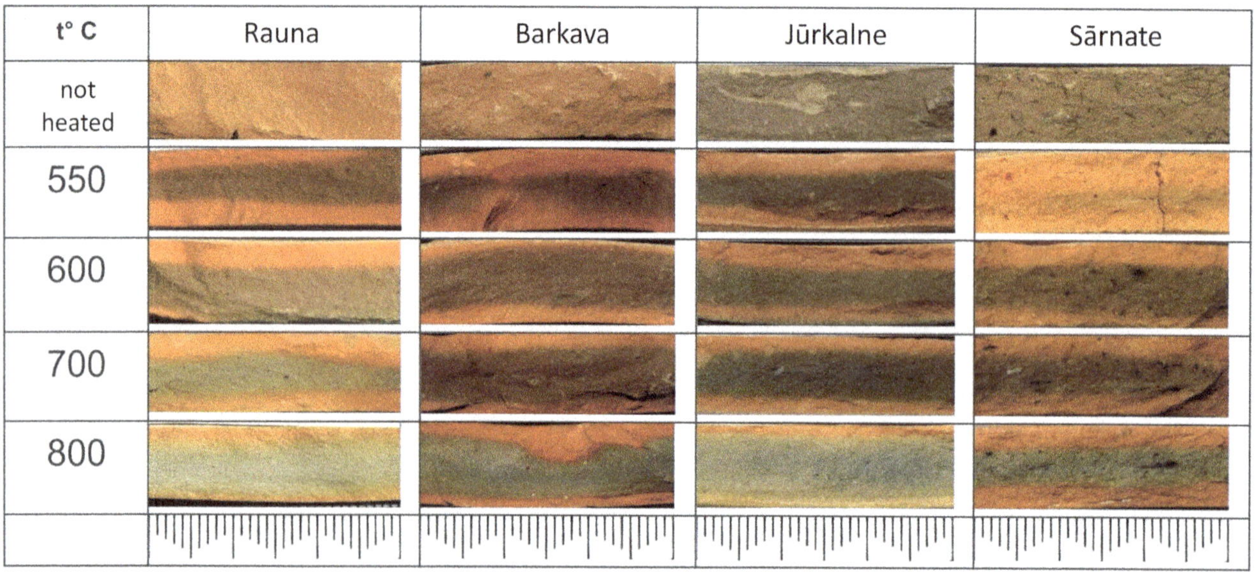

Fig. 8: The appearance of the fracture surface of fabric under different firing temperatures. Bonfire firing test No. 11 (Rauna clay) and No. 12 (Barkava, Jūrkalne and Sārnate clays).

50

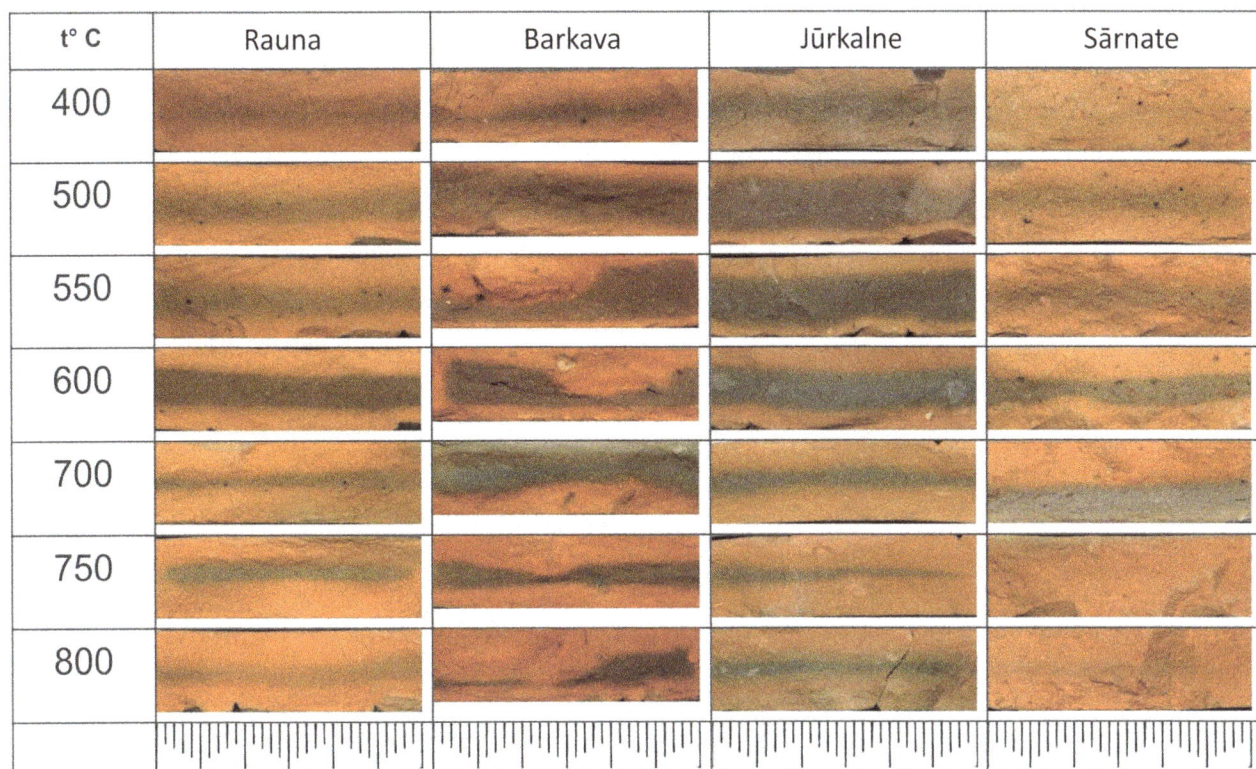

t° C	Rauna	Barkava	Jūrkalne	Sārnate
400				
500				
550				
600				
700				
750				
800				

Fig. 9: The appearance of the fracture surface of fabric under different firing temperatures. Bonfire firing test No. 13.

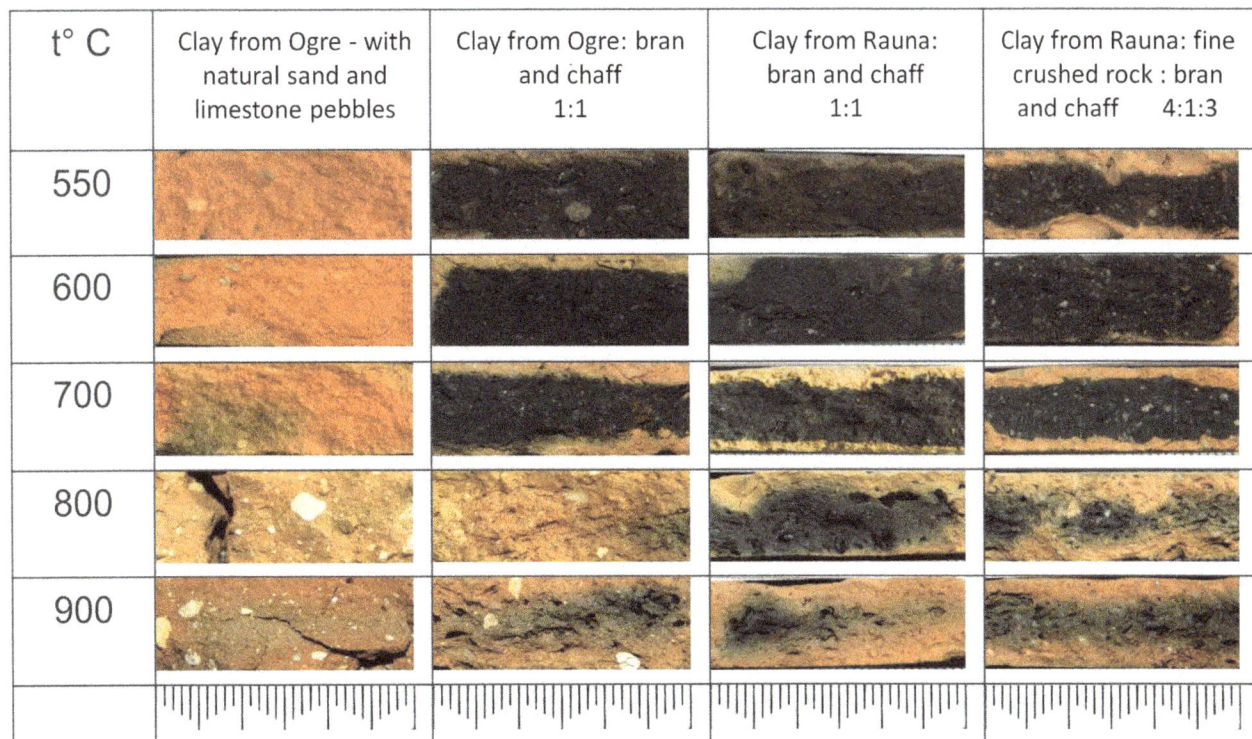

t° C	Clay from Ogre - with natural sand and limestone pebbles	Clay from Ogre: bran and chaff 1:1	Clay from Rauna: bran and chaff 1:1	Clay from Rauna: fine crushed rock : bran and chaff 4:1:3
550				
600				
700				
800				
900				

Fig. 10: The appearance of the fracture surface of fabric with various inclusions and under different firing temperatures. Bonfire firing test No. 11.

(CaO) or lime, which upon coming into contact with air humidity becomes slaked and grows approximately three times in volume, cleaving or crumbling the ware of the product (Kuršs and Stinkule 1997, p.96). Fig. 10 shows the decomposition of Ogre clay samples removed from the firing at the temperatures of 800 and 900°C.

By comparing the results of the experiments with the Iron Age pottery summarized in Fig. 11, one may try to interpret the traces of the firing process seen on the archaeological material. The intense dark colouring that a part of the sherds displays can be the result of high concentration of small organic particles in the fabric. This means that the

Ķente hill fort	Ušuru Lake fort	Tērvete hill fort	Grobiņa settlement Vārtaja settlement

Fig. 11: The appearance of the fracture surface of fabric of middle and late Iron Age pottery.

temperature was not high enough to completely burn the organic substances (compare Fig.10) and that there was an insufficient supply of air during the firing process, i.e. reduction environment makes the fabric saturated with carbon (Fig. 11:8, 9, 15, 16, 22, 23, 26, 27, 28).

Part of the sherds are intensely dark on the side which had been part of the inside surface of the vessel, while the other side, the one which had been part of the vessel's outer surface, is lighter. It may be assumed that such vessels had been fired and left to cool off in an upside down position (Fig. 11:2, 10, 17, 24, 25).

Sherds which have the dark colouring concentrated in the middle part of the fabric with both surfaces displaying a more or less lighter colouring, suggest that air flow had been less restricted during the firing process of the respective vessels. As of yet we cannot accurately describe such pottery firing details, however, this ceramic firing temperature most likely did not exceed 700°C (Fig. 11:3, 4, 5, 6, 7, 11, 12, 18, 19). All the analysed sherds also display traces of use: soot or other residue of cooking. This

indicates that the sherds are not burned repeatedly by the vessel breaking, so have retained the original features of firing.

Figure 11 also contains information on sherds that do not display any clear traces of use: they had undergone erosion or repeated firing (Fig. 11:13, 14, 20, 21). They are evenly light or show light traces of reduction in the form of slate-blue colouring in the middle of the fabric.

Conclusions

The results of this study demonstrate that the experimental studies and laboratory analysis complement each other well in studying archaeological pottery. Experimental and analytical comparison of the results led to a number of conclusions:

No essential differences in the maximum firing temperatures were detected among different types of pottery in the archaeological material.

As revealed by the comparison of the results of experiments and analysis, the prevalent pottery firing temperature could have been in the interval 600–700°C.

The firing was conducted during a short time interval otherwise the fabric would have obtained evenly light colouring, even at a low firing temperature. At higher temperatures, as well as heating for a long time, the organic admixtures of fabrics completely burned out and ceramics obtained a yellow-reddish oxidized colour.

Some of the pots seem to have been placed upside down during and/or after the firing.

Experiments with this firing method allow us to recognise similar features as those observed upon the archaeological ware surfaces. Perhaps, then, a similar method has been used in Middle and Late Iron Age pottery firing. However, the visual comparison of experimental samples showed that the organic admixtures are much more important than was previously known. The reducing environment which creates the typical dark coloration of the Iron Age pottery fabric core is caused by charring of the organic admixtures.

In this study, it was possible to view only a small part of the pottery firing process and the research will continue.

Acknowledgements

This work has been supported by the European Social Fund within the project "Support for Doctoral Studies at University of Latvia". The authors are grateful to Eva Eihmane for translating the article.

Bibliography

Barley, N. (1997) Traditional Rural Potting in West Africa. Ed. by Freestone I. and Gaimster D., *Pottery in the Making. World ceramic traditions*, 140–145. London: British Museum Press.

Birzniece, E., Vītiņš, E. and Šķiņķe, A. (1964) *Pārskats par apdedzināto seno māla lausku analīzēm* [Survey of the analysis of fired archaeological potsherds]. No. AA 918. National History Museum of Latvia, Department of Archaeology.

Dumpe, B. (2009) Senākās podniecības krāsnis Latvijā. *Pa somugru pēdām Baltijas jūras krastā. Starptautiskās zinātniskās konferences materiāli, 2009. gada 23. aprīlis, Turaida*, 67–75. Rīga: Zinātne.

Dumpe, B., Bērziņš, V. and Stilborg, O. (2011) A dialogue across the Baltic on Narva and Ertebølle pottery. *Early Pottery in the Baltic – Dating, Origin and Social Context. International Workshop at Schleswig from 20th – 21st October 2006. Berichte der Römisch-Germanischen Kommision. Band 89*, 409–441. Darmstadt/ Mainz: Philipp von Zabern.

Dumpe, B. and Stivrins, N. (2015) *Organic Inclusions in Middle and Late Iron Age (5th – 12th century) Hand-Built Pottery in Present-Day Latvia*. Journal of Archaeological Science. 57, 239–247.

Hamer, F. and Hamer, J. (2004) *The Potters Dictionary of Materials and Techniques. Fifth edition*. London: A&C Black, Philadelphia: University of Pennsylvania Press.

Iordanidis, A., Garcia-Guinea, J., and Karamitrou-Mentessidi, G. (2009) Analytical Study of Ancient Pottery from the Archaeological Site of Aiani, Northern Greece. *Materials Characterization vol. 60 issue 4 (April, 2009.)* 292–302, DOI:10.1016/j.matchar.2008.08.001.

Kuršs, V. and Stinkule, A. (1997) *Latvijas derīgie izrakteņi*. Rīga: Latvijas Universitāte

Loze, I. – Лозе И. А. (1979) *Поздний неолит и ранняя бронза Лубанской равнины*. Рига: Зинатне.

Maritan, L., Mazzoli, C., Nodari, L. and Russo, U. (2004) *Second Iron Age Grey Pottery from Este (northeastern Italy): Study of Provenance and Technology. Applied Clay Science 29, no. 1 (February 2005)*, 31–44. DOI:10.1016/j.clay.2004.09.003.

Rice, P. M. (1987) *Pottery Analysis. A Sourcebook*. Chicago – London: Univesity of Chicago Press.

Sedmalis, U., Šperberga, I. and Sedmale, G. (2002) *Latvijas minerālās izejvielas un to izmantošana*. Rīga: RTU Izdevniecība

Shepard, A. O. (1959) *Ceramics for the archaeologist*. Washington: Carnegie Institution of Washington.

Stubavs, A. (1959) Arheoloģiskie izrakumi Ķentes pilskalnā un apmetnē 1958. gadā. *Referātu tēzes zinātniskai sesijai veltītai 1958. gada arheoloģiskām un etnogrāfiskām ekspedīcijām Latvijas PSR teritorijā*, 24. Rīga: Latvijas PSR Zinātņu akadēmijas Vēstures un materiālās kultūras institūts, Latvijas PSR Kultūras ministrija.

Stubavs, A. (1976) *Ķentes pilskalns un apmetne*. Rīga: Zinātne.

Šnore, E. (1957) Asotes pilskalna krāsnis. *Arheoloģija un etnogrāfija. 1. laid.*, 5-20. Rīga, Latvijas PSR Zinātņu akadēmijas izdevniecība.

Šnore 1961 – Шноре, Э. (1961) *Асотское городище*. Рига: Зинатне.

The Prehistoric Ceramics Research Group, 2010. *The Study of Prehistoric Pottery: General Policies and Guidelines for Analysis and Publication*.

Urtāns, V. (1967) Daugmales ekspedīcijas rezultāti 1966. gadā. *Zinātniskās atskaites sesijas referātu tēzes par arheologu, antropologu un etnogrāfu 1966. gada pētījumu rezultātiem*. 41–42. Rīga: Zinātne.

Urtāns, V. (1974) Izrakumi Aizkraukles senvietu kompleksā. *Zinātniskās atskaites sesijas materiāli par arheologu un etnogrāfu 1973. gada pētījumu rezultātiem*. 74-77. Rīga: Zinātne.

Vītiņš, E. and Šķiņķis, E. (1963) *Pārskats par Kivtu apmetnes seno māla trauku analīzēm* [Survey of the analysis of the archaeological pottery from Kivtu settlement]. No. AA 917. National History Museum of Latvia, Department of Archaeology.

Vītols, P. and Vītiņš, E. (1962) *Pārskats par seno trauku lausku analīzēm* [Survey of the analysis of archaeological potsherds]. No. AA 916. National History Museum of Latvia, Department of Archaeology.

The Making of Tatinger Pitchers and Transmission of Technology

Maggie Fredriksson[1] and Thomas Eriksson[2]

[1] *Maggies Keramik, Äspelundsvägen 15, 395 94 Rockneby, Sweden*

Maggie.fredriksson@gmail.com

[2] *The Laboratory of Ceramic Research, Lund University, Sweden*

Thomas.eriksson@geol.lu.se, theriksson63@gmail.com

Abstract: The Tating or Tatinger pitchers have been in focus for many reasons: their exclusivity, production and distribution. A main theme has been if the pitchers could be associated with Christian mission. The starting point for this study is the manufacture of the vessel and especially the application of the tin-foil on the vessels. The method of application is closely related to the application of tin-foil in Carolingian Book Illuminations. A transmission of ideas, handicrafts, methods and symbolic values is discussed.

Key words: Viking age; Tatinger pitchers; Decoration; Handicraft; Experimental archaeology; Transmission of technology

Introduction

The background to the article is that Kalmar county museum asked the ceramist Maggie Fredriksson to make some pitchers—the so called Tatinger- or Birka-pitcher. Fredriksson became very curious of what the ordinary find known as Tatinger ware originally looked like and so got in touch with archaeologist Thomas Eriksson. The article is based on the practical work involved in making a replica. The application of the metal-foil was particularly tricky. The practical side also gave some ideas of how this new form of decoration could evolve.

Background

The West-European pitchers with their decoration of tin-foil have, for a long time, been a source for discussion about function, origin, and production. The first Scandinavian attempt to reconstruct this mode of handicraft was made by Dagmar Selling (Selling 1951; Selling 1955). Selling made a full description of the type and attributed it to the Rhineland during the first half of the 9th century. Furthermore, she made an explanation of the decoration which she thought was finished with the addition of tin-foil attached using a glue made of antler (Selling 1951, p. 280). Since her first study, more thin-sections have been made on this type, AI:a1 according to Selling's own definition (Selling 1955, p. 13). The analysis shows that the clay used in Tatinger ware is not homogenous but consists of different clays with different amounts of silt and sand. Most of them are made of clay, in which the levels of calcareous are low but the amount of iron-oxides varies The used coarse clays made it possible to wheel-throw the vessels without the addition of temper (Brorsson 2010; Selling 1955). In other words, it might be wrong to see the Tatinger pottery as one single ware with one single origin. Nevertheless, the production of the vessels probably originates from a region of the Rhineland, and one proposition is the Eifel-area around the town of Mayen in the Carolingian Empire (Steuer 1987, p. 136). Within the empire, Tatinger ware can be found within debris layers in towns. These finds have been taken as evidence for a non-liturgical function of the vessel (Steuer 1987). The most southern example is found outside the Merovingian and Frankish basilica of Saint-Dénis in Paris (Loveluck 2013, p. 117). Other scholars have claimed that the jugs worked as liturgical vessels and that they are connected to the first Christian mission of Scandinavia (Selling 1955, p. 294).

The distribution of Tatinger-ware outside the empire is concentrated to ports, towns, and centres such as Birka and Helgö in central Sweden, Tating and Haithabu in Germany, Oslo-area and Borg in Lofoten in Norway, southern Scotland, three places on the east coast of England, and the Saint Petersburg-area of Russia (Holand 2001, p. 48, 99; Holand 2003; Selling 1951). Many of the Swedish finds come from graves at Birka. The contexts of the finds are often wealthy contexts, such as high-status graves or chieftains' farms. They are often connected to rich female burials. These women has been interpreted as members of the first Christian society and the jugs as vessels for wine used in the rituals around the funeral. (Staecker 2009, p. 323).

Basis for the reconstruction: the potter's description

The basis for the reconstruction is one of the best preserved pitchers in Sweden from the famous chamber grave BJ 854 at Hemlanden, Birka, Uppland (SHM 34000, FID. 106987). The vessel was made of fired earthenware and was wheel-thrown, polished, and fired in a kiln without an inflow of oxygen (Selling 1955). After the firing the vessel was decorated with a pattern made of tin-foil, applied with some kind of animal glue. The melting point of tin is 232° C so the tin cannot have been applied and fired in the kiln.

In my own interests as a ceramicist who produces wares in different ways compared to a potter who only uses the throwing wheel, I had a closer look at this ware and tried to make a replica of it (Fig. 1). The ordinary pitcher was made of earthenware and had been fired in an outdoor-kiln without an inflow of oxygen, which makes the clay turn black. In the absence of such a kiln, the replica pitcher was made using dark brown—almost black—clay when throwing the ware, and throughout the design and the fixing of the handle and the nozzle. After almost complete drying, the surface of the ware was polished with a flat stone to make it a little waterproof and glossy. An electric kiln replaced the outdoor-kiln. The top temperature in the kiln was about 1000° C. A piece of tin-foil measuring 0.1 mm and two different animal glues were used to apply the pattern. The tin-foil used in this experiment was made in Germany by a modern technique. The main focus was how the foil could be applied to the body. Archaeologist Dagmar Selling has written a detailed report about the Tatinger ware where she describes the order in which the different pieces of pattern were applied to the pitcher (Selling 1951). She also noted that the animal glue in this case was probably made of horn, skin, or fish products.

To apply the pattern took quite a long time (Fig. 2). I had to calculate the size of each piece, cut them accordingly with a sharp knife (as scissors did not make the required beautiful edges on each piece), put glue on each one, and finally place them on the pitcher. First I tried using resin of spruce which I melted in a metallic pot before dipping the tip of a knife into it and adding it to the piece of tin-foil. This did not work because the resin dried too quickly. I then tried some pure egg yolk but this did not stick so well. The next step was to try the melted horn glue, to put it on the pieces, and to finally apply them. However, it was a little difficult to keep the melted glue at the right texture. It also smelled very badly!

The pattern on the first pitcher was applied by horn glue, which had the texture of small hard pieces before melted, and the second by fish glue (produced in a modern way) that had a perfect texture directly out of the bottle. In both cases the tin-foil-pattern was attached well enough to stay on the pitcher, if treated in a gentle manner.

The potter's reflection

Sitting in my studio, applying this beautiful pattern, my fantasy took me for a ride back to the past, to the place and the time when the pitcher was made. What did it look like in the studio? Who was the potter? Was he/she working alone? What happened when the order of the pitcher was made? And who was the order made by? What did the person say? 'How do you do? I would like to order a pitcher decorated with a tin-foil-pattern please!' Did the same person make both the ware and the pattern, or was it another craft worker belonging to a better class in the

Fig. 1: Maggie Fredriksson in her study. Photo by Christer Lundberg.

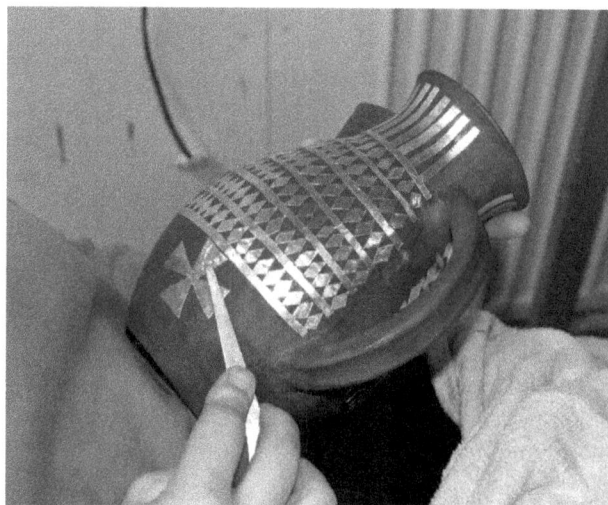

Fig. 2: Applying the tin-foil to the body. Photo by Christer Lundberg.

Table 1. Approximate process time of different stages in the making of one pitcher

Timescale approx.	
Throwing the ware	15 minutes
Design and fixing the handle and the nozzle	30 minutes
Polishing the surface	30 minutes
Drying and firing	One week
Preparing the tin-foil pattern (cutting and matching the pieces)	45 minutes
Application of the pattern	5 hours
Summary	**7 hours**

society and living further down the street who was allowed to do it? Would a Christian become the only one with monopoly to work with the pattern itself, if it was rated as a holy object?

The finds of Tatinger wares seem to have different patterns of rhombs, lines, and even placing of the crosses. The pitcher that is the basis for this experiment is beautifully finished at the top but rougher in the bottom, as though someone has cut it with a knife.

Both the pitcher's top and nozzle edges are covered in silver-like pattern. Further down the pitcher the pattern is more open and suddenly ends sharply. Below there are three crosses. Why are they placed this low down? What was the message of these patterns?

Could the roughly cut lower part of the pitcher correspond to the non-Christians 'down' here on earth, whilst the glittering top represented the new belief 'up' in heaven? When wine was poured from the pitcher, was its upside down form symbolic of the non-Christians and the crosses becoming Christians as the pitcher was turned up to heaven, whilst the glittering and divine top of the pitcher was turned to face the earth where the new beliefs and religion had taken root?

Technological transmission: the archaeologist's reflection

Covering a ceramic vessel with metal foil was a completely new trait in North-European pottery during the 9th century. The method of covering the pitchers with tin-foil gave them a sophisticated and elegant appearance. The contrast between the black polished areas and the shining silver-coloured tin gives the pottery a very special and distinguished look. The explanation for the new occurrence of this technique of metal foil on pottery cannot be simply a potter's wish of making a fancy ware. The idea must have come from a source outside the potter's technical sphere.

The production of Tating-pottery begins in the Rhineland during the second half of the 8th century, i.e. during the so-called Carolingian Renaissance. One of the most important features during this period was the production of illuminated books such as Gospels, Bibles, and Psaltars. The art of book illumination began to flourish during the 8th century. One of the main types of decoration was the use of gold and tin-foil to give pages a heavenly, shiny appearance. The use of tin-foil in books is described by the monk Theophilius Presbyter (c. 1070–1125) in his *Schedula diversarum atrium* (1847, p. 31–33). According to Theophilius (and other sources), tin foil was sometimes covered with a varnish containing saffron, among other things, to imitate gold foil. This type of false gold was called *Auripetrum* (Merrifield 2012, XCVIII–IV; Gettens and Stout 2012, p. 160). The method of affixing the tin-foil and/or gold-foil onto the pages of books is very similar to the result from Maggie Fredriksson's experiment.

Mayen, the presumed area for the Tating production, is situated near the Rhine, between Aachen and Ingelheim, two of the strongholds of the Carolingian Empire and its culture. It is very likely that some kind of transmission of ideas and handicraft between the artisans of book illumination and potters has taken place in this area. One even dares to say that book illumination, with its older

traditions, is essential for the developed use of tin-foil on pottery.

A central theme for understanding the novelty of this type of decoration is transmission (Eerkens and Lipo 2007). In a typological perspective the occurrence of the Tatinger pitchers cannot be explained without two major transmissions. In the Merovingian period the bag-formed vases with stamped incisions became popular in the 6th century. The most common décor element was rhomboid/diamond-shaped stamps, that also occurred in the contemporary metal object (Corsten 1995; Petré 1984, p. 104–109). This type of vessel was common in the Rhineland but also in the rest of the Germanic world, from Lombardy in the South to Scandinavia in the North (Bierbrauer 2008; Stjernquist 1992; Nerman 1967; Clercq and Taayke 2004; Gudesen 1980, p. 69). The diamond stamps became transformed to the tin-foil pattern in the Rhine-valley under influences of book illumination. The iconography from the latter art also contributed, with the cross a common appearance on the lower body of the vessels. The type of cross is the so called Croix Pattée, with equal-long cross-arms with triangular forms. It is also found on illuminated manuscripts, for instance on the frontispiece of the Lindau Gospel but also on Merovingian and Carolingian coinage.

The context of a pitcher for wine, mead, or beer is difficult to interpret. On one hand it was embedded with Christian signs and a technique borrowed from the most pious handicraft of them all, namely the production of sacred texts. In Sweden, it has been suggested that the vessels should be seen as ritual vessels. One probable suggestion is that this type of vessel has even been used in Holy Communion (Gräslund 2001, p. 60–62; Zachrisson 2011, p. 101). On the other hand, however, this type of vessel is found in secular contexts in the Rhine valley.

To understand the pitchers and their appearance in chieftain's halls, graves, and towns in the pagan or earliest Christian contexts in Scandinavia, we probably have to return to the Carolingian Empire. The drinking, especially of wine, did get a new Christian context during the Merovingian period. The Church tried to monopolize ritual wine-drinking through the Communion. But drinking became more popular among laymen at holidays of different Saints. In the beginning, during the Merovingian period, the Church tried to oppose the excess of drinking. During the Carolingian period the Church tried to channel the feasting and drinking. One way of doing that was to always give food and drink as alms to the poor during feasts. The second way was to formalize the drinking through the establishment of Carolingian guilds. One of the most important issues for the attention of the guilds was the organization of *Minne-trinken* (memory drinks) during funerals (Hen 1995, p. 146–9). This type of commemoration feasting was also easy to accept in Scandinavia where there was a long domestic tradition of the so-called *Erfi*. This was also a ritualistic way of drinking to commemorate dead persons in the Norse tradition (Sundqvist 2000, p. 239–

246). It is probably in this context that we shall understand both the pitchers inside the Empire and outside it. This explanation is perhaps better to explain the occurrence of Tatinger ware in both graves and halls. The pitchers were precious and shiny vessels for serving wine, beer or mead in the halls. They were embedded with Christian power but were not liturgical vessels.

Summary

Working on the reconstruction of the pitchers resulted in new knowledge and understanding of the manufacture of the vessels. The pitchers cannot be seen as ordinary non-religious pitchers. The manufacture of these vessels testifies that a technical and ideological transmission of know-how from the artisans of illuminated books to the potters crafting the vessels took place. The result was a silver-shining pitcher with implicit, and sometimes even explicit, Christian signs. We cannot be certain of their function and are cautious of interpreting them as jugs for Communion. Rather, we should probably see the pitchers as expressions of a new Christian Minne-trinken tradition.

Bibliography

Bierbrauer, V. (2008). "Alboin adduxit Langobardos in Italia" Langobarden nach der Einwanderergeneration: Verliert die Archäologie ihre Spuren im 7. Jahrhundert? In: J. Bemmann & M. Schmauder, eds *Kulturwandel in Mitteleuropa: Langobarden – Awaren – Slawen: Akten der Internationalen Tagung in Bonn vom 25. bis 28. Februar 2008.* Kolloquien zur Vor- und Frühgeschichte. Bonn: Habelt, ss 467–489.

Brorsson, T. (2010). *The pottery from the early medieval trading site and cemetery at Gross Strömkendorf, Lkr. Nordwestmecklenburg: Forschungen zu Gross Strömkendorf III*, Wiesbaden: Reichert.

Clercq, V. de and Taayke, E. (2004). Handgemachte Keramik der späten Kaizerzeit und des frühen Mittelalters in Flandern (Belgien). Das Beispiel der funde Friesischer Keramik in Zele (O-Flandern). In: M. Lodewijckx, eds *Bruc Ealles Well: Archaeological Essays Concerning the Peoples of North-West Europe in the First Millennium AD.* Acta Archaeologica Loaniensia Monographiae. Leuven: Leuven University Press, 57–72.

Corsten, M. (1995). *Die stempelverzierten Metallgegenstände der Merowingerzeit*, München: Drucken & Binden.

Eerkens, J.W. and Lipo, C.P. (2007). Cultural Transmission theory and the Archaeological Record: Providing Context to Understanding Variation and Temporal Changes in Material Culture. *Journal of Archaeological Reseach*, (15), 239–274.

Gettens, R.J. and Stout, G.L. (2012). *Painting Materials: A Short Encyclopedia*, Courier Corporation.

Gräslund, A.S.(2001). *Ideologi och mentalitet: om religionsskiftet i Skandinavien från en arkeologisk horisont*, Uppsala: Institutionen för arkeologi och antik historia.

Gudesen, H.G. (1980). *Merovingertiden i Øst-Norge: kronologi, kulturmønstre og tradisjonsforløp*, Oslo: Universitetets Oldsaksamling.

Hen, Y., 1995. *Culture and Religion in Merovingian Gaul: A.D. 481-751*, Leiden: Brill.

Holand, I. (2003). Chapter 9E. Pottery. In: G. S. Munch, O. S. Johansen, and E. Roesdahl, eds *Borg in Lofoten: a chieftain's farm in North Norway.* Arkeologisk skriftserie. Bøstad: Lofotr – Vikingmuséet på Borg Tapir Academic Press, 199–212.

Holand, I. (2001). *Sustaining life: vessel import to Norway in the first millennium AD*, Stavanger: Arkeologisk museum i Stavanger.

Loveluck, C. (2013). *Northwest Europe in the Early Middle Ages, c.AD 600–1150: A Comparative Archaeology*, Cambridge University Press.

Merrifield, M.P. (2012). *Medieval and Renaissance Treatises on the Arts of Painting: Original Texts with English Translations*, Courier Corporation.

Nerman, B. (1967). Den mellersta och yngre Vendeltidens gotländska keramik. *Fornvännen*, 1967, 93–94.

Petré, B., (1984). *Arkeologiska undersökningar på Lovö*, Stockholm: Almqvist & Wiksell International.

(Presbyter.), T. (1847). *Theophili, qui et Rugerus, presbyteri et monachi, libri III. de diversis artibus: seu, Diversarum artium schedula*, J. Murray.

Selling, D. (1951). Problem kring vikingatida keramikkannor. *Fornvännen*, 275–297.

Selling, D. (1955). *Wikingerzeitliche und frühmittelalterliche Keramik in Schweden*, Stockholm.

Staecker, J. (2009) The 9th-century Christian mission to the North. In: A. Englert & A. Trakadas (eds), *Wulfstan's Voyage. The Baltic Sea region in the early Viking Age as seen from shipboard. Maritime Culture of the North 2.* Roskilde. 309–329.

Steuer, H. (1987). Der Handel der Wikingerzeit zwischen Nord- und Westeuropa aufgrund archäologischer Zeugnisse. In: K. Düwel, eds. *Untersuchungen zu Handel und Verkehr der vor- und frühgeschichtlichen Zeit in Mittel- und Nordeuropa.* Göttingen: Vandenhoeck & Ruprecht, 113–197.

Stjernquist, B. (1992). An Iron Age site at Kverrestad, in south-east Scania, with finds of pottery with stamped decoration. *Meddelanden från Lunds universitets historiska museum*, 9, 105–129.

Sundqvist, O.(2000). *Freyr's offspring: rulers and religion in ancient Svea society*, Uppsala: Teologiska institutionen, Univ.

Zachrisson, T.(2011). Arkeologin bakom Rimbert: om Hergeirs och Gautberts kyrkor och borgen i Birka. *Fornvännen*, 100–112.

Suttung's Mead and Jugs with Tubular Handles in Sweden

Thomas Eriksson

The Laboratory of Ceramic Research, Lund University, Sweden

Thomas.eriksson@geol.lu.se, theriksson63@gmail.com

Abstract: The jugs with tubular handle are a quite peculiar type of vessel with a rather unpractical combination of handle and spout. They are dated to c. 100–600 AD and found scattered around in Northern and Central Europe. There are many different interpretations of the vessels. The island Gotland is a region where the jugs are common. Some of the stamped decors on the Gotlandic jugs might explain the symbolic background to these vessels. Stamps in form of birds, feather-like and wavy patterns may be connected to the myth about how man and the gods acquired the mead of wisdom. Even the drilling of a tunnel through the handle can be seen as a ritual recreation of one of the most central myths in Norse Religion.

Key words: Roman Iron Age; Migration period; Merovingian period; Tubular Handle; Jugs; Measuring of volume; Germanic pottery; Scandinavia; Ritual recreation of myths in production; Mythology; Drinking and feasting; Typology; Symbols in decoration

Introduction

Jugs with tubular handles are one of the most distinctive forms of ceramic vessels during the Roman Iron Age (1–400 AD) and the Migration period in Europe (400–550/600 AD). The jugs, with their rather non-functional combination of a handle with a channel, have puzzled a lot of archaeologists. Several suggestions of the function of the jugs have been presented. The vessels have been interpreted as puzzle vessels (sw. *gyckelkrus*), lamps, jugs, vessels for brewing alcoholic beverages and ritual vessels for libation (Stjernquist 1955, 1977; Hegewisch 2003, p. 44–48; Hoftun 1998). The design of the handle and the entire vessel form raises questions about transmission of table-manners, rituals, ideas and even myths, as well as possible trade-routes, exchange of vessels, movements of potters and mode of production. Is the chorological distribution a result of moving vessels within a network of exchange of goods? Or is it merely a result of ideas expressed in vessels? If the latter is the case, what kind of ideas travelled over time and space? Is it possible to interpret the vessels by differences in forms, sizes and decoration?

The focus in this study is on the Swedish material with a broader survey of continental Europe and the rest of Scandinavia. In particular, the vessels from the islands of Gotland and Öland, here called the 'insular material', might tell us more of the ideological background of the vessels. Iconography and interpretations of decor can be important for understanding the vessels' contexts and may reveal some new aspect which has not previously been discussed.

The iconography on some of the Gotlandic vessels involves birds and patterns that can be interpreted as snakes. Those symbols, together with the drilled hole in the handle, can be seen as a materialization of the myth about Suttung's magic mead. The drilling of the hole and the drinking through it can be seen as a symbolic recreation of the acquisition of the mead of wisdom and poetry.

The material

This type of vessel is spread around the shores of the Baltic Sea, the North Sea and water-systems in modern Germany, Poland, Denmark, Norway and Sweden, with one example in Anglo-Saxon England and a cluster in Central Europe (Fig. 1). The focus of this article is on the Swedish material. At least 51 vessels with tubular handles have been found in Sweden. There are probably even more vessels in the material from Gotland which are not included in this study. At least 30 vessels have been found in Norway and at least the same number in Denmark. The continental material from Poland and Germany compromises more than 60 vessels (Hegewisch 2003). More interesting is the spread of similar jugs at Crimea during the 3rd and 4th century AD and their later spread into modern Hungary, Austria and the Czech Republic. The jugs have also combined spout with handle and are associated with contexts interpreted as Hunnic, Alanic or Gothic. (Bóna 1991, p. 263 and abb. 34). The vessels from Central Europe often have a sprout with an extension on top of the handle and form, and decoration that differs from the Scandinavian material. Some, but not all, characteristics of the Swedish vessels from Tranemo in Västergötland and Ösmo in Sörmland resemble those of the kind found in Central Europe. The form and decoration of the vessel from Ösmo has its closest parallel in vessels from Grimmen in Vorpommern (Eggers and Stary 2001, Taf. 240). The closest Swedish parallell in comes from Östra Vemmenhög in eastern Scania

The chorological distribution of the vessels is very interesting (Fig. 6). The material from northern Germany

Fig. 1: Three vessels from the southeastern part of Sörmland (Södermanland). Two small vessels from graves in Torp, Sorunda parish dated to c. 500–600 AD (period D2–E1). They are made in insular style. The taller jug is found in a C2–C3 grave from Vansta in Ösmo parish. It is made in a more South-Scandinavian/Continental style (photo: T. Eriksson).

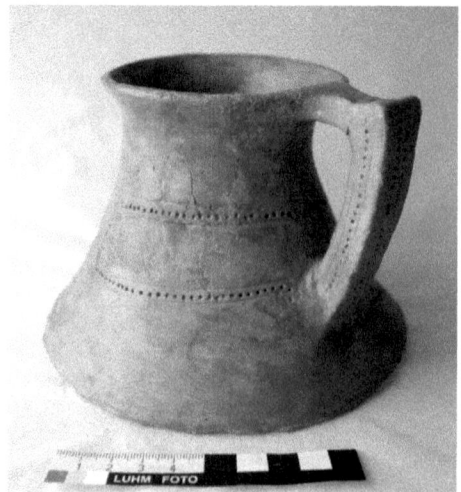

Fig. 2: The upper part of one of the oldest examples from Sweden- A vessel with meander decor from grave 22 on the Simris grave-field, Scania. The jug has a decoration of dotted meander (photo: T. Eriksson).

and Poland is rich, especially in Niedersachsen, Schleswig-Holstein, Vorpommern and Pomerania. The type of handle is common in southern Norway up to Opland and Sogn og Fjordane. The Norwegian spatial distribution corresponds to the Swedish; there are no tubular handles found north of the River Dalälven and no vessels in northern Norway. However, there are some Swedish counties that lack this type, even though the material is rich in other decorated vessels during these periods. This is a fact in Bohuslän and, to a certain degree, in Norrland. The counties that have the richest material are the island of Gotland and, to a lesser extent, the island of Öland. The Gotlandic material is probably even more extensive with many vessels not included in this study. The vessels found on Öland come from the north, i.e. the part that is closest to Gotland. The distinctive decoration of the vessels on the insular material makes them easy to recognize. Stamped decors are the most prominent feature on all kinds of the vessel type in this tradition.

The Danish material is scattered on the Danish islands but large areas of Jutland are lacking vessels with tubular handles. Vendsyssel in the north is the exception where a cluster of vessels were found. The rest of Jutland has a rich in decorated vessels with other forms during the Roman Iron Age (periods C1–C3) and the Early Migration period (period D1) (Ringtved 1986). This makes the absence of tubular handles even more interesting.

Dating

Tubular handles seem to be an invention in northern Germany or Poland according to dateable graves. The earliest continental examples come from the Early Roman Iron Age, period B1 (Hegewisch 2003). The oldest Scandinavian finds are from southeastern Scania and Denmark and can be dated to period C1a (150/160–220

AD) (Stjernquist 1955, p. 12 and Pl. XV:1–3). The Scanian find is a vessel with meander-decor from Simris (Fig. 2). The type of decor is old-fashioned at this stage and belongs to the Early Roman Iron Age, period B. There are often difficult-to-date the vessels in the graves on the mainland of Sweden due to a lack of dateable artefacts found in their original context.

The tradition of making tubular handles is spread over the entire area during the C2–C3 period. It seems that the tradition disappears in Denmark at the end of the 4th century. In Sweden and Norway, the tradition continues until the beginning of the 5th century. In the mainland of Sweden, north of Scania and on Öland and Gotland, the tradition begins also around 200 AD and continues until c. 600 AD, i.e. the end of the Vendel Period. The tradition is strongest on Gotland and Öland during the Migration period. On Gotland the tradition appears to fade out during the beginning of the Vendel Period (Period E) (Fig. 3, 4, 5).

Chorology and contacts

A starting point for the study is that the distribution of vessels reveals different networks and contacts expressed in material culture. The absence of special features, such as the tubular handle, can be seen as a refusal to share ideas, rituals or table manners. There are, of course, lots of source-critical problems connected to absence of features. It is always a possibility that the features are found but not included in the study. Furthermore, there is always a possibility that the material is not statistically significant to make such statements, or that we will find the missing vessel in future excavations. The material from Jutland and Bohuslän, in western Sweden, is so rich that absence is statistically significant. Consequently, the absence may reveal some kind of lack of contact and lack of common rituals between, for instance, Bohuslän and its neighbours in Norway and Västergötland. Pottery from Bohuslän

Periods and Regions

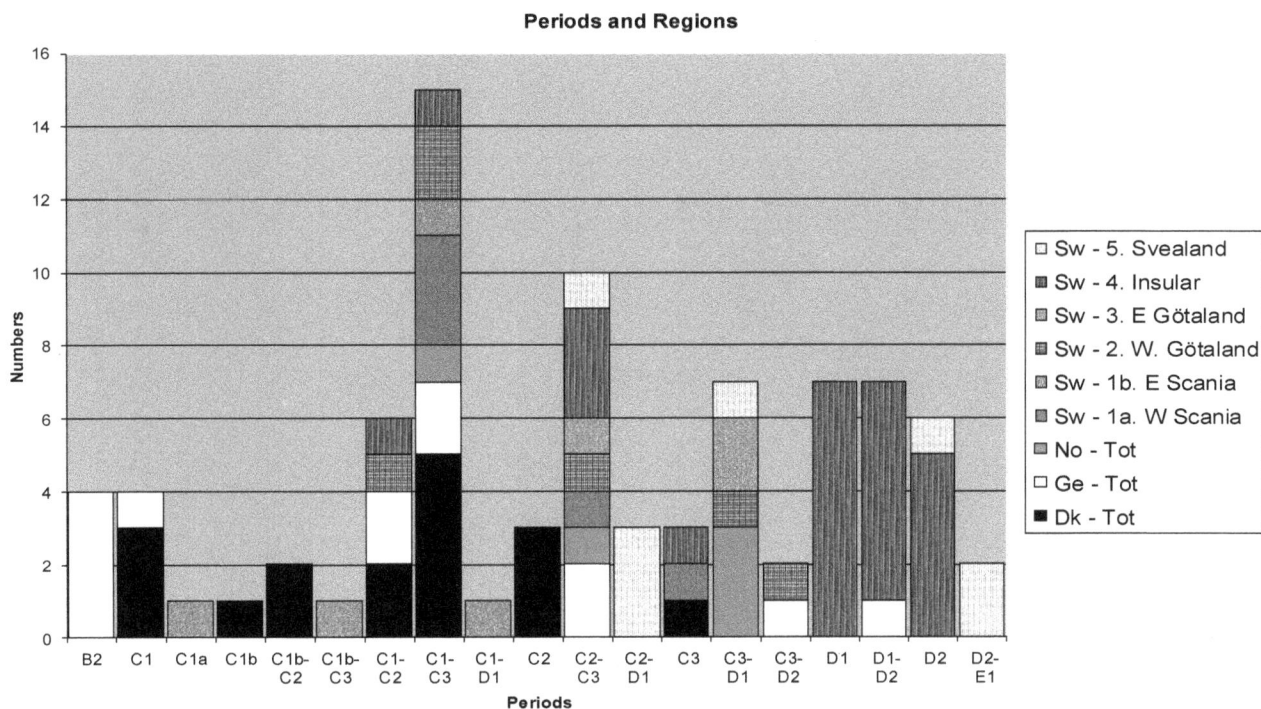

Fig. 3: Datings in different regions. The material outside of Sweden is not complete but gives an impression of the innovation and spread of the type.

has, in other aspects, a very Norwegian character during these periods. The absence of tubular handles, then, may have an important role for the interpretation of contacts between the regions. The same may be said about the non-existent networks between Vendsyssel and the rest of Jutland and Schleswig-Holstein. Rather, the vessels found at Vendsyssel indicate a connection with southern Norway, even though the vessel shapes have more similarities to the contemporary material in eastern Denmark, Scania and Vorpommern.

Contexts

The majority of vessels are found in graves, but that should not leave us to look upon them primarily as funeral vessels. On the contrary, tubular handles are also found in settlements and within houses. Some examples are from the house foundation II at Helgö in Lake Mälaren, Uppland. Helgö is remarkable as no grave was found to contain decorated vessels despite the extent decorated vessels in the settlement debris at the site. The connections between the ceremonial halls, the finer pottery (including tubular handles), and other drinking utensils are obvious in Helgö. The correlation stresses on a more ritual behaviour with this kind of vessels in the halls (Arrhenius and Holmqvist 1964; Zachrisson 2004; Herschend 1998, p. 25, 31, 2001, p. 48)

Unlike some other artefacts, there is no clear connection between vessel types found in graves and gender. If a traditional division is made concerning gender and artefacts found in the graves (i.e. weapons buried with males; numerous fibulae with females), the distribution of the vessels is about fifty-fifty in the twelve cases examined

in Sweden. If ostheological attributes are added—and very few are made—two females and one man have been buried together with a jug. An interesting fact is that three children have been buried with this type of vessel. Some of the smallest vessels are found in graves for children. This is a contradiction if we understand the jugs to be personal vessels of the deceased for serving alcoholic beverages. However, we cannot assume that Iron-Age man had the same attitude to juveniles drinking alcohol as we have today. Perhaps we ought to see the vessels in the graves of young people as a symbol for feasting rather than evidence of juvenile drinking. The assumption that tubular handles belonged to a female sphere have no support in the Swedish material (Hoftun 1998). They might have been used for libation but they belonged to a more common sphere which was connected to males, females and children.

If the rest of the grave-goods are considered, we can see that most graves do not belong to the richest nor the poorest members of society. It is more common to find weapons, fibulae and other vessels in the graves than the rest of the material. Some of the graves in the Malaren Basin (Svealand, i.e. Uppland, Västmanland and Sörmland) are particularly rich, especially the graves from Skuttunge, Skuttunge parish in Uppland and Vansta, Ösmo parish in Sörmland (Arbman 1932; SHM inv. 34572). It must be emphasized that decorated pottery in the Mälaren region is very uncommon: out of approximately 250 graves from the Migration period in the Mälaren region only 30 contained some kind of decorated ceramic vessel. Consequently, this type of pottery is very unique. Other parts of Sweden, like Västergötland, Scania, Gotland and Öland, have a richer

UPPLAND

SHM 34861
Up, Danmark sn
Danmarks by RAÄ 100:1
A161 F318:8

SHM 18675
Up, Skuttunge sn
Skuttunge prästgård, RAÄ 50

SHM 21559:3
Up, Stavby sn
Husby

UMF
Up, Uppsala sn
Studentholmen RAÄ 88
St?b

SÖRMLAND

SHM 34492
Sö, Sorunda
Torp 6:72 RAÄ 309:1
A7, F42

SHM 34492
Sö, Sorunda
Torp 6:72 RAÄ 309:1
A7, F43

SHM 34572
Sö, Ösmo
Vansta 5:2 RAÄ210
A2 F36

SHM 26015:4
Sö, Ösmo
Älby RAÄ 165:1
A41

VÄSTERGÖTLAND

SHM 7494D
Vg, Norra Lundby sn
Amundstorp Överstegården

SHM 11481:B1
Vg, Näs sn
Västra Mobäcken

SHM 11481:B1
Vg, Näs sn
Västra Mobäcken

SHM 31244
Vg, Tranemo sn
Önnesmo RAÄ 41
A6 F35

SMÅLAND

Klm 12654
Sm, Kalmar
Svaneberg, Tjuvbackarna
RAÄ 1? A46

Jlm -
Sm, Norra Ljunga
Örsbyholm 1:8 RAÄ 41
A2:2 F5

HALLAND

SHM 23511
Ha, Ysby
Hov RAÄ 38?

BLEKINGE

SHM 9499:20
Bl, Edestad
Leråkra

SCANIA

LUHM 25789
Sk, Bodarp sn
Bodarp 3

LUHM 30019:100
Sk, Flackarp sn
Trolleberg 1:1 RAÄ 42
A23 Kärl 2

LUHM 28756-8
Sk, Maglarp sn
Maglarp 23:1, Albäcksbacken
RAÄ 6, A8B Kärl 1

LUHM 26806
Sk, Smedstorp sn
Gårdslösa 3 RAÄ 5-9, 28
A73C

LUHM 26806
Sk, Smedstorp sn
Gårdslösa 3 RAÄ 3-9, 28
A14

LUHM 29155
Sk, Simris sn
Simris
Grav 22 kärl 2

LUHM 29155
Sk, Simris sn
Simris
Grav 90 kärl 2

LUHM 28573
Sk, Tottarp sn
Djurslöv 4 RAÄ 34
A2 kärl 2a

LUHM
Sk, Trollenäs sn
Gullarp 2:2 RAÄ 4
A2

SHM 12088
Sk, Östra Vemmenhög sn
Dybeck, Tofthögarna

5 cm

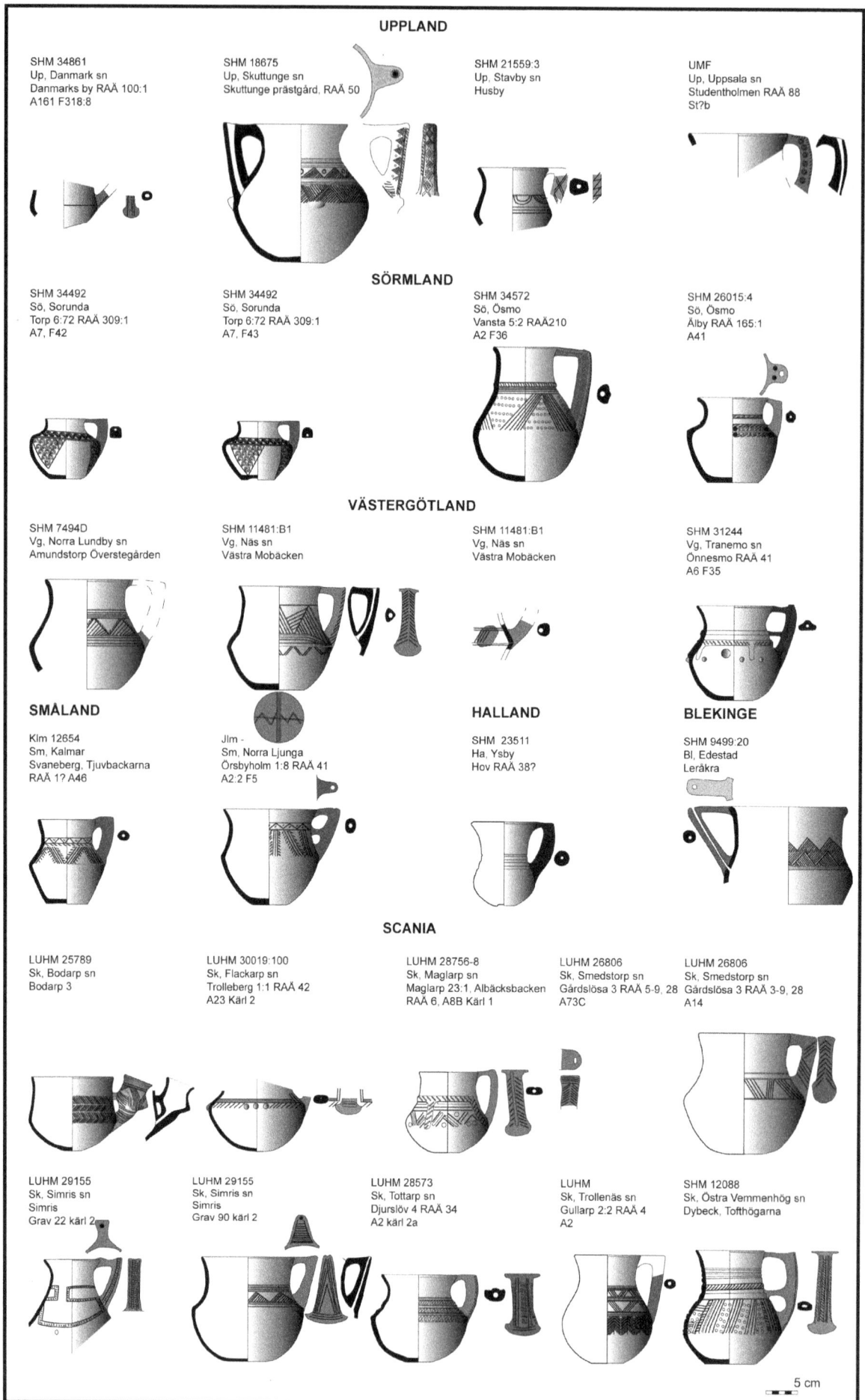

Fig. 4: Vessels with tubular handles from the mainland of Sweden (drawings and reconstructions: T. Eriksson).

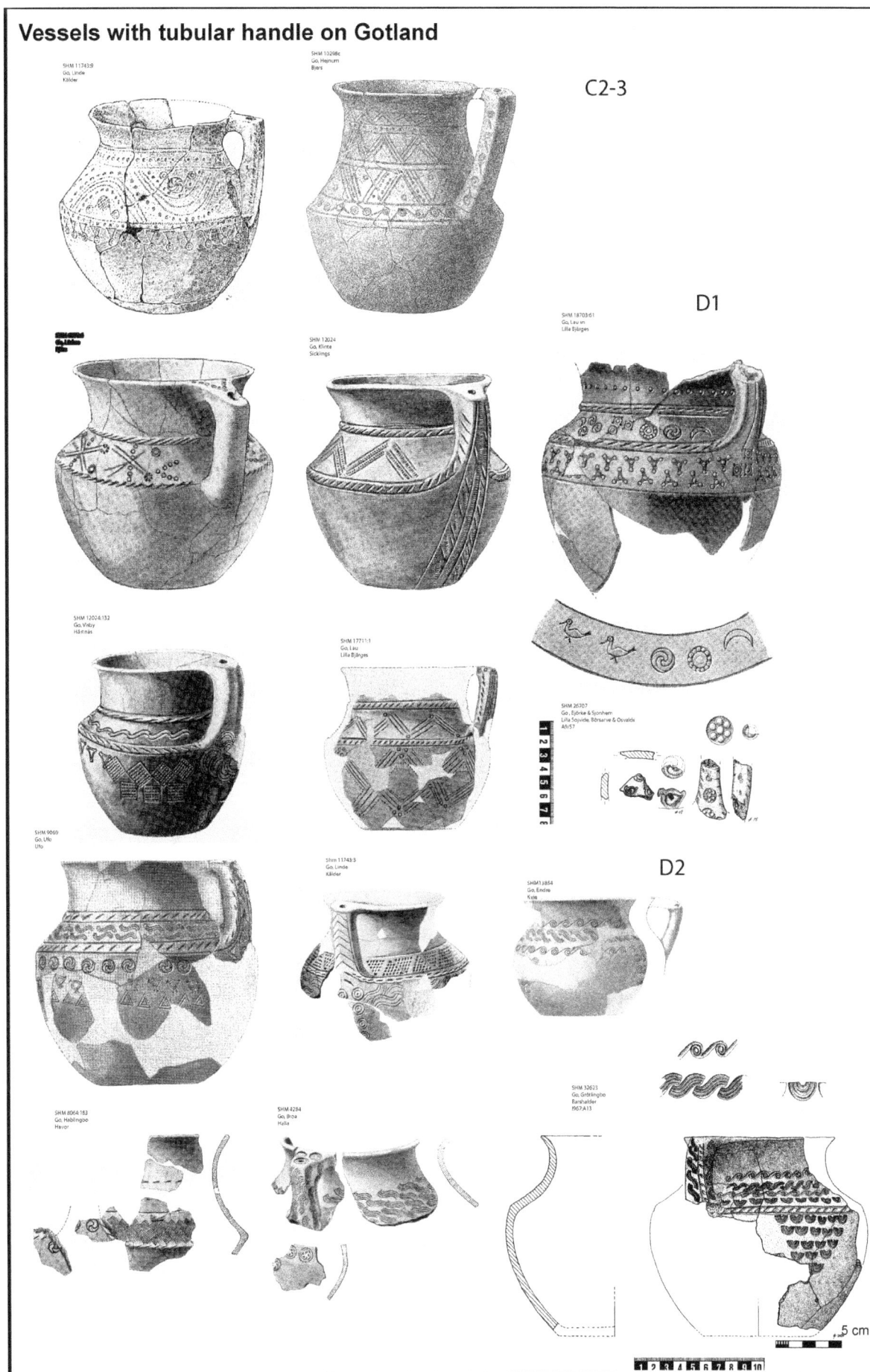

Fig. 5: Vessels with tubular handles from Gotland. Notice the stamps with deltoid forms, the creeping S-forms and the birds (drawings: Almgren and Nerman 1923; Nerman 1935, 1979; Cecilia Bonnevier, Historiska museet).

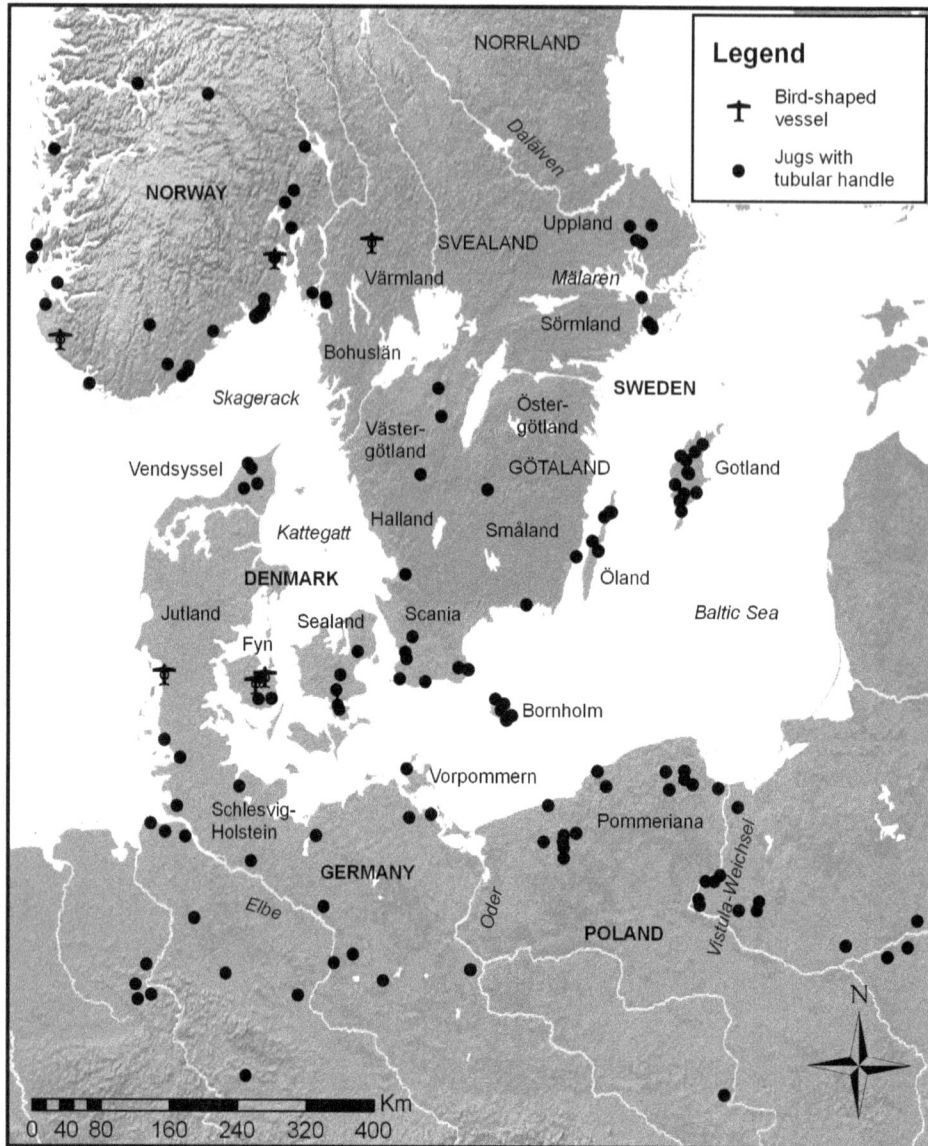

Fig. 6: Map of the distribution in Northern Europe of vessels with tubular handles (data: Albrectsen 1968, 1971; Almgren and Nerman 1923, 1935, 1969; Bøe 1931; Hegewisch 2003; Løchsen Rødsrud 2012; Magnusson 1946; Oldenburger 2010; Stjernquist 1955, 1977; Ringtved 1986; Nørgård Jørgensen 1991; Klindt-Jensen et al. 1996; Beskow-Sjöberg and Hagberg 1991; Beskow-Sjöberg and Arnell 1987; Hagberg and Beskow-Sjöberg 1996; Rasch and Fallgren 2001; Nerman and Lundström 1975. Map: T. Eriksson).

ceramic culture with many decorated vessels once buried in the graves.

There is also evidence of jugs with tubular-handle being used alongside other types of vessel to form a set for drinking and eating from. Vessels of glass, decorated or undecorated pots and bark-vessels are not uncommon in combination with the jugs.

Insular and other styles in eastern Sweden

According to the stylistic variations in Scandinavia two primary regions can be considered in the decorated material. There is, of course, a lot of variation inside these regions but two main traditions can be seen. In western Scandinavia we can find vessels with more rounded profiles and handles which are situated with the upper part at the neck and the lower part on the shoulder. Decorations are

made of linear motives such as chevrons, zigzag-lines and modelled elements like cordons and buckles. This tradition can be found in Norway, western and northern Sweden and Denmark, with the exception of the island of Bornholm. Western Scania belongs to this main tradition too.

The other tradition is an eastern Scandinavian one, found on Bornholm, Gotland, and Öland and in eastern Scania. The vessels tend to have a carinated profile. The handles begin on the rim and end on the shoulder. In eastern Scania and on Bornholm the decorations are dominated by horizontal lines or groves. On Gotland and Öland a very special tradition develops during the Early Roman Iron Age (1–160/180 AD) and evolves into a very elaborate and rich tradition during the Late Roman Iron Age and Migration period. This is, of course, the stamped decors, a tradition that is very easy to recognize and has its richest blooming on Gotland with a contemporary parallel in Anglo-Saxon

England. The style on the islands is probably endemic and has its roots in the Sösdala style. The decor there consists mainly of stamps which correspond to the metalwork, especially in silver and gold during the period (Andersson 1995; Poláskova 1997, 1998, 2001).

Gotland is outstanding in its number of vessels with a richness in stamps and vessel forms, and yet the material has never been summarized in whole (Almgren and Nerman 1923; Nerman 1935, 1969; Nerman and Lundström 1975). The distribution indicates that Gotland is the main region for producing this style. The amount of decorated vessels is much smaller on Öland and has been published in its entirety (Beskow-Sjöberg and Arnell 1987; Beskow-Sjöberg and Hagberg 1991; Hagberg and Beskow-Sjöberg 1996; Rasch and Fallgren 2001). A study of stamp identities shows that at least in one case the same potter made vessels found on both islands (Poláskova 1998, p. 26).

The contacts between Öland and Gotland seem to disappear according to the entire ceramic material dating to the end of period D2. Vessels with Gotlandic style do not appear at all on Öland during the Vendel period but were still to be found in the Lake Mälaren region. Another interesting fact is that no insular vessels are found on the southeastern shore of Sweden, i.e. in Blekinge, Småland and Östergötland. In Svaneberg, Kalmar parish in Småland, one jug with a tubular handle has been found in a rich grave (Klm12654). The distance to Öland is very short and the island is almost visible from the grave, but the jug has a typical decor for the region with its closest parallels in the interior of the county (Örsbyholm, Norra Ljunga parish in Småland). The lack of insular vessels may reveal some kind of antagonism between Gotland, Öland and Svealand versus Småland and Östergötland. In any case, the contacts are not as vivid as the connection between Svealand and

Gotland. The ceramic material seems to suggest that Småland had more connections with Västergötland than with Östergötland (Eriksson in press). The material reveals direct contacts between some regions and a lack of contact between others. The pottery can be seen as materialisations of different ethnicities within Scandinavia. Seen in a wider perspective this may reveal political alliances and antagonisms between regions.

How much did they drink?

In the past archaeology was limited to measuring diameters, thickness, height etc. Today we can use calculations of volumes, which is the most important measurement to understand vessels. All drawings in this study are made in Adobe Illustration, and a special script written to measure volumes helps to give an impression of the vessels' maximum content in litres (http://www.olapersson.com/thing/volume-in-illustrator). The volumes in litres are important for understanding whether the vessel was used for private drinking or to serve liquids during communal feasting. In a more advanced economy where liquids were sold, the volumes became standardized. One example is the Roman and Byzantine system with units of measurement such as Sextarius and Pinakion.

No obvious system of units is visible in the Swedish material, perhaps evidence of a culture of home-brewing rather than commercial markets. The jugs found have contained between 0.43–2.38 litres (Fig. 7). The smallest vessels seem to have been more for individual use or for very precious liquids. The largest jugs were probably used for serving or for more communal drinking.

There is a striking correspondence to be found between size of vessels and quantity of grave-goods: the most

Maximum volume of vessels with tubular handles in quartiles

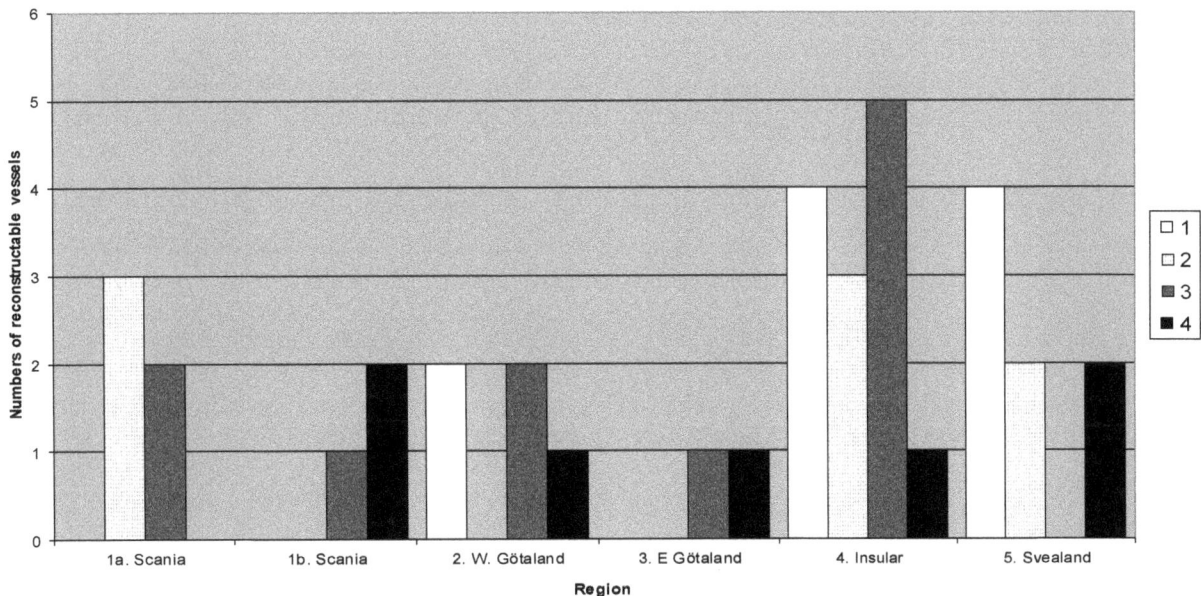

Fig. 7: Vessel sizes in litres in different regions. Quartile 1: 0.43–0.7 litres. Quartile 2: 0.86–1.61 litres. Quartile 3: 1.66–2.38 litres. Quartile 4: 2.55–5.00 litres.

Wealth and volume

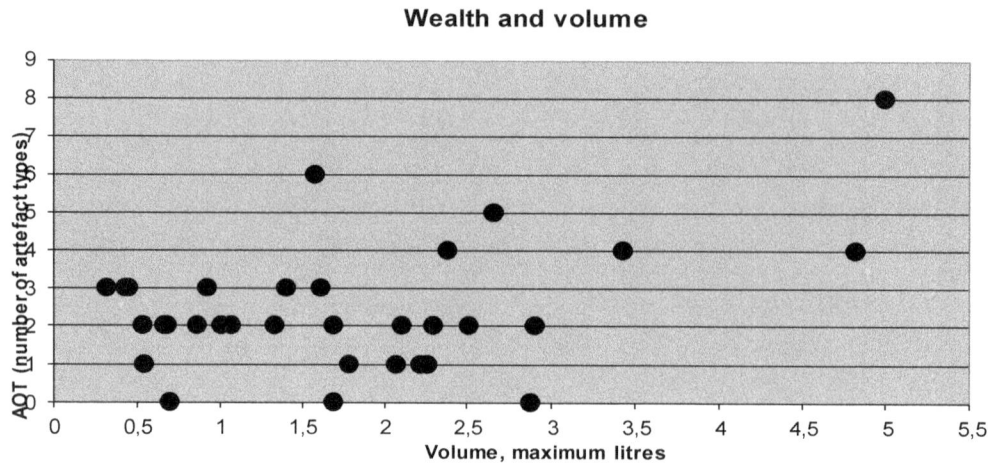

Fig. 8: Diagram with maximum volume of vessels in litres versus number of artefact types in graves. A strong correlation between rich graves and voluminous vessels is visible.

voluminous vessels are all found in richer graves, alongside weapons (Fig. 8). Such grave-goods are normally associated with males. The two biggest vessels are found in the rich weapon-graves in Skuttunge, Uppland, from period C2 and in Edestad, Leråkra, Blekinge, period C3 (Arbman 1932, 157f; Nicklasson 1997, 90, 242, 262f).

The insular vessels are often particularly small. They seem to be for more private consumption. Vessels with a volume of more than 1.66 litres (quartiles 3–4) must have been used for communal feasting or rituals. There is also a strong correlation between rich graves and large vessels. All graves containing more than three artefact types have vessels with a maximum volume of more than 1.66 litres. This can be interpreted in two possible ways. The first is that the rich deceased have been given more mead or other liquids. The second possibility is that the large volume represents an ideology where rich men and women were supposed to be generous hosts and hostesses in life and the after-life. This is a mentality clearly visible in old Norse literature, mythology and other finds, like the contemporary bracteates (Andrén 1991, p. 248–252; Enright 1996; Behm-Blancke 1979; Rundkvist 2011; Herschend 1998).

Typology

A way to study the possible contacts of the past and perhaps even the vessels that might have been transported between these contacts is to study vessel forms and decor thoroughly. The easiest way to compare the vessels is simply to observe the relation between rim-diameter and height. A standard jug for serving usually has a relatively greater height and a smaller rim-diameter. The relations can be seen in Table 1. The insular material has a very strict relation to the measures (Fig. 11). The relation is approximately 1.3x rim-diameter in most cases. In Denmark and Norway both high jugs and more bowl-like forms are to be found. The material shows both as having a wide range of forms and, more importantly, a big regional difference. It is only in Svealand (Lake Mälaren region) that the material is very similar to another region, namely that found in Gotland (Fig. 9, 10).

In order to make the analysis more detailed a stricter study of vessel forms must be used. A new typology is under construction to make a new division based on the entire Swedish material of decorated vessels (Eriksson forthcoming). The vessels have been classified into four main groups based on the relation between vessel height and rim-diameter (Table 1). Only three of the forms are used together with tubular handles: Forms 45–100. The main secondary features have concerned the height of breaking point versus total height and the relation between maximum vessel-diameter/rim-diameter. An important feature has also been the form of the vessel—whether it is carinated with sharp angles or has a more rounded profile (Eriksson forthcoming).

The spatial distribution can be seen in two maps. The tallest forms, Form 45, are spread over the entire area. The carinated Form 45:1Bk is spread over the southern part of the Baltic in periods B and C. There are, for instance, strong connections between Scania, Vendsyssel, Bornholm, Gotland and Vorpommern (Fig. 9).

Form 75 is a jug-like vessel with a somewhat broader body and rim than is present in the former group (Fig. 10). Some interesting facts can be seen in the spatial distribution. Form 75:1k is found in Scania, Fyn and Västergötland. The two vessels from the latter county are very similar in form and decor; they could even have been made by the same potter, but are found at a distance of 30 km from one another. A jug with an usual form from Hov, Osby parish in Halland, has its closest counterparts in western Norway (Form 75:1r). The insular material is very homogenous. It seems to be made in a strict and uniform tradition. This can point towards a more centralized production. The material of insular character in Mälardalen is somewhat deviant than the material in Gotland. Its creation can be interpreted as the result of Gotlandic potters having moved to Svealand or that the production came from a workshop on Gotland with preoccupation of export rather than for domestic use. Form 100, jugs with a more bowl-like shape, are not common. They belong to the southern area of the Baltic, with few examples found in Norway.

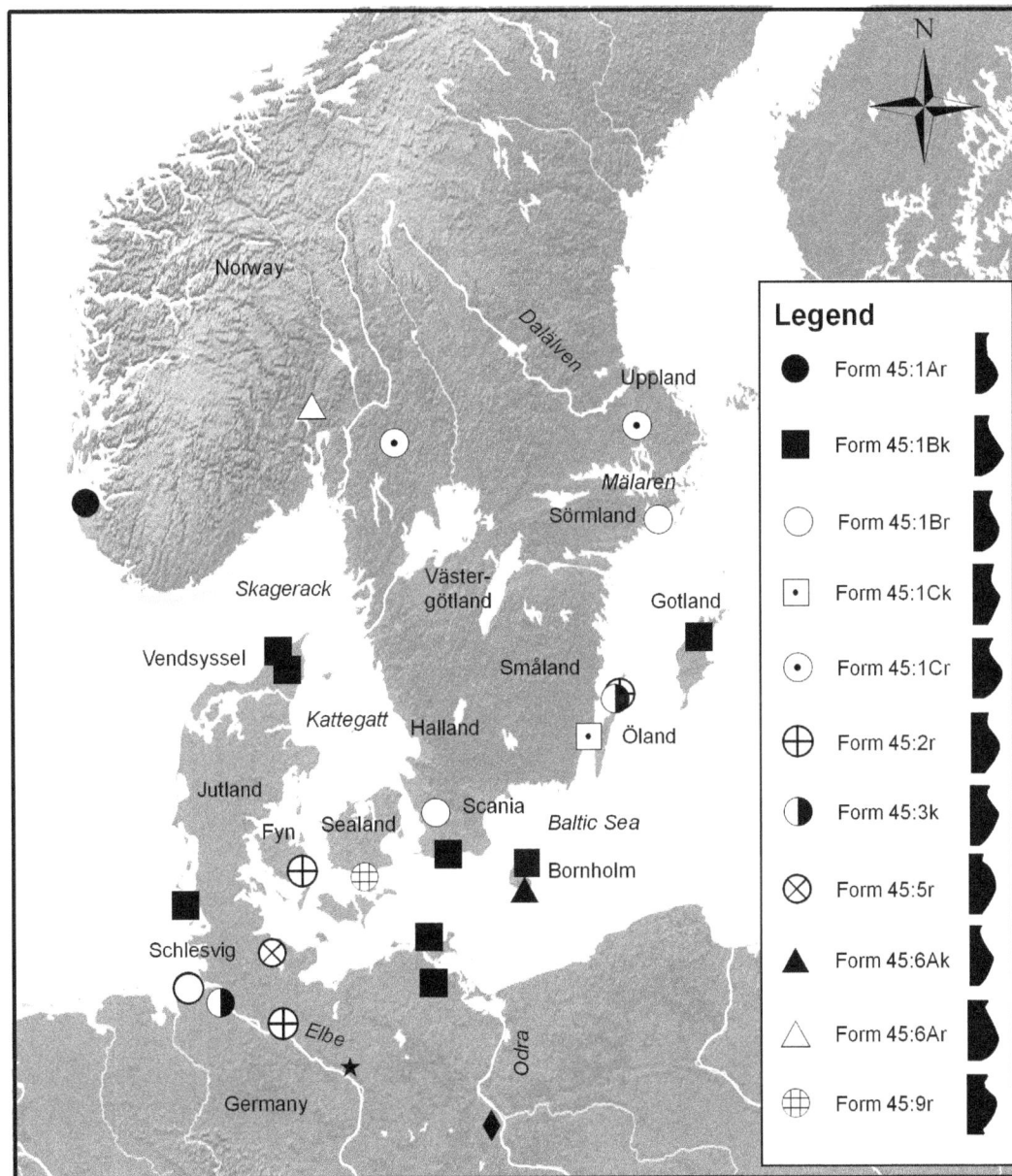

Fig. 9: The distribution of vessel forms with a tall and slender body. There are similarities in the material from the Danish islands and northern Germany. Form 45:1Bk can be seen as an old form spread over large areas in regions in the Southern Baltic Sea. The classification of vessels outside Sweden is not complete in Fig. 9 and 10 (map: T. Eriksson).

If the distribution of forms and vessel-size ratios is summarized in one graph, it is easy to see that the vessels have been locally made on the whole (Fig. 11). What is most striking is the uniformity in the insular material. The disparity in the whole material is evidence that the jugs were not exported, but rather were the result of an idea or tradition that spread. It must have been a tradition so strong that it survived at least four centuries in different areas of Northern Europe in spite of a rather impractical design. To make an interpretation of that idea we must study the decor, especially the insular types.

Myths materialized in clay?

One of the central myths in Norse mythology concerned the story of how man had acquired poetry and wisdom. The myth is best recorded by Snorri Sturlason in his *Skáldskaparmál*

or 'Language of poetry' in the Prose Edda. It tells us about the god Kvasir, the wisest god of them all. He was born from the saliva of two groups of gods. The two groups, Aesirs and Vanirs, made peace by spitting in a vessel and that gave life to him. Kvasir was killed by two dwarves who mixed his blood with honey in a cauldron and two vats (the vessels were named *Óðrerir, Són* and *Boðn*). This brew became the mead of poetry. Anyone who drank the magical mead would be inspired with poetry and wisdom.

The mead was hidden in a mountain and protected by a giant named Suttung and his daughter, Gunnlöð. The god Odin heard about the mead and his desire for the drink was born. He disguised himself as a farmhand and called himself Bölverkr (bad work) and took service with Suttung's brother, Baugi. In order to get the hidden mead he convinced Baugi to help him:

67

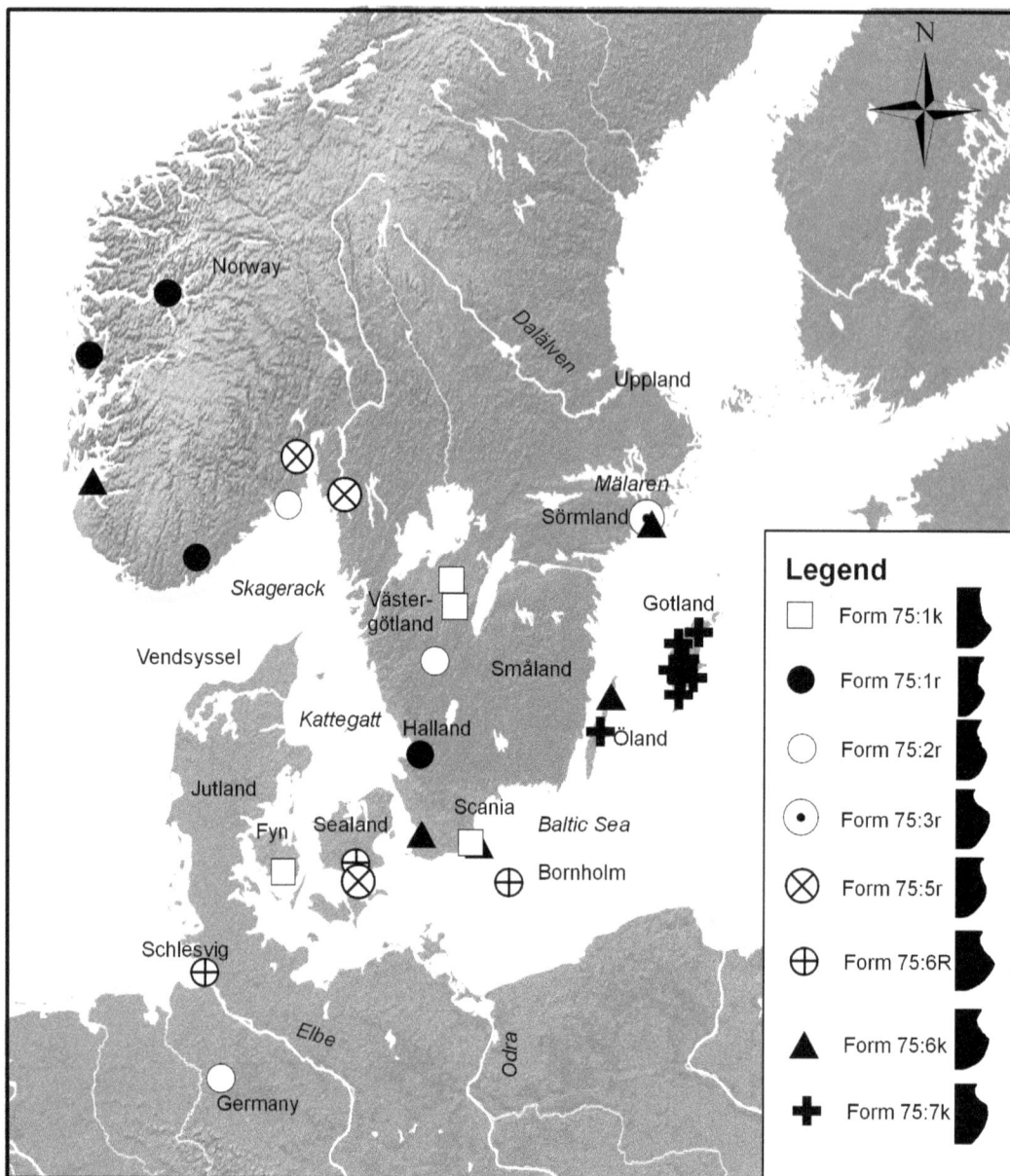

Fig. 10: Map with broader forms of jugs, Form 75. Local cluster can be seen in southern Norway, Västergötland and Scania. The small jug from Halland has its closest relatives in western Norway. The classification of vessels outside of Sweden is not complete in Fig. 9 and 10.

Table 1: Main vessel forms in Swedish material

Type	Relation rim-diameter versus vessel height
Form 45	45.0-74.9 %
Form 75	75.0-99.9 %
Form 100	100.0-139.9 %
Form 140	>139.9 %

they might find means to get at the mead; and Baugi agreed readily. Thereupon Bölverkr drew out the auger called Rati, saying that Baugi must bore the rock, if the auger cut. He did so. At last Baugi said that the rock was bored through, but Bölverkr blew into the auger-hole, and the chips flew up at him. Then he discovered that Baugi would have deceived him, and he bade him bore through the rock. Baugi bored anew; and when Bölverkr blew a second time, then the chips were blown in by the blast. Then Bölverkr turned himself into a serpent and crawled into the auger-hole, but Baugi thrust at him from behind with the auger and missed him. Bölverkr proceeded to the place where Gunnlöd was, and lay with her three nights; and then she gave him leave to drink three draughts of the mead. In the first draught he drank every drop out of Ódrerir; and in the second, he emptied Bodn; and in the third, Són; and then he had all the mead. Then he turned himself into the shape of an eagle and flew as furiously as he could. (Skáldskaparmál 6)

Odin succeeded to return with the mead to Àsgard. After that, mead, wisdom and poetry were given to the humans. The motive might also be seen on one of the picture-stones on Gotland. On Hammars III in Lärbro parish, a large bird containing a human figure is fronted to a female carrying a cup and a man, perhaps representing Gunnlöd and Odin. The *Hávamál*, in the Poetic Edda, refers also to

Regions and sizes of vessels

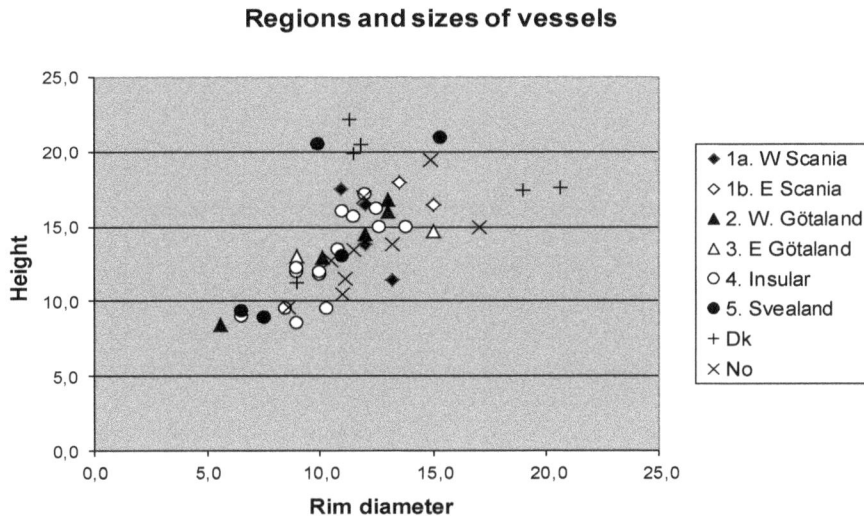

Fig. 11: Diagram with regions and vessel sizes in Scandinavia. The material from Denmark and Norway is not complete.

the myth in verses 101–110 about Suttung's mead-hall and is emphasized again on the drill *Rati*. The word probably means 'right into' or 'traveller'. The latter is one of many circumlocutions (*kenning*) for Odin himself.

The motive with the drill and the drilling is central to the story and might be central for understanding the tubular handles. The construction of this type of ewer is remarkable; the vessel lacks an ordinary spout as found on most ewers, and instead, the handle is made into a spout by drilling a hole. The construction is made in the opposite direction to all normal pitchers, jugs and ewers in antiquity and during the Iron Age. The construction cannot be made for functional reasons; the vessels would have been difficult to pour from.

Two animals are connected to the myth: one snake and two eagles. The eagle is also known in other Indo-European myths. The theme with the holy drink, the eagle stealing it and the snake is also known from the Vedic traditions with the soma and the eagle Garuda (Jakobsdóttir 2002; Jennbert 2011, p. 209). He brought the holy drink Soma together with Indra to the gods (Veda 4:26-7). In Greek mythology Ganymede was the cup-bearer to the god and he was brought to Olympus on Zeus taking shape of an eagle.

Iconography on insular vessels

In traditional, mainly pre- or proto-literary societies, emphasis is often placed on non-written narratives like rituals, gestures, symbols and objects (Kyhlberg 2012, p. 11). Myths were often recreated in rituals and objects (Pettersson 1972, p. 226–229). Mircea Eliade (1967, p. 23) wrote: 'In imitating the exemplary acts of a god or of a mythic hero, or simply by recounting their adventures, the man of an archaic society detaches himself from profane time and magically re-enters the Great Time, the sacred time.'

Perhaps we have to look upon the tubular handles as a result of a ritual recreation of the myth of Suttung's mead.

The drilled hole in the handle may symbolize the drilling of Baugi and Odin into the mountain to get the hidden mead. It is a ritualistic way for the producer/potter to recreate myth. In the next stage the consumer had to know how to drink the holy mead to receive wisdom, poetry and status. A participant that did not succeed in drinking without getting wet must have bred the malicious pleasure in the mead-hall. The accentuation of mead as a symbol for wisdom and good behaviour was then materialized in the puzzle-vessel.

The richest repertoire of different symbols and signs in Scandinavia is to be found on the insular pottery from ca 100–700 AD. This type of stamped decor, with close similarities to the contemporary decor in terms of the use of silver, gold and bronze, is outstanding in the Baltic Sea area. The symbols are most often geometric and enigmatic. Some of them are so common that they must be seen as some kind of iconic symbols. There no clear human representations among the stamps but there are zoomorphic signs that appear on some rare vessels. The animal is some kind of bird. Of greater interest is that this type of bird-stamp is found on jugs with the tubular handle (i.e. SHM 9069 grave find from Gotland VWZ 620; SHM 18703:63 Lau parish, Lilla Bjärges, VWZ fig. 66; SHM 26707 Sjonhem and Björke parish, Sojvide grave 9/57) (Fig. 5 & 13). One explanation of the bird is that it represents Odin as an eagle. Birds are appearing in many different contexts during the Migration period on Gotland but only on vessels with tubular handles. There are also bird-shaped vessels during the Roman Iron Age and Migration period in Western Scandinavia (Løchsen Rødsrud 2012, p. 52, 114, 131; Albrectsen 1968, p. 281; Magnus 2012, p. 25–28). Only one bird-vessel is found in Sweden, in Köla parish in western Värmland (Fig. 6 & 12). It could be seen as a ritualistic vessel—a ceramic form of Odin containing the holy mead. It is even possible to drink through the drilled hole on the head of the Köla vessel. It is probably the easiest way of sipping liquids from it and it must have suggested mythical connotations in the significant ritual of drinking. Even the ternary vessels, where mead was made in the myth, might be seen in the material from Norway and

Bornholm. Bowls composed with three separate containers are found there (Løchsen Rødsrud 2012, p. 223).

One of the most extraordinary examples of a jug with a tubular handle is found in the rich so-called gold-grave from Regöly, Pénzesdomb, Komitat Tolna in Hungary. It is interpreted as a Hunnic princess grave and the jug has a rim in the form of a head of an eagle or falcon (Bóna 1991, p. 270 and taf. 17; Menghin et al 1987, p. 194). The ethnic interpretation may be troublesome, but the mix of Roman, Hunnic and Germanic features is interesting and can be considered as distinguishing features for the period. The Hunnic and East-Germanic influences are under discussion and the ideological impact in Scandinavia is a fact (Hedeager 2011). The eagle-headed vessel is perhaps the best example of the ideological background for this type of vessel even though it does not belong to a Scandinavian sphere.

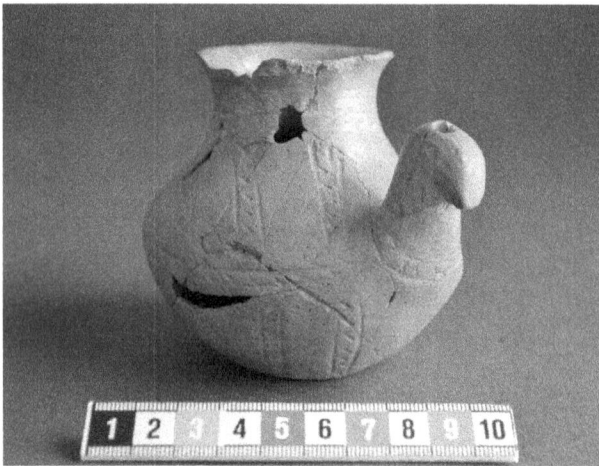

Fig. 12: The bird-shaped vessel from Grannerud, Lövåsen, Köla parish in Värmland. The shape can perhaps be interpreted as representing Odin in the form of an eagle. The head may be seen as a tubular handle (photo: T. Eriksson).

One animal is still missing from the myth. It is, of course, the snake, or its relative, the dragon. They are main characters in Norse mythology and are easy to recognize in later animal art, especially during the Vendel and Viking periods. There are some geometric patterns on the pottery from the Roman Iron Age and Migration period that can be interpreted as snakes. One of the main patterns is the chevron and the zigzag-fields on the pottery. Some examples of herring-bone patterns are also found. They are situated on the upper part of the vessel. One suggestion is that they represent the level of the liquid inside the vessel. During the Early Roman Iron Age the meander-pattern is common, and is represented on the earliest vessel from Simris, Scania. All of those features can also be interpreted as creeping snakes around the body or the handle. The meander and the later patterns, such as the chevron and the zigzag, may also represent the snake. The interpretations of liquid level and snake may not be contradictory. A main theme in animal art and poetry (Fig. 4 & 5).

A main theme in animal art and poetry was the ambiguity of terms and symbols. The appreciation of complex and ambiguous circumlocutions, the so called kennings, consituted the nucleus of old Norse art and poetry (Neiß 2004). An example on pottery could be the zigzag lines. I could stand both for snakes, vipers and the surface of a liquid, i.e water or mead. The snake-like patterns are clearly visible when we consider the creeping movements of snakes, a movement which is captured on the vessels. All those patterns are known from anthropological sources to represent snakes. (Boas 1955, p. 89–91) Some examples are also shown on Gotlandic vessels. One of the oldest vessels on Gotland, SHM 10298c from Bjers in Hejnum parish, dated to period C1–2, has zigzag-lines on the neck but also on the handle. Another example with the same zigzag-patterns comes from Sicklings in Klinte parish, dated to period D1 (SHM12024). The zigzag-pattern on the handles might be taken as a representation

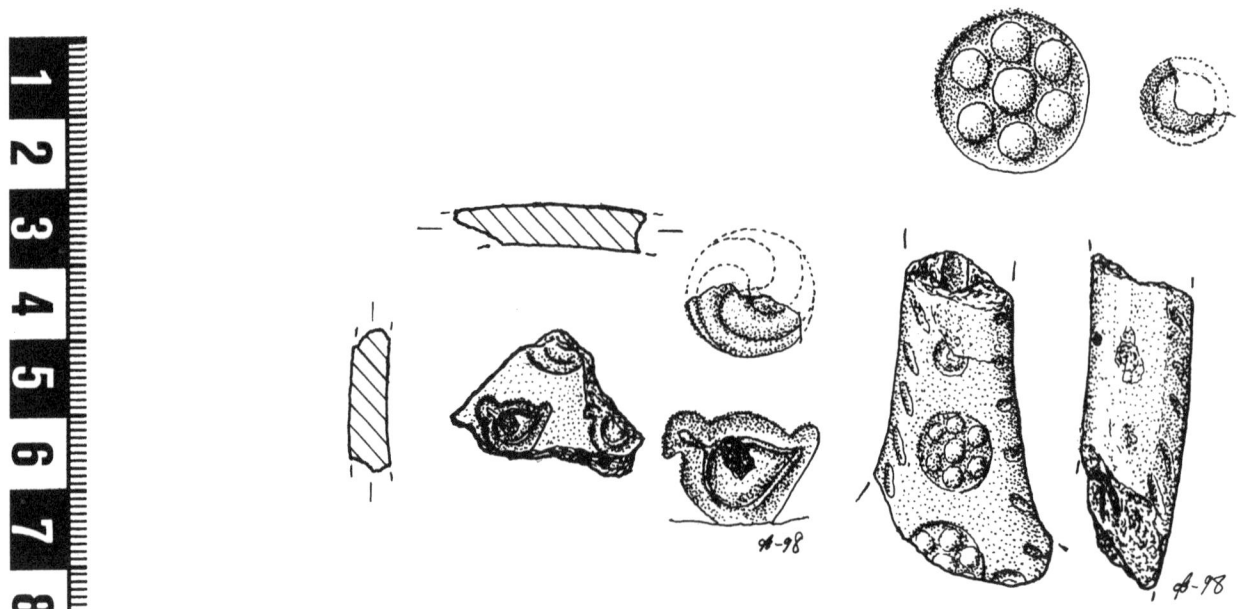

Fig. 13: Bird-stamps on a vessel with a tubular handle from Björke parish, Gotland (drawing: Cecilia Bonnevier, SHM).

of the snake creeping in the anger-hole, searching for mead.

Animals and anthropological depictions on pottery are very rare in the entire North-European tradition. However, there are still some exceptions in Anglo-Saxon and north-German pottery during the Migration period. A dozen *kegelhalsgefässe* from the gravefield at Süderbrarup in Angeln have motives upon reliefs of birds, snakes, humans and four-footed animals. The snakes are particularly popular and can be interpreted as representing Odin in different forms, together with his wolves (Bantelmann 1988, p. 60, taf. 56, 59, 60, 68 and 75). The pot from grave 547 even has decorations that can be interpreted as wings (Bantelmann 1988, taf.75).

Some of the later smaller vessels from Gotland provide an even more complex picture of the myth. It is a group of vessels found, for example, on the grave-field of Barshalder in Grötlingbo parish (SHM 32623) (Fig. 14), and which have also been found in graves in the mainland of Sweden, in Torp, Sorunda parish in Sörmland (SHM 34492). They

can all be dated to the end of the Migration period and the beginning of the Vendel period. It is possible to see them as the climax of a tradition that was dying out. The vessels are decorated with creeping S-patterns along the neck and the handle and wave-bands over the upper part. The body has hanging triangles filled with stamps with U-form. The same kind of triangular fields with U-patterns can be seen on contemporary Frankish book-illuminations and Langobardic gold-works (http://expositions.bnf.fr/carolingiens/itz/24/05.htm; Backes and Dölling 1969, p. 20, 65). In both regions they are representing wings of birds. In a somewhat imaginative decipherment of the iconography on the vessels, the whole myth of the theft of the mead can be seen. The drilling into the vessel, the snake that creeps in and the bird that brings the gift of wisdom to gods and humans.

Another stamp commonly found on the Gotlandic ceramic drinking vessels from the Migration period is the triangular impression with curved sides, a deltoid (sw. *treudd*). The form is mostly known as a special type of stone-setting on the mainland of Sweden, and more rarely in Denmark and

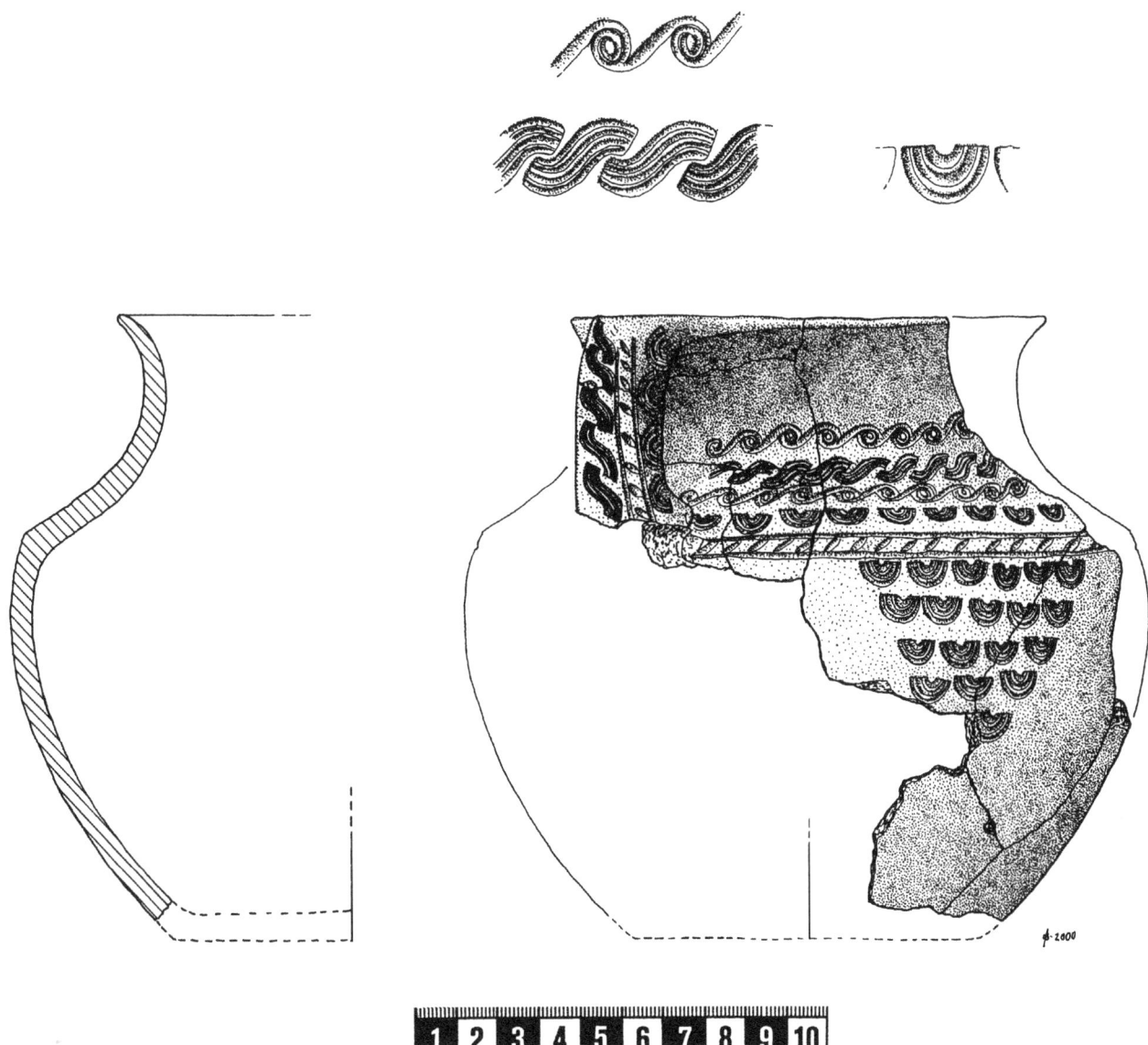

Fig. 14: The vessel from grave A13, Barshalder, Grötlingbo parish, Gotland (drawing: Cecilia Bonnevier, SHM).

Decors, regions and periods

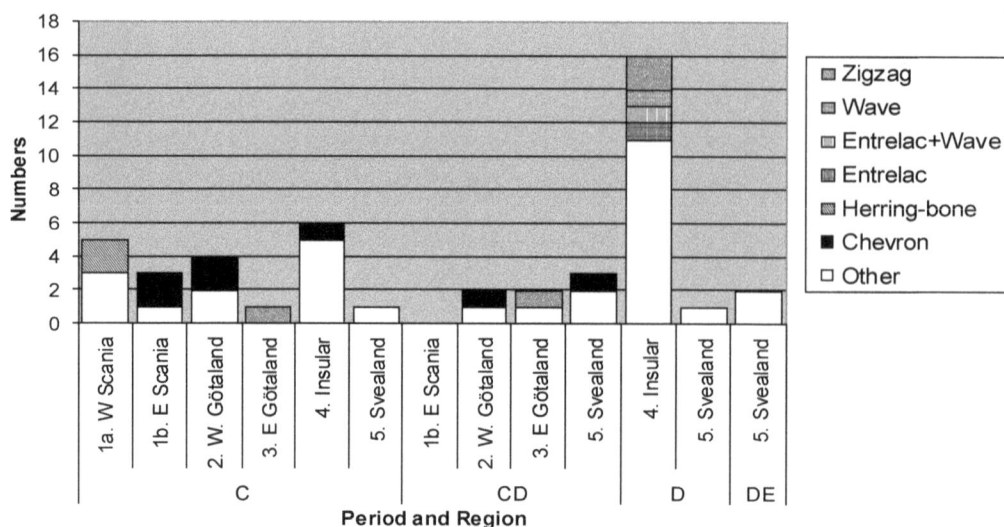

Fig. 15: Diagram with main decors on vessels with tubular handles in Sweden.

Norway. In Sweden they are often situated on grave-fields and can be dated to c. 300–700 AD. It is quite common that they lack ordinary graves as might be attested by finds of cremated bones or inhumations. Furthermore, this type of stone-setting is completely missing on Gotland. But it appears on the finer ceramic vessels on Gotland in the form of stamped decors and on, for example, dress-pins (Fig. 5). One of the more recent interpretations of the stone-settings is that they symbolize the ash Yggdrasil, the immense and cosmological tree with three roots. Each root is connected to a well. The first root is in the Urðarbrunnr, where the Norns are spinning the fate of every being. The second is in Hvergelmir, in Niflheim, and the last reaches Mimisbrunnr, the well were the giant Mimir kept all knowledge of the world and where Odin sacrificed one of his eyes to receive wisdom and intelligence. On the pottery the sign often has one or three endings in the form of stamped circles. Again the sign might be a symbol for the drink that gives wisdom and poetry.

Concluding remarks

The vessels with tubular handles are a heterogeneous group of vessels, with a production era that spans almost half a millennia. The production is usually local, with a distribution of perhaps less than 100 km in most cases. One exception is the Gotlandic vessels that are spread to Öland and Svealand. The connection between the Swiar and the Gotlanders is important for the understanding of development of the Swiar power. It is known from other archaeological and literary sources, such as the Guta saga. The saga tells us about Avair Strabain who made a treaty with the Swiars during the Iron Age (Nerman 1923). The connections between the Svealand and Gotland can be seen in many archaeological sources from the Early Roman Iron Age and onwards (Andersson 1995; Eriksson 2009, p. 145).

The Gotlandic connection to the eastern and central part of Continental Europe was crucial for the regions around the

northern part of the Baltic Sea. One of the most important rituals to forge the bonds to create exchange of goods, alliances and friendship was to drink and show how to behave. The jugs and bowls with tubular handles were probably one of the most important vessels for correct behaviour in the halls and recreating the myths of the drink of wisdom. The handle was a kind of puzzle-vessel, but with a clear connotation of power and ritual, and was embedded with magical power: the mead taken from Suttung by Odin himself. The idea of the rather unpractical tubular handle has a distribution around Northern and Central Europe that must be explained by an ideological context rather than a practical one.

The different styles and the spatial distribution reveal interesting networks and also the lack of contacts. Absence of specific items is, of course, always connected to a lot of problems according to source criticism. The chorological spread of different vessels with tubular handles may even tell us about different networks and groups with different rituals and material culture. A main division of the material is the East Scandinavian material culture in Svealand, Öland, Gotland, that has more in common with Bornholm and Poland than it has with the western part of Scandinavia. There are also different subgroups within this group. The same kind of subdivision into regional styles can be seen in western Scandinavia. The style in Västergötland is spread into Småland but not to Östergötland. Tubular handles also seem to be lacking in large parts of Jutland and Bohuslän.

Acknowledgements

This article is financed by the Gustav VI Adolfs fond för svensk kultur, Magn. Bergvalls stiftelse, Åke Wibergs Stiftelse and Lars Hiertas Stiftelse. The author is very grateful for this support.

Bibliography

Albrectsen, E. (1968). *Fynske jernaldergrave. 3. Yngre romersk jernalder*, Odense.

Albrectsen, E. (1971). *Fynske jernaldergrave. 4. Gravpladsen på Møllegårdsmarken vid Broholm*, Odense.

Almgren, O. and Nerman, B. (1923). *Die ältere Eisenzeit Gotlands*, Stockholm. Kungl. Vitterhets- historie- och antikvitetsakad. Wahlström & Widstrand.

Andersson, K. (1995). *Romartida guldsmide i Norden*, Uppsala: Dept. of Archaeology, Uppsala Univ.

Andrén, A. (1991). Guld och makt – en tolkning av de skandinaviska guldbrakteaternas funktion. In: C. Fabech and J. Ringtved, ed. Samfundsorganisation og regional variation. Norden i Romersk Jernalder og Folkevandringstid.Nordisk jernaldersymposium 1 1989 Sandbjerg Slot. Höjbjerg, p.245–256.

Arbman, H. (1932). Två främmande inslag i vår äldre järnålders keramik. *Fornvännen*, 1932(27), p.151–167.

Arrhenius, B. and Holmqvist, W. ed. (1964). *Excavations at Helgö*, Stockholm: Kungl. Vitterhets- historie- och antikvitetsakad. Almqvist & Wiksell International.

Backes, M. and Dölling, R. (1969). *Art of the dark ages*, New York: Abrams.

Bantelmann, N. ed. (1988). *Süderbrarup: ein Gräberfeld der römischen Kaiserzeit und Völkerwanderungszeit in Angeln. 1, Archäologische Untersuchungen*, Neumünster: Wachholtz.

Behm-Blancke, G. (1979). Trankgaben und Trinkzermonien im Totenkult der Völkerwanderungszeit. *Alt-Thüringen*, (16), pp.171–227.

Beskow-Sjöberg, M. and Arnell, K.-H. (1987). *Ölands järnåldersgravfält. Vol. 1, Alböke, Köpings, Räpplinge, Löts, Egby, Bredsätra och Gärdslösa socknar*, Stockholm: Riksantikvarieämbetet och Statens historiska museer.

Beskow-Sjöberg, M. and Hagberg, U.E. (1991). *Ölands järnåldersgravfält. Vol. 2, Högsrum, Glömminge, Algutsrum, Torslunda, Långlöt, Runsten, Norra Möckleby och Gårdby*, Stockholm: Riksantikvarieämbetet och Statens historiska museer.

Boas, F. (1955). *Primitive art*, New York. Dover.

Bóna, I. (1991). *Das Hunnenreich*, Stuttgart. Theiss.

Bøe, J. (1931). *Jernalderens keramikk i Norge*, Bergen. Bergens Museum.

Eliade, M. (1967). *Myths, dreams and mysteries: the encounter between contemporary faiths and archaic realities*, New York. Harper Torchbooks.

Enright, M. J. (1996). *Lady with a mead cup: ritual, prophecy, and lordship in the European warband from La Tène to the Viking Age*, Dublin. Four Courts Press.

Eggers, H.J. and Stary, P.F. (2001). Funde der Vorrömischen Eisenzeit, der Römischen Kaiserzeit und der Völkerwanderungszeit in Pommern. Beiträge zur Ur- und Frühgeschichte Mecklenburg-Vorpommerns. Band 38. Archäologischen Landesmuseum für Mecklenburg-Vorpommern. Lübstorf.

Eriksson, T. (2009). *Kärl och social gestik. keramik i Mälardalen 1500 BC-400 AD*, Uppsala. Uppsala universitet.

Hagberg, U. E. and Beskow-Sjöberg, M. (1996). *Ölands järnåldersgravfält. Vol. 3, Vickleby, Resmo, Mörbylånga,* *Kastlösa, Sandby, Stenåsa och Hulterstad*, Stockholm. Riksantikvarieämbetet och Statens historiska museer.

Hedeager, L. (2011). *Iron age myth and materiality. an archaeology of Scandinavia AD 400-1000*, London. Routledge.

Hegewisch, M. (2003). Röhrenhenkelkannen. Anmerkungen zu einer kaizer- und völkerwanderungszeitlischen Gefässform. *Ethnographisch-archäologische Zeitschrift*, 44(1), p.43–61.

Herschend, F. (2001). *Journey of civilisation. the Late Iron Age view of the human world*, OPIA 24. Uppsala. Department of Archaeology and Ancient History [Institutionen för arkeologi och antik historia], Univ.

Herschend, F. (1998). *The idea of the good in late Iron Age society*, OPIA 15. Uppsala. Dept. of Archaeology and Ancient History [Institutionen för arkeologi och antik historia], Univ.

Hoftun, O. (1998). Kultisk keramikk i jernalderen. *Fornvännen*, 1998(93.2), p.81–88.

Jakobsdóttir, S. (2002). Gunnlǫð and the precious mead. In: P. Acker and C. Larrington, ed. *The Poetic Edda. essays on Old Norse mythology*. Routledge medieval casebooks. New York. Routledge, p. 27–58.

Jennbert, K. (2011). *Animals and Humans. Recurrent Symbiosis in Archaeology and Old Norse Religion*, Nordic Academic Press.

Klindt-Jensen, O., Bech, J.-H., Bender Jørgensen, L., Walton Rogers, P., Trier, J., Sellevold, B. J., Alexandersen, V. and Trolle Lassen, T. (1996). *Slusegårdgravpladsen IV. Bornholm fra 1. årh. f. til 5. årh. e.v.t*, Højbjerg. Jysk Arkæologisk Selskab.

Kyhlberg, O. (2012). *Den långa järnåldern. sociala strategier, normer, traditioner*, Uppsala. Department of archaeology and ancient history, Uppsala University.

Løchsen Rødsrud, C. (2012). *I liv og død. Keramikkens sosiale kronologi i eldre jernalder*, Oslo. Kulturhistorisk museum. Universitet i Oslo.

Magnus, B. (2012). Lykken er som en liten fugl…In: *Frá haug ok heiðni. Tidskrift for Rogalands arkeologiske forening*. Nummer 1. 2012, p. 25–28.

Magnusson, M. (1946). Two skeleton graves from the Roman Iron Age produced at Gullarp no.5. *Meddelanden från Lunds universitets historiska museum*, 1946, p.96–105.

Menghin, W. Springer, T. and Wamers, E. ed. (1987). *Germanen, Hunnen und Awaren. Schätze der Völkerwanderungszeit. die Archäologie des 5. und 6. Jahrunderts an der mittleren Donau und der östlich-merowingische Reihengräberkreis*, Nürnberg. Germanisches Nationalmuseum, Nürnberg & Museum für Vor- und Frühgeschicte der Stadt Frankfurt am Main.

Neiβ, M. (2004). Midgårdsormen och Fenrisulven, två grundmotiv i vendeltidens djurornamentik. Kontinuitetsfrågor i germansk djurornamentik, I. In: Fornvännen 2004, p. 9–24.

Nerman, B. (1969). *Die Vendelzeit Gotlands. 2, Tafeln. die Zeichnungen von Harald Faith-Ell*. Stockholm. Kungl. Vitterhets-, historie- och antikvitetsakad.

Nerman, B. (1935). *Die Völkerwanderungszeit Gotlands*, Stockholm.

Nerman, B. (1923). *En utvandring från Gotland och öns införlivande med Sveaväldet*, Uppsala.

Nerman, B. and Lundström, A. (1975). *Die Vendelzeit Gotlands. im Auftrage der Kungl. Vitterhets-, historie- och antikvitetsakademien. 1.1, Text*, Stockholm. Akad.

Nicklasson, P. (1997). *Svärdet ljuger inte. vapenfynd från äldre järnålder på Sveriges fastland*, Stockholm. Almqvist & Wiksell International.

Nørgård Jørgensen, A. (1991). Kobbeågravpladsen, en yngre jernaldergravplads på Bornholm. *Aarbøger for nordisk oldkyndighed og historie*, 1991, p.123–183.

Oldenburger, F. (2010). Et usædvanligt lerkar fra yngre romersk jernalder fundet på Sydsjælland. *Aarbøger for nordisk oldkyndighed og historie*, p.97–108.

Pettersson, O. (1972). *Tro och rit . religionsfenomenologisk översikt*, Stockholm. Almqvist & Wiksell.

Polásková, Z. (2001). Gåtfulla tecken i lera. "besläktad" stämpelornerad keramik från Gotland och Öland. In: Vi får tacka Lamm. ed. Magnus, B & Lamm, J. P. Studies 10. p. 149-155. Stockholm. The Museum of National Antiquities.

Polásková, Z. (1998). *Stämpelornerad keramik från järnåldern på Gotland. Stämpelidentitet, handstilar, verkstadstraditioner.* Stockholm. Stockholms Universitet. Institutionen för arkeologi.

Polásková, Z. (1997). Stämpelornerad keramik på Gotland. verkstäder och dekortraditioner. In: T*ill Gunborg. Arkeologiska samtal.* ed. Åkerlund. A. & Janzon, G. Stockholm, p.253–8. Stockholm. Institutionen för arkeologi, Stockholms univ.

Rasch, M. and Fallgren, J.-H. (2001). *Ölands järnåldersgravfält. Vol. 4, Böda, Högby, Källa, Persnäs, Föra, Smedby, Södra Möckleby, Ventlinge, Segerstad, Gräsgård och Ås*, Stockholm. Riksantikvarieämbetet och Statens historiska museer.

Ringtved, J. (1986). Jyske gravfund fra yngre romertid. Tendenser i samfundsudviklingen. *Kuml.* Årbog for Jysk Arkæologisk Selskab. Aarhus. Aarhus University Press, p. 95–231.

Rundkvist, M. (2011). *Mead-halls of the Eastern Geats. elite settlements and political geography AD 375-1000 in Östergötland, Sweden*, Stockholm : Visby: Kungl. Vitterhets historie och antikvitets akademien ; Eddy.se.

Stjernquist, B. (1977). Neue funde von Gefässen mit röhrenformigem Henkel. *Studien zur Sachsenforschung*, p.405–414.

Stjernquist, B. (1955). *Simris. [1], On cultural connections of Scania in the Roman iron age*, Lund.

Zachrisson, T. (2004). The holiness of Helgö. In: Excavations at Helgö 16. Exotic and sacral finds from Helgö. Stockholm. Kungl. Vitterhets historie och antikvitets akademin.

http://www.olapersson.com/thing/volume-in-illustrator/
Volume in illustrator – calculate the volume of a revolved solid in illustrator
[Accessed 30-12-2014]

http://expositions.bnf.fr/carolingiens/itz/24/05.htm
Le décor Carolingien
[Accessed 30-12-2014]

Ceramic Evidence from Non-ferrous Metallurgy in the Mälaren Valley during the Viking Age

Daniel Sahlén

Stockholm University, Department of Archaeology and Classical Studies,
Archaeological Research Laboratory

daniel.sahlen@arklab.su.se

Abstract: Studies of non-ferrous metallurgy in the Viking Age, predominantly from casting activities, have chiefly looked at specialised production contexts, while less specialised production has rarely been discussed in any detail. As a consequence, we know very little about the organisation and context of production outside larger pre-urban/trading sites. The purpose of this article is to discuss the evidence of non-ferrous craft production at a range of sites within region the Mälaren valley. It highlights that non-ferrous metallurgy was a widespread phenomenon during the Viking Age, but shows clear differences in the extent and context of the production.

Key words: The Mälaren valley – Craft organization – Technical ceramics

Introduction

Studies of non-ferrous metallurgy in the Viking Age, predominantly from casting of copper and silver alloys, have chiefly looked at specialised production contexts (e.g. at Birka) and linked this to the development of urbanisation and socioeconomic specialisation (Clark and Ambrosiani 1991; Callmer 2003). The presence of less specialised production is known (Callmer 1991; Ljungkvist 2012, p. 190-91), but this does not form part of the general narrative of production in the Viking Age. As a consequence, we know very little about the organisation and context of production outside larger pre-urban/trading sites.

The purpose of this article is to present some preliminary results from the ongoing project, Metalworking Crafts in Context, looking at the ceramic evidence of metallurgical production in the Mälaren valley during the Viking Age. Technical ceramics are the most reliable evidence of non-ferrous metallurgy (Bayley 1989; Martinon-Torres and Rehren 2014), while metallic waste products, hand-tools and furnace structures are ambiguous find categories which could relate to other craft activities or, in some cases, trade (Bayley 1991; Pedersen 2000). Phase one of Metalworking Crafts in Context was financed by Berit Wallenbergs Stiftelse and was an initial study to contextualise the production of non-ferrous metals in the Viking Age in two separate regions, Skåne and the Mälaren valley. This article discusses the material from one of these regions with the goals of defining different types of sites and characterising the ceramic material as a find category.

In this study, the Mälaren valley is defined as the area around the lake Mälaren in east central Sweden (Sporrong 2008), focusing on developments around Birka and Sigtuna. The chronological emphasis of the project falls on the Viking Age, loosely following the traditional chronology AD 800– 1050, but includes sites with materials which are at least partly Viking Age in date.

Ceramic evidence of metallurgical production

Recent research has been able to identify an increasing number of non-specialised sites with evidence of non-ferrous production from different archaeological periods. This follows an increased interest in domestic contexts and the expansion of contract archaeology, but there is also an improved awareness of production processes and their material remains. Earlier research identified non-ferrous production mainly from the occurrence of moulds and crucibles, and the identification of a workshop building, but later research has indicated that non-ferrous production can leave a range of different materials and that the link to an actual workshop building is the exception rather than the norm (Armbruster 2004; Gustafsson 2012; Sahlén, forthcoming). The evidence discussed here derives from an extensive study of excavation reports and published sources, and materials published online in the National History Museum artefact database and The Swedish National Heritage Board database, *Fornsök*. Only sites classified as production sites by the excavators or in the publication of the material have been included since an independent classification of site activities was beyond the scope of the current work. As a consequence, there might be additional excavated sites where production was also carried out but currently not classified in this way.

The term technical ceramics, or sometimes metalworking ceramics, includes various ceramic tools employed for the production and processing of metals and metal alloys (Freestone and Tite 1986; Martinón-Torres and Rehren 2014). The main categories are crucibles and moulds, but also include structural parts of furnaces and other specialised artefacts used for particular processes.

From a ceramic perspective, crucibles – vessels used for high temperature and chemical processes – have been the most discussed find variety in this category (Bayley and Rehren 2007; Sahlén 2013). The main type is the metal-melting crucible used in casting of non-ferrous metals, but other types of importance are scorifiers, cupels and heating trays used for the refining or purification of metals (Söderberg 2004; Bayley and Rehren 2007). Crucibles during prehistoric and early medieval contexts are typically made in ceramic materials, although crucibles made in stone are known from the Viking Age and the medieval period, but are rare. The dominating Viking Age shape is the small open crucible (Fig. 1), with or without a handle or a spout, which is known from diverse sites (Pedersen 2010; Lamm 2008; Sahlén 2012), but is chronologically non-diagnostic since this type was used also in earlier periods. The size varies from 3-7cm in height and around 5cm in diameter, but larger examples are also known. Other shapes are known, but a full study of Viking Age types is missing. The ceramic crucible is often described as sandy to course sandy, tempered with sand or crushed quartz (Sahlén 2013), but little work has been carried out to investigate the technology of Viking Age crucibles. Vince (2011, p. 305-307), comparing crucibles from Kaupang (Norway) and Birka, noted some petrographic similarities between the material from the two sites. He argued that this relationship at least indicated a shared technology between the two sites, but did not rule out the use of similar sources of clay.

Viking Age casting moulds were made from stone or clay, and a few moulds in metal are known. Moulds in stone – mainly soapstone, schist or sandstone – were particularly used for casting of ingots and simple forms, such as Thor hammers and crosses, but also for simple ornamental objects. In most cases these were used as open moulds, but in some cases were supplied with a cover. Ingot moulds of soapstone are a characteristic Viking Age artefact found mainly at larger trading sites, but also at minor sites in the North Atlantic. Two types of clay moulds were used during the Viking Age: two-part moulds and investment moulds (cire perdue). Clay moulds were used particularly for casting of personal ornaments, for example brooches or pins (Fig. 2). Investment moulds are made around a model of wax which is then heated up and poured out, and the metal is poured into the space within the clay package (Lønborg 1998, p. 16-17). Two-piece clay moulds are made in two halves and are held together with an outer layer of clay, mainly for the production of pins and brooches. Moulds of clay are typically made from sandy/fine sandy clays or are alternatively tempered with a large amount of fine sand/silt and organic matter (e.g. Vince 2008). Studies of materials from other periods have shown a difference in the fabric between two-part moulds and investment moulds (Sahlén 2011, 203), but this has not been assessed for Viking Age finds.

The other main types of technical ceramics are tuyères and clay used in the construction of the furnace and hearths. The bowl furnace was the main metallurgical furnace structure from the Iron Age and the early medieval period, but structures used for smithing and non-ferrous crafts were simpler hearths with an external air supply (McDonnell 2001). Little is often left of these structures, but it would have been a small open structure charged with charcoal, sometimes dug into the ground and lined with clay. A

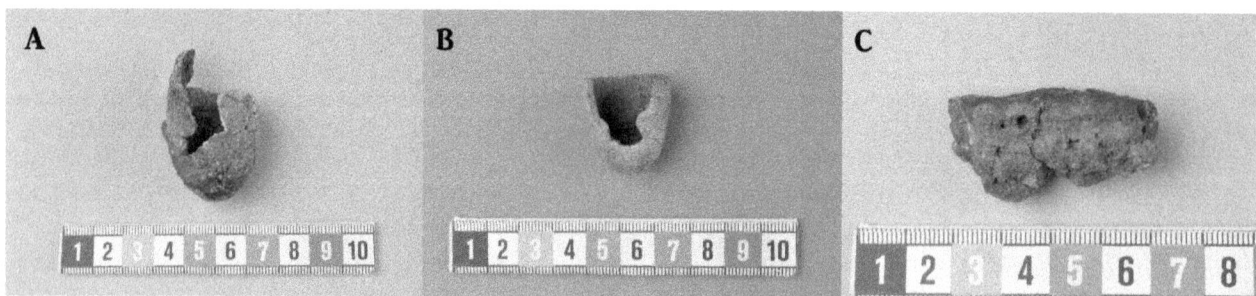

Fig. 1: Examples of crucibles from Birka, (Photograph: Daniel Sahlén Copyright: SHMM). A, almost complete crucible (FID1000674); B, almost complete crucible (FID998747); close-up on crucible fragment, showing degree of vitrification, ceramic texture, and metal staining of the ceramic material.

Fig. 2: Almost complete clay mould for the production of an oval brooch from Birka (Photograph: Daniel Sahlén, Copyright: SHMM). A: casting side; B: backside; C: sidewise.

tuyère connected to bellows could be used as an air supply to make it possible to reach higher temperatures.

There has been surprisingly little technological work on technical ceramics from the Viking Age. Most work on moulds has looked at their preparation and use (e.g. Zachrisson 1966; Brinch Madsen 1984) and, in relation to crucibles, on identifying their association to particular metals or metallurgical process (Söderberg 2004; Bayley and Rehren 2007). A few petrographic analyses of moulds and crucibles have been published (Vince 2006, 2008), but these are often part of larger studies and the main aspect has been to provenance the material, while the material's technology has only been discussed in schematic terms.

The sites

In total 14 sites have been identified with evidence of casting during the Viking Age in the Mälaren valley. The context and size of these sites varies considerably and there is an even spread of sites throughout the area in focus (Table 1, Fig. 3). This demonstrates that non-ferrous

metalwork was more common in the Mälaren valley than has previously been acknowledged and similar patterns can be observed in other areas in the Viking World (e.g. Callmer 1991; Gustafsson 2013).

Table 1 summarises the ceramic evidence of non-ferrous production in the Mälaren valley during the Viking period, but note that the sites range from the early Viking Age to the early medieval period and many of the sites do not need to be contemporary. It is possible to define three categories of sites: Sites with extensive remains from metalworking suggesting a craft specialisation (site category 1); Sites with limited amounts of debris, but where the evidence for the production is clear, mainly through the presence of ceramic debris (site category 2); Sites with little or ambiguous remains and where the identification of an actual production is not certain (site category 3). This classification is not strictly a definition of site types since the characterisation of site categories 2 and 3 is mainly based on what was found, and this has to a large degree depended on how and to what extent each site was investigated. In addition, the sites' production contexts have been noted in Table 1 (PC);

Table 1: List over sites with evidence of casting in the Mälaren valley

No.	Site	Date	Site type	Cat	Ceramic debris and production context					
					Cbl	SC	TPM	StM	Misc	PC
1	Birka	VA	Pre-urban/trading place	1	E	S	E	S	E	W
2	Ekhammer	IA/VA	Settlement	3	R	---	---	---	---	L
3	Farsta gärde	VA-EM	Terrace house, smithy	3	---	---	---	---	---	L
4	Fornsigtuna	VP-VA	Hall building	2	R	---	---	---	---	Mi
5	Helgö	VP-VA	Large workshop area	2	S	---	S		S	W
6	Hjulsta	VA	Settlement	2	R	---	---	---	S	Mj
7	Mälby	VA-EM	Settlement	2	---	---	---	---	S	Mj
8	Pollista	VA	Settlement	2	S	---	---	---	---	M
9	Rissne	VA	Settlement/grave	2	E	---	---	---	---	L
10	Säby gård	VA	Settlement and ritual complex	2	R	---	S	---	S	Mj
11	Sanda	VA	Undefined	3	---	---	---	---	---	L
12	Sigtuna	VA-EM	Urban	1	E	S	E	E	E	W
13	Strömsnäs	VA	Without context	3	R	---	---	---	---	S
14	Valsta	VA	Grave complex	3	---	---	R	---	---	L

Key – Cat.: site category; IA: Iron Age; VP: Vendel period; VA: Viking Age; EM: early medieval; Cbl: crucibles; SC: specialised crucible; TPM: two-piece moulds; StM: stone mould; Misc: miscellaneous (mainly ceramic materials part of the furnace structure); E: extensive; R: rare; S: some; PC: Production context; W: workshop; L: limited; Mi: minor; Mj: Major; S: sporadic. The dates of most sites are uncertain, except for Birka and Sigtuna, why the periods have been listed rather than absolute dates.

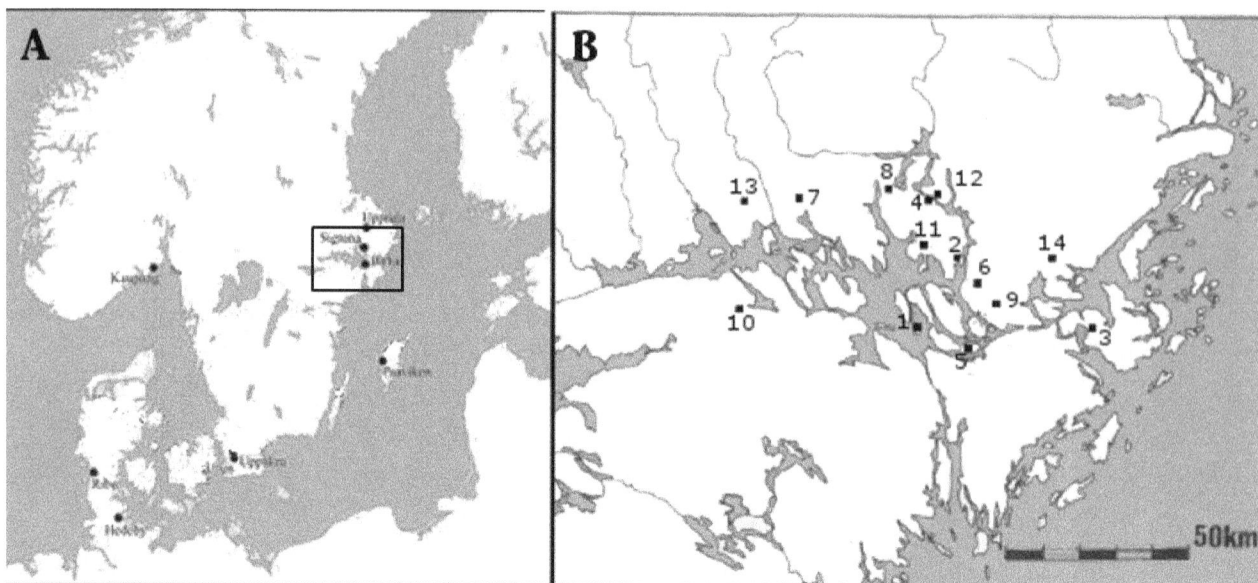

Fig. 3: A, Map over Viking Age Scandinavia, including sites discussed in this article. The Mälaren valley is marked with a box; B, Map over the Mälaren valley, with site locations marked out (for site numbers see Table 1).

this is a classification of the evidence of production at the different sites and includes an assessment of production debris and structural remains. This classification is preliminary and based on a system developed from the study of production contexts in late prehistoric Scotland (Sahlén, forthcoming). The quantity of crucibles, moulds and other ceramic materials (mainly furnace lining) has been defined using a descriptive nomenclature: rare, some and extensive to give an indication of the production intensity at the different sites.

There is obviously a clear difference between Birka and Sigtuna and the other sites listed in Table 1. Birka and Sigtuna were two early urban sites with extensive evidence of different specialised crafts and sporadic production in a workshop setting, while the other sites are mainly large farmsteads. The ceramic materials from site categories 1 and 2 are discussed briefly below, while the metallurgical material from all three categories and a full review of the sites will be presented in a future publication.

The ceramic materials

In most cases only limited amounts of ceramic debris are recorded, excluding the assemblages from Birka (Jakobsson 1996) and Sigtuna (Nordin 1990) where extensive amounts of moulds and crucibles were found. At Birka, the largest production site, around 25,000 mould fragments and 10,000 crucible sherds and solder packages were identified (Ambrosiani 2013, p. 237-38). This is two orders of magnitude larger than the 279 mould fragments found at Säby Gård, the site with most extensive ceramic assemblage in category 2 (Table 1). Crucibles are the chief material at the sites discussed here, but moulds and fragments of furnace lining are found at some places (Table 1). The number of crucible sherds can often be informative for an actual number of vessels since it can be possible to distinguish between different shapes

and morphological features. In contrast, the number of mould fragments is not a good indicator of the number of actual moulds. Mould fragments are often much abraded and it is rarely possible to join individual fragments or to recreate a whole mould. This is due both to the fragile nature of moulds and that the mould is deliberately broken after use to remove the casted object. Still, a count of the number of mould fragments and identified mould patterns can give an indication of the extent of production and range of materials produced at the site. A crucible may very well have been used several times before it collapsed (cf. Eklöv Pettersson 2011) and does not give a clear idea of the extent of production.

The lack of moulds at excavated sites has led some researchers to discuss alternative moulding materials, particularly sand, but there is little evidence of such practices in the archaeological record. Clay moulds have been found at five sites (Birka, Helgö, Säby Gård, Sigtuna, and Valsta; Table 1), but the mould fragment found in the filling of a Viking Age grave at Valsta is probably intrusive and from the production in the Vendel period. Stone moulds are found at two sites, Birka and Sigtuna, and make up the largest portion of mould material at Sigtuna (Nordin 1990, p. 74). The casted objects are mainly decorative items such as brooches and pins, but metal ingots were also casted in the stone moulds from Birka and Sigtuna. The moulds from Säby Gård are interesting since they are for the casting of oval brooches (Dunér and Vinberg 2006), an artefact also manufactured at Birka (Ambrosiani 2013, p. 239-40). A petrographic analysis of the moulds from the two sites and pottery from the area around Säby Gård was carried out as part of the post-excavation assessment of the material from Säby Gård (Vince 2008). The purpose of the analysis was to assess if the clay was made from the same clay at the two sites and to test if the moulds were made at Birka and brought to Säby Gård. The petrographic analysis was unable to demonstrate if the moulds from Birka and Säby

Gård were made from the same clay since the mineralogy did not show any diagnostic features.

The evidence from hearth structures at the sites discussed here are ambiguous and seems more associated with ferrous metalworking, but the same hearths might have been used both for ferrous and non-ferrous production. A hearth structure was found in the west side of the terraced house at Farsta Gärde (structure A16, Andersson 2004, 13), which seems associated to smithing and possibly the working with copper alloys. The hearth measures approximately 3m in diameter and contains large amounts of fired cracked stones, charcoal, vitrified and glassy clay, slag and fragments and droplets of copper alloys, tin and lead. The position of the hearth within the building is unusual since the casting activities are often found outside a building or without connection to an actual building.

Discussion and conclusions

The main purpose of this article was to discuss the evidence of non-ferrous craft production in the Mälaren valley based on the ceramic debris and it presents preliminary results from the ongoing project Metalworking crafts in context at Stockholm University. The study has highlighted that non-ferrous metallurgy was widespread in the Mälaren valley during the Viking Age, but clear differences in the extent of the material remains from the different sites are apparent. Ceramic evidence for non-ferrous metallurgy was divided into four different categories (Table 1): melting crucibles, processing vessels (e.g. scorifiers, cupels and heating trays), clay moulds, and ceramic materials associated with furnace structures. The occurrence of stone moulds was also noted in Table 1. Non-ferrous production was identified at 14 sites (Table 1 but ceramic materials were only discovered at 12 sites and the amount of material discovered at the different sites varies considerably.

The material diversity at the different sites in the Mälaren valley is telling for the different types of production carried out. The extent of the material, the duration of the production and the range of different non-ferrous crafts carried out at Birka and Sigtuna indicate that the production at these two sites was both specialised and extensive following the main narrative of non-ferrous production in the Viking world. It is possible to identify different independent locations of production at both Birka and Sigtuna. Production at Birka has been discovered at several different locations (cf. Hedenstierna-Jonson and Holmquist Olausson 2006; Ambrosiani 2013), suggesting different production contexts. The production at Sigtuna is located at several minor workshops (Wikström 2011), possibly an organisation typical of early medieval production. In contrast, the material seen at the other sites presented here show a more limited and shorter production; although part of the variability derives from differences in the excavation of the sites. This difference in production contexts is also seen in the variability of the material, where the material from Birka and Sigtuna appears more specialised with a wide range of crucibles for different purposes and different

types of moulds. This suggests that at least two sets of production were established in the Mälaren valley during the Viking Age, one more specialised and one sporadic. Similar patterns have been seen in other areas, for example Skåne (Callmer 2003). This seems to indicate that non-ferrous production, and probably also other crafts, saw an increased specialisation during the Viking Age, though local non-specialised production continued outside the major sites.

This conclusion raises a number of questions concerning the consumption of metals and the presence of craft knowledge. For example: Were the crafts at these smaller sites linked to trade or local consumption? Were the crafts carried out by settled or itinerant craft workers? How common were skills in casting and forging of non-ferrous metals in the Viking Age society? It has not been possible to answer these questions from the present dataset, but these questions are explored in an ongoing project.

It is interesting that moulds and crucibles – the main types of ceramic evidence from casting production – are fairly sparse at most sites, excluding Birka, Sigtuna and to some extent Säby Gård. A similar pattern is noted by Callmer in his review of casting sites in southeast Skåne during the Viking Age (2003, p. 355). Callmer found seven sites with evidence of casting in his region of interest. Most of the sites showed only limited amounts of moulds and/or crucibles, while the material at Åhus II showed a considerable amount of material. This difference in materials quantities is partly related to the method of excavation, but the contrast between the large amount of material found at Birka and Sigtuna and the small amount or absence of materials at the other sites suggests that there were also different production practices and how the production was organised. Future analyses of the ceramic and metallurgical material at these sites are ongoing and will illuminate this relation further.

The patterns discussed in this article are tentative and more work is needed to test some of these conclusions. Comparison with similar distribution of production sites in other regions would clarify if the observations made in the Mälaren valley are representative of the Viking society or typical of socioeconomic central regions. Technical analysis of metal and ceramic debris has been initiated to assess the variability in the use of metal and craft techniques, which will be important to make assessments about the nature of the production at the different sites.

Bibliography

Ambrosiani, B. (2013). *Stratigraphy. Vol. 1, Part one: the site and the shore, part two: the bronze caster's workshop*. Stockholm: The Birka Project, Riksantikvarieämbetet.

Andersson, K. (2004). Tidigmedeltida verkstadsbebyggelse vid Farsta Gärde, Arkeologisk delundersökning av boplats RAÄ 40, Farsta, Gustavsbergs socken, Värmdö kommun, Uppland, Stockholms Läns Museum, Rapport 2004: 9.

Armbruster, B. (2004). Goldsmiths' tools at Hedeby. In Hines, J. Lane, A. and Redknapp, M. (eds), *Land Sea, and Home, Society for Medieval Archaeology,* Monograph, 109–23.

Bayley, J. (1989). Non-metallic evidence of metalworking. In Maniatis, Y. (ed.) *Archaeometry: proceedings of the 25th international symposium,* Amsterdam: Elsevier, 291–303.

Bayley, J. (1991). Anglo-Saxon non-ferrous metalworking: A survey, *World Archaeology,* 23: 115–30.

Bayley, J. and Rehren, T. (2007). Towards a functional and typological classification of crucibles. In La Niece, S., Hook, D. and Craddock, P.T. (ed.) *Metals and Mines: Studies in Archaeometallurgy.* London: Archetype, 46–55.

Brinch Madsen, H. (1984). Metal casting: Techniques, production and workshops. In Bencard, M. (ed.): *Ribe Excavations 1970–76.* Vol 2. Esbjerg.

Callmer, J. (1991). Platser med anknytning till handel och hantverk i yngre järnålder. Exempel från Södra Sverige. In Mortensen, P. & Rasmussen, B. M. (eds.), *Fra Stamme til Stat i Danmark 2. Høvdingesamfund og Kongemagt.* Jysk Arkæologisk Selskabs Skrifter 22:2, Højbjerg.

Callmer, J. (2003). North-European trading centres and the Early Medieval craftsman. Craftsmen at Åhus, northeastern Scania, Sweden ca. AD 750-850+. In Hårdh, B. and Larsson, L. (eds.) *Central Places in the Migration and the Merovingian Periods: Papers from the 52nd Sachsensymposium.* Lund: Almquist &Wiksell, 125–57.

Clarke, H. and Ambrosiani, B. (1991). *Towns in the Viking age.* Leicester: Leicester University Press.

Dunér, J. och Vinberg, A. (2006). Barva – 2 000 år vid Mälarens södra strand E20, sträckan Eskilstuna–Arphus Södermanland, Barva socken, UV Mitt, Rapport 2006: 20.

Eklöv Pettersson, P. (2011). En hållbar utveckling? – Hållbarheten för bronsålderns keramiska deglar, Master Dissertation, Lund University.

Freestone, I.C. and Tite, M.S. (1986). Refractories in the ancient and preindustrial world, In Kingery, W.D. (ed.) *High Temperature Ceramics – Past, Present and Future, Ceramics and Civilization 3,* Columbus, Ohio, 35–63.

Gustafsson, N.B. (2012). Beyond Wayland – thoughts on early medieval metal workshops in Scandinavia, *Historical Metallurgy* 45: 90–101.

Gustafsson, N.B. (2013). In the wake of the hoards – glimpses of non-ferrous metalworking through the finds of the Gotland hoard projects, *Fornvännen* 108: 1–11.

Hedenstierna-Jonson, C., and Holmquist Olausson, L. (2006). The Oriental Mounts from Birka's Garrison: An expression of warrior rank and status, *Antikvariskt arkiv,* 81.

Jakobsson, T. (1996). Bronsgjutarna på Birka – en kort presentation. In Forshell, H. (ed.), *Icke-Järnmetaller: Malmfyndigheter och Metallurgi, Föredrag från Symposium på Jernkontoret den 16 mars 1995,* Stockholm: Jernkontorets Bergshistoriska Utskott, 71–75.

Lamm, K. (2008). Crucibles and cupels from Building group 3. In H. Clarke and K. Lamm (eds), *Excavations at Helgö XVII, 171–208.* Stockholm: KVHAA.

Ljungkvist, J. Handicrafts. In Brink, S. and Price, N. 2008. (eds) *The Viking World,* 186–192.

McDonnell, J.G. (2001). Pyrotechnology. In Brothwell, D.R. and Pollard, A.M. (eds.) *Handbook of Archaeological Sciences.* Chichester: John Wiley and Sons, 493–505.

Nordin, A-C. (1990). Bronsgjutning. In Tesh, S. (ed.), *Makt och människor i kungens Sigtuna. Sigtunautgrävningen 1988–1990.* Sigtuna, 73–75.

Oldeberg, A. (1966). *Metallteknik under vikingatid och medeltid,* Stockholm: Seeling.

Pedersen, U. (2010). I Smeltedigelen, Finsmide i Vikingtidsbyen Kaupang, PhD Thesis, University of Oslo.

Sahlén, D. (2011). Ceramic technology and technological traditions The manufacture of metalworking ceramics in Late Prehistoric Scotland, unpublished PhD thesis, University of Glasgow.

Sahlén, D. (2012). Crucibles and moulds from Udal, North Uist, macroscopic and X-Ray Florescence analyses, initial assessments, Interim Report 2012, The Udal Project.

Sahlén, D. (2013). Selected with care? – the technology of crucibles in late prehistoric Scotland. A petrographic and chemical assessment, *Journal of Archaeological Science,* 40: 4207–4221.

Sahlén, D. (forthcoming). Production as activity – defining the context of casting production in late prehistoric Scotland, *European Journal of Archaeology.*

Sporrong, U. (2008). Från vikingatida hövdingadömen till en kraftfull region i europagemenskapen. In *Kungl. Vitterhets Historie och Antikvitets Akademiens årsbok,* 2008: 177–94.

Söderberg, A. (2004). Metallurgical ceramics as a key to Viking Age workshop organisation, *Journal of Nordic Archaeological Science,* 14: 115–24.

Vince, A. (2008). Petrological and chemical analysis of mould fragments, in Dunér, J. and Vinberg, A. 2006. Barva – 2 000 år vid Mälarens södra strand E20, sträckan Eskilstuna–Arphus Södermanland, Barva socken, UV Mitt, Rapport 2006: 20, bilaga 57.

Vince, A. (2011). Charaterisation studies of pottery, industrial ceramics and fired clay. In Skre, D. (ed.) *Things from the Town. Viking Age Artefacts from the Kaupang Settlement.* Kaupang Excavation Project Publication Series, vol 3, Århus: Aarhus University Press, 305–09.

Wikström, A. (2011). *Fem stadsgårdar: arkeologisk undersökning i kv. Trädgårdsmästaren 9 & 10 i Sigtuna 1988-90.* Sigtuna: Sigtuna museum.

Zachrisson, I. (1960). *De ovala spännbucklornas tillverkningssätt,* Tor VI: 207–37.

www.ingramcontent.com/pod-product-compliance
Lightning Source LLC
Chambersburg PA
CBHW061304270326
41932CB00029B/3461